HOUSE & HOME REPAIRS

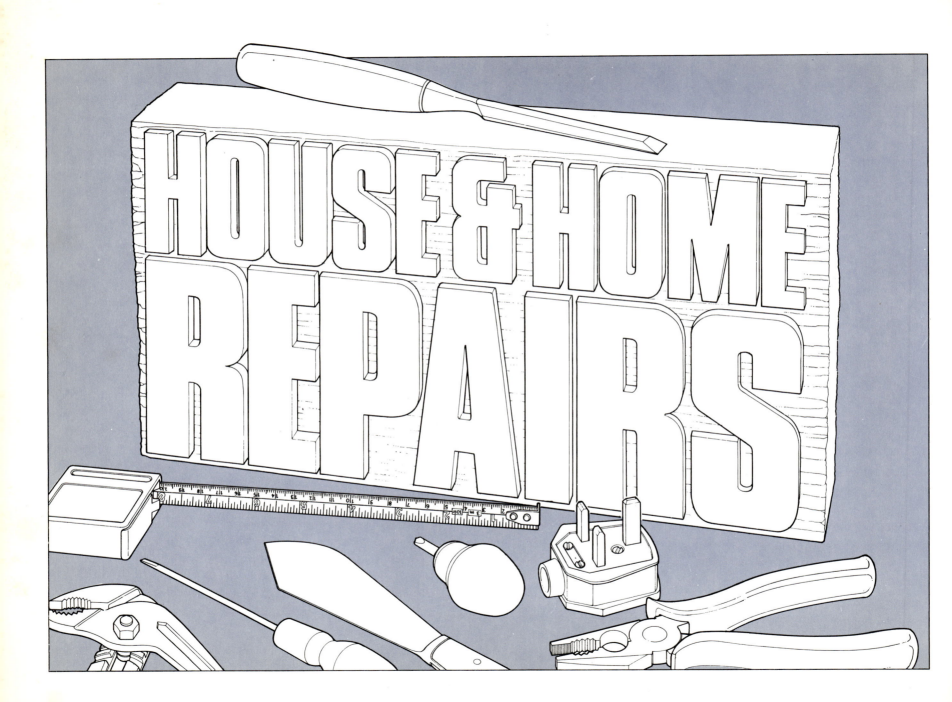

HOUSE & HOME REPAIRS

Ward Lock Limited · London

First published in Great Britain in 1983
by Ward Lock Limited, 82 Gower Street,
London WC1E 6EQ, a Pentos Company.

Layout by Bob Swan

Text filmset in Plantin Light
by MS Filmsetting Limited, Frome, Somerset

Printed and bound in Spain by Graficromo, S.A.,
Cordoba

British Library Cataloguing in Publication Data
Gundrey, Elizabeth
  House & home repairs.
  1. Dwellings—Remodeling
  I. Title   II. Gundrey, Walter
  643′.7   TH4816

ISBN 0-7063-6201-2

Note The bold numbers in the margins
refer to illustrations.

'Insulation', pages 146–155 of 'Painting
and Decorating', and 'Floors and
Flooring' were contributed by Walter
Gundrey, who also edited the book.

Contents

5 PAINTING AND DECORATING

6 FLOORS AND FLOORING

Introduction

For those of little skill

To call a tradesman to one's home these days costs several pounds, no matter how trifling the job that has to be done. This is particularly hard on people of limited means – and it is often quite unnecessary.

This book is about jobs that can be undertaken by a complete amateur. They call for no previous experience or skill, and need a minimum of very ordinary tools. The book is written in everyday language, avoiding technical jargon wherever possible.

The main essential is to have the right tools – few of them but well chosen (see the beginning of each section).

Tenants and leaseholders

Unless you own the freehold of your house, some repairs may be the landlord's responsibility rather than yours. This is particularly likely to be the case in flats where certain services are common to more than one home. Examples are drains, the cold water supply, staircase lighting, and gutters and downpipes. It is normally up to the landlord to repair 'common parts', such as staircases or paths, in a shared building, and to see to things like the roof which are part of the main structure of any rented property. If the landlord fails to keep these repaired, any Citizens' Advice Bureau or Legal Advice Centre will tell you what to do. Be careful about undertaking any repairs to such things yourself: in particular, you would be liable for any damage you might do.

Fixtures within your home are also the landlord's property, but an obligation to keep them in good order is normally the tenant's: examples are baths, basins, sinks, WCs, taps, electric circuits and water heaters. If you go further and put in improvements, these become the landlord's property: examples are new doorbells or WC seats – unless you were to replace the old ones when you move out.

Your insurance policy

You (or your landlord) should have a policy covering the building, and you should also have one that covers its contents. One policy may combine both. Your building policy will be in the hands of your building society if your house is mortgaged.

Such policies cover fire, flood, theft and some other disasters too.

You may be able to claim for the cost of putting right the following mishaps – whether you do them yourself or not. Outbuildings, gates and so forth are likely to be covered too. But don't expect a claim to succeed if the cause of the damage is really old age or neglect; and claim immediately the damage occurs, starting on the repair only if it is so urgent that it cannot await the insurance company's reaction.

Flooding from cracked tank or pipes. (Damage to carpets, or even dry rot, may qualify for a claim, but not replacement of the tank or pipes. Keep the damaged goods as the insurance company may want to inspect them.)

Flooding from cracked basin, WC, etc. (The replacement of these will probably be covered, but not if you caused the crack while carrying out repairs.)

Flooding from blocked drain, rusted gutters, etc. (Less likely to qualify because blockages are usually due to negligence).

Damage to underground cables and pipes is covered in some policies.

Damage to landlord's fixtures (a contents policy may protect tenants against claims or the cost of repairs).

Woodworm is not ordinarily covered but special insurance can be taken out against this risk provided your house is free of infestation when you first apply.

If a tenant, you are also likely to have rights under your landlord's insurance policy for the structure as a whole: see above.

Many policies require the policyholder to foot the bill for the first £15 or so of certain types of repair.

Repairs and your mortgage

When you get a mortgage loan you may have part of it withheld until (for example) dry rot or a defective damp-proof course are put right. Find out whether your building society will or won't accept do-it-yourself repairs before embarking on such things.

The society will require you to keep the house in good repair. It will also require you to ask permission before making any major alteration, such as changing from one type of window to another (you may find you need permission from the local council too).

If you have it in mind to improve the house in some way, an extra loan may be available to cover the cost.

Repairs and grants

Local councils do not ordinarily give grants for repairs or decorations – except, sometimes, when these are inseparable from grant-aided improvements such as putting in a bath, WC, etc., or if they bring an old house up to modern standards (putting in a damp-proof course, for example). Grants are also available towards the cost of home insulation. Some councils are more flexible than others, but there are always many strings attached to grants and usually weeks or months of delay before you may start work. Full details are in leaflets obtainable from your local council.

When you cannot do it yourself

There is nothing to beat personal recommendation when it comes to choosing a builder or other craftsman. Failing that, membership of a trade association is often some guarantee of reliability. Avoid the type of man who turns up unannounced at the front door with some 'bargain' offer.

Unless a craftsman belongs to a firm, it is best to phone outside working hours. Get an estimate for any small job before he starts: this is not so binding as a written quotation, but is a good deterrent to overcharging later. For big jobs, get written estimates from several – one might quote twice as much as another, but might be providing a more elaborate or better quality job, so read and compare descriptions carefully. Those who advertise an emergency service are apt to be expensive.

If you have a complaint that cannot be resolved, take it to the consumer protection department of your local council or to one of the trade associations named below if a member of theirs is involved. If it is a dispute with an electricity board and you can get no satisfaction, take the matter up with the local consultative council – the address is in the telephone book under electricity, or obtainable from the local board.

In an emergency, the water authority or even the police may give you names of plumbers. Some water authorities will not only turn off the supply but even change tap washers or ball-valves (free or at a moderate charge).

Hiring gear – big or small

To find a firm that will hire you anything from a screwdriver upwards, look in the yellow pages of the telephone directory under 'hire', 'contractors' or 'plant' or in the National Plant Hire Guide which many libraries have. The Hire Association, 12 Voluntary Place, Wansted, Essex, can supply addresses. Terms vary enormously. Not all firms give instructions for using complex equipment, and it's wise to check the condition it's in and the length of flex if it's electric.

More advice

Here are some addresses that may come in useful when you want major work done:

Asphalt and Coated Macadam Association (25 Lower Belgrave St., London SW1) will advise on any estimates and specifications you get for paths or drives.

British Ceramic Tile Council (Federation House, Stoke on Trent) will recommend tilers (wall and floor, not roof).

British Wood Preserving Association (62 Oxford Street, London W1) will recommend firms to treat rot, worm or damp.

Federation of Master Builders (33 John Street, London WC1) admits only well qualified builders to membership. So does National Federation of Building Trades Employers (82 New Cavendish Street, London W1)

Felt Roofing Contractors Association (Boltro Road, Haywards Heath, Sussex) is for non-tiled roofing work.

Glass Federation (6 Mount Row, London W1) will investigate complaints against member-firms who do double-glazing, etc.

National Cavity Insulation Association (Bremar House, Sale Place, London W2) vets member-firms' wall insulation work and will see that complaints are settled.

National Federation of Roofing Contractors (15 Soho Square, W1V 5FB) will take up any complaints against firms which are among their members.

National Institute of Electrical Installation Contracting, 93 Albert Embankment, SE1 will provide lists of house-wiring contractors; so will Electrical Contractors Association, 55 Catherine Place, SW1.

Radio, Electrical and TV Retailers' Association, 100 St Martins Lane, WC2N 4BD will suggest expert firms for appliance repairs.

Manufacturers are usually very ready to advise on problems and often have good free booklets. Monthly magazines like *Do It Yourself*, *Practical Householder* and *Homemaker* not only have helpful articles but run enquiry departments. *Handyman Which?* publishes comparative test reports on tools and materials. It is available to subscribers to *Which?* (Consumers' Association, 14 Buckingham Street, London WC2).

In addition, there are trade associations through which you can obtain advice on the choice and correct use of materials. Here are some useful addresses:

Asbestos Cement Manufacturers' Association, 602 Castle Lane West, Bournemouth, BH8 9UF.

Brick Advisory Service, 26 Store Street, London WC1E 7BT.

British Wood Preserving Association, 62 Oxford Street, London W1N 9WD.

Cement & Concrete Association, 52 Grosvenor Gardens, London SW1.

Chipboard Promotion Association, 7a Church Street, Esher, Surrey.

Electrical Association for Women, 25 Fouberts Place, London W1V 2AL.

National Council of Building Material Producers, 26 Store Street, London WC1E 7BT.

Steel Window Association, 26 Store Street, London WC1E 7BT.

Tile Advisory Service, 1 Brook House, Bushey Heath, Herts.

Timber Research Association, 26 Store Street, London WC1E 7BT.

If you do not find what you want here, try your nearest Building Centre. The London one is at 26 Store Street, London WC1E 7BT. A visit is more likely to get results than a written enquiry.

Many big cities have such centres, where you can see displays of fittings, materials and equipment, and obtain sheaves of brochures. Those in London, Cambridge, Bristol and Manchester have very good bookshops that sell do-it-yourself books.

The Department of the Environment and the Building Research Establishment, which has a paint division, both publish numerous leaflets on specific subjects obtainable (for a charge) from HMSO, 49 High Holborn, London WC1V 6HB. These cover such subjects as condensation, electric circuits, and the painting of difficult materials.

Metrication

Volume

Paint and similar things are now sold by the litre (l) or millilitre (ml). 1ml is one thousandth of a litre; 1cl (centilitre) is one hundredth of a litre.

Common sizes are:

$\frac{1}{4}$ litre (250 millilitres)	about $\frac{1}{2}$ pint
$\frac{1}{2}$ litre (5 ml)	about 1 pint
1 litre	about $1\frac{3}{4}$ pints
$2\frac{1}{2}$ litres	about $\frac{1}{2}$ gallon
5 litres	about 1 gallon

Weight

Dry materials are sold in kilograms (kg) or grams (g) which are one-thousandth of a kg.

1kg = about $2\frac{1}{4}$ lb.
$\frac{1}{2}$ kg = about 1 lb.

Length

Wood and boards are now measured in metres (m) and millimetres (mm). 1mm is one-thousandth of a metre; 1cm (centimetre) is one-hundredth of a metre.

Standard lengths of softwood boards go from 1.8m up to 6.3m (that is, 1m 800mm; 6m 300mm).
Standard widths are 75–150mm.
Standard thicknesses are 16–38mm.

Standard sizes for posts, rails, etc. are 25 × 25 or 38 or 50mm.

Tool sizes are mostly metric now and so are nail sizes, but so far screws are still being measured in inches.

Glass and tiles are measured in mm.

1mm = about $\frac{1}{25}$ in.
1cm = about $\frac{2}{5}$ in.
1m = about 3ft 3in.

A steel rule or steel tape with both millimetres and inches on it is a necessity now.

1
Plumbing

Typical water supply system

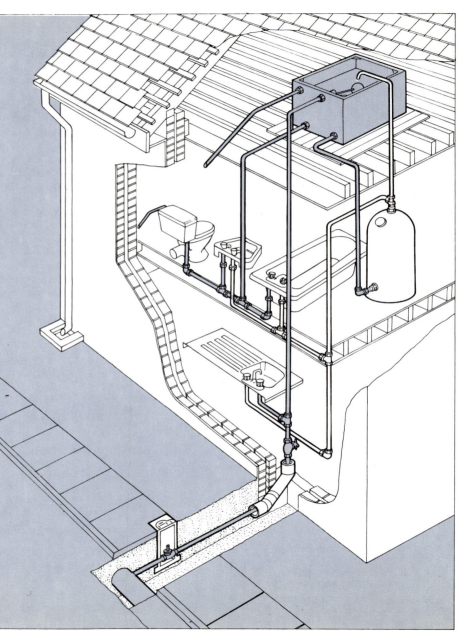

The cold water supply

Whose responsibility?

The water authority is liable only for the public supply running beneath the road and its responsibility ends at the stopcock through which the water enters your service pipe under the ground. This stopcock, usually in a small pit below the pavement but possibly in your garden or cellar, may need a special water authority key to turn it off and on. The water authority is also responsible for sewers, although the actual work involved in looking after them may be done by the local council.

The main service pipe

Normally this gives no trouble unless gardening operations have left it with much less than a metre of soil above, in which case frost may crack it. It ordinarily enters the house via the kitchen floor (at this stage it is usually referred to as the rising main). If it is not embedded in a solid floor but is exposed to the cold air beneath floorboards, it should have been insulated against frost when it was installed.

Turning off the main supply

You should be able to see the rising main under the kitchen sink or elsewhere and, just above floor level, there is usually a stopcock on it which can be turned by hand if the entire water supply needs to be cut off: for instance, if a pipe or tank leaks; while carrying out certain repairs; or when leaving the house vacant for a long period (insurance policies can be invalidated by failing to do this). Above the stopcock may be a drain-cock, operated by a spanner, the purpose of which is to empty the rising main, an operation rarely needed. It has a ridged nozzle so that a hosepipe can be attached.

  If you drain off the water supply, also turn off or rake out the boiler or water heaters before these run dry. When turning the water on again, be sure to turn it full

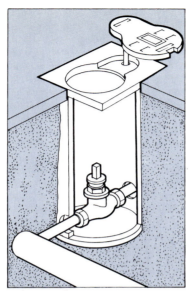

main stopcock

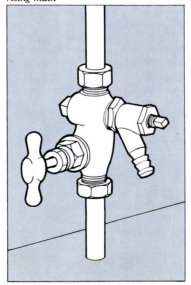

rising main

on – otherwise water pressure will be reduced, with an adverse effect on a shower, automatic washing-machine, the filling of the WC, etc. Because stopcocks can become immovable through prolonged disuse, it is a good idea to turn them off and on again occasionally and to grease the stem. (For methods of releasing stiff ones, see page 20.)

  To empty the water system it is, of course, necessary not only to cut off the incoming supply but also to turn taps on and flush the WC, in order to drain the indoor pipes.

Indirect supply

Although in some homes all cold taps and WCs are supplied straight from the rising main, today most water authorities allow only a kitchen cold tap and possibly a non-storage type of water heater (such as an Ascot) to be supplied by branch pipes from it, with all the rest of the water carried up to be stored in a cold-water tank (usually in the attic or occasionally on a flat roof, because the higher it is, the better will be the water pressure and the less likely is its noise to be heard in the house). The reason for this indirect method is largely that it cuts down any risk of contamination getting drawn back into the public supply. It also keeps water pressure constant in the house, and ensures a supply for a while even if the mains water is cut off.

  From this tank will descend at least one pipe, with branches serving bathroom taps and WC, while a second will serve any storage-type water heater (such as an electrically heated cylinder). A third may serve a shower. These pipes may have their own isolating stopcocks, usually near the tank, so that if you want to drain only the cold supply to the bathroom you can do so.

  If these pipes do not have their own stopcocks, you can cut off the supply to the cold tank by either using the main stopcock under the sink or tying up the arm of the floating ball in the tank, which will close its intake pipe.

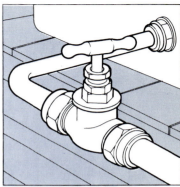

stopcock on pipe from cold tank

tying up ball float

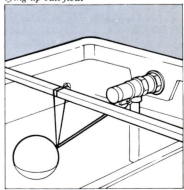

Tools and materials

Undoing connections

The hardest part of plumbing repairs is often getting things undone. With prolonged disuse, screw-threads are apt to seize up, particularly if rust, hard-water scale or paint have worsened matters. Tapping, or pouring boiling water over them, may help. Paint stripper can be used, or a blow-lamp if adjacent surfaces are protected with wet cloths.

Choosing the right tools is essential. Spanners must be exactly the right size for the job, and must grip without slipping. The wrong tools can spoil the shape of nuts, maul and distort pipes, and damage chromium. These pages show the choice available, and which to use for which job.

To help with really stubborn cases, there are dismantling lubricants in cans or aerosols. After applying one of these, give a tightening-up movement to crack any rust or scale before attempting to undo the part. If this does not suffice, give another application and allow it to soak in for a few minutes.

If all else fails, a hacksaw blade may cut through a bolt.

Reassembly

When reassembling things like taps and waste-traps, grease the screw-threads with Vaseline to keep them movable in future.

Where water pipes are concerned, the usual method was to apply a special compound and hemp to the screw-thread before assembling it. This seal does not harden, so that the joint can be unscrewed at a future date if need arises. A newer alternative involving less mess is to wind round the screw-thread a fine tape made of PTFE. This makes an absolute seal but easily comes away if the joint has to be unscrewed later (apply the tape in the same direction as the screw-thread). Plastic joints, though needing no sealing, have screw-threads which tend to jam if not turned carefully: do not force them.

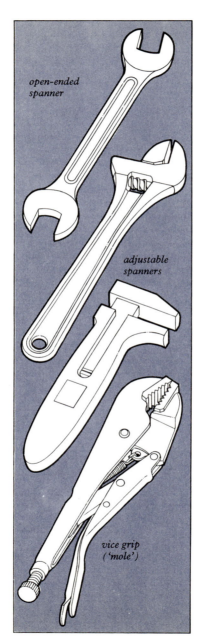

open-ended spanner

adjustable spanners

vice grip ('mole')

Tools and materials

Spanners

Nuts and other components need spanners to fasten and unfasten them. Because nuts come in a variety of sizes, some spanners have adjustable jaws. They are sometimes referred to as wrenches.

The commonest fixed-jaw spanners are open-ended. Ring spanners, which exert more force and can be used in more confined spaces, are sometimes useful for plumbing jobs. Some spanners have a ring at one end and an open end at the other.

Unfortunately, several systems of nut sizes are in use in Britain, and often they are not clearly marked. The only way out of this dilemma is to take the nut to the tool shop (or motor accessory shop) when you go to buy a spanner. Do not buy spanners in large sets containing many sizes you will never need. You may find it helpful to have duplicates – one to hold and the other to turn. Over-long (and over-thick) spanners can be a nuisance in confined spaces, although the longer the spanner, the more force you can exert on it.

Although there are many patent adjustable spanners, the simple crescent-jawed or square-jawed type remains the best for most purposes. A thumb-screw moves one of the jaws until the right size is reached – up to 20–30mm, depending which size you buy.

To hold pipes and other circular things, you may need a pipe wrench. A Stillson is a common type, and is made in a range of sizes. Also useful is a vicegrip, like a pair of large pliers that can be locked.

Pliers

Pliers have square jaws to grip most things, a curved portion to hold pipes or nuts, and a cutting portion with which to sever wires. (Some have another wire cutter too – a small groove on the outside.) 175cm (7in) pliers are popular size, smaller ones will be more convenient in confined spaces. Thin jaws are often handier, too. Long-nosed pliers will often be needed.

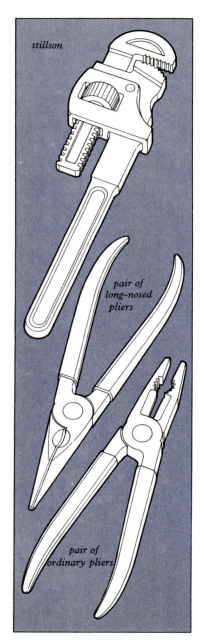

stillson

pair of long-nosed pliers

pair of ordinary pliers

Tools and materials

Fillers for gaps and cracks

Epoxy putty
Strong, hard, smooth, heatproof. White (can be painted). Usable for cracks in pipes, basins, etc. See page 25.

Plastic steel
Epoxy plus steel particles. Very strong, hard, smooth, heatproof. Fine for metal pipes.

Silicone rubber
Resilient, strong, smooth. White or coloured; shiny. Best choice for gaps around baths and sinks. Can even be applied under water.

Vinyl adhesive
Specifically for cracks in things like plastic gutters and rainwater pipes.

Non-setting mastics or sealants
Are usable for joints which may one day need to be opened up again, but mainly for filling gaps subject to some movement. Plastic-based ones are white or grey; bitumen-based ones, for outdoor use, are usually black.

Often **waterproof building tapes** are a good solution to cracks and gaps. Some have a top surface of aluminium foil. (More about these on pages 25 and 39, Water-pipes and Gutters.)

Some tap types

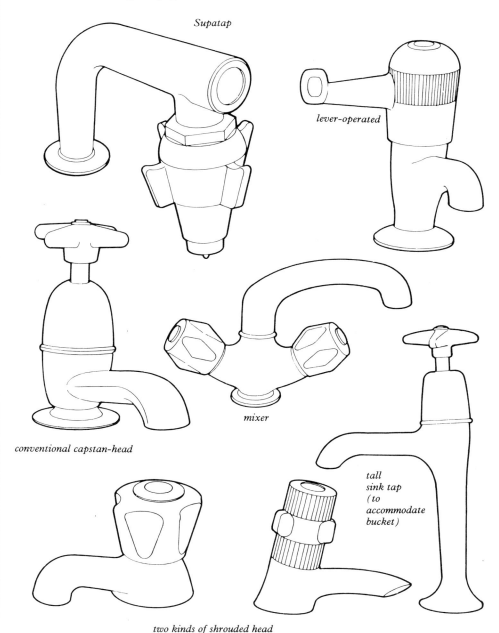

Supatap

lever-operated

conventional capstan-head

mixer

tall sink tap (to accommodate bucket)

two kinds of shrouded head

Taps – dripping

Note Many water authorities will repair dripping taps without charge

Cause
Washer deteriorated

Tools and materials needed
Washer: 20mm (¾in) for most bath and mixer taps, 15mm (½in) for most sink and basin taps
Small spanners
Probably large spanner and dismantling lubricant (see page 20)

Method
1 Turn off water supply as follows: for a kitchen cold tap, use main stopcock; for any other, see page 19. You do not need to empty the hot-water cylinder when re-washing a hot tap because the water comes only from the top of the hot cylinder. Turn taps on to drain the pipes.

2 With the tap in the full-on position, remove handle by loosening the screw at the side and then tapping the handle upwards. If it will not move, raise the tap cover and jam a piece of wood or large spanner below, then screw the handle down and lever it off with the wood. Hot water may help to get the tap cover unscrewed by hand. If the tap handle is impossible to shift, it can be left in place if a spanner can be slid beneath the raised tap cover.

3 If a large spanner has to be used to unscrew the tap cover, use sticky-tape or a cloth to protect the metal. Not all tap covers are screwed on clockwise.

4 Having removed the tap cover, use a spanner to undo the large hexagonal nut (hold the body of the tap firmly). Remove the top gear.

5 Pull out the jumper (a brass stem): there may be a split-pin to remove first. Undo its nut. Replace the old washer with a new one of the same size.

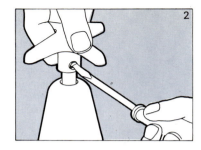

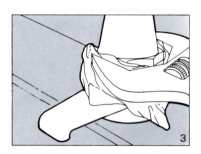

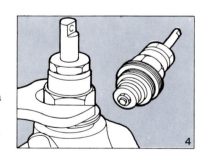

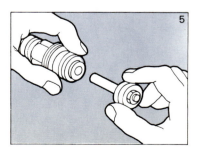

Taps – dripping

6 If even dismantling lubricant will not shift the nut, a new jumper complete with washer may have to be bought.

7 When reassembling the tap, grease all screw-threads (Vaseline or even lard will do) and do not over-tighten. Take particular care with plastic ones as it is easy to jam the screw-thread.

8 If dripping still continues, this means the valve seating below the jumper needs replacement. A plastic seating and jumper unit can be bought, to force down on to the existing seating. Screw the tap handle hard down.

Shrouded heads
To remove the combined cover and handle, prise out the plastic disc on the top to reveal a screw. When this has been unscrewed, a firm tug will pull the head off. Some have no screw but simply pull off; others have a screw at the side.

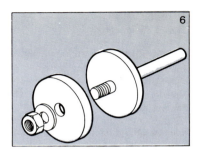

removing a shrouded head

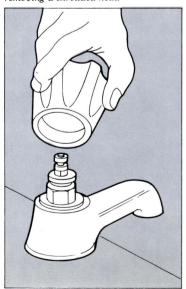

Taps, swivel – dripping

Cause
Washer deteriorated

Tools and materials needed
Long-nosed pliers
Washer(s)

Method
1 There is no need to turn off the water supply. Unscrew or lever up the shroud at the foot of the nozzle.
2 Use the pliers to take out the circular copper clip and slide it up the nozzle.
3 With the nozzle removed, replace the washer (or washers) with new ones. Wet the foot of the nozzle before replacing it.

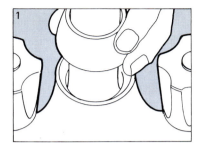

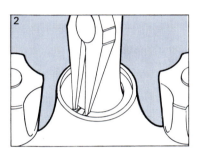

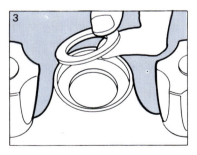

Supataps – dripping

Cause
Washer deteriorated

Tools and materials needed
Spanner
Washer-jumper

Method
1 There is no need to turn off the water supply. Partly open the nozzle and unscrew the nut with the spanner. Detach the nozzle by unscrewing (the water will stop flowing).
2 Press nozzle on table-top to free the anti-splash device that is at the bottom of it, or push it out with a pencil.
3 Lever the washer-jumper out from the anti-splash device, brush the latter clean, and put in a new washer-jumper.
4 Put the anti-splash back in the nozzle and screw the nozzle back in place until almost closed (water will start to flow again). Tighten nut, then close the nozzle completely.

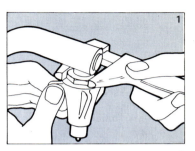

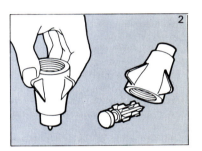

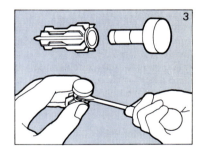

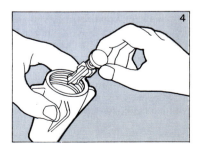

Taps and stopcock – leaking or stiff

Symptoms
Leaking round the spindle
Tap or stopcock hard to turn on and off

Cause
Any of these may be due to deteriorated gland packing, or loosened gland-nut. (Gland packing in a tap may be affected by water forced back into the tap by a hose connected to it; or by detergent having entered from the top and washed the grease out of it.)

Tools and materials needed
Small screwdriver
Spanners
New gland packing (i.e., string or wool, and Vaseline)

Method
1 With the tap fully on, remove the handle and tap cover (see page 22).
2 Turn the gland nut (at top) clockwise half a turn, using a spanner. Test, and if this has not ended the leak, try another half-turn.
3 If this does not solve the problem, remove the nut completely, pick out the packing and replace it with new string smothered in Vaseline. Wind this round two or three times (do not over-stuff) and press it down with the screwdriver tip.
4 Reassemble the tap.

Symptom
Stopcock leaking. (This should be repaired without delay, for fear of dry rot.)

Method
Repair in the same way as a tap – see page 22. In the case of a main stopcock, the water authority should be asked to cut off the water supply to the house – or to do the repair for you.

Note Some modern taps have a plastic O-ring on the spindle instead of gland packing; this is easier to replace than string.

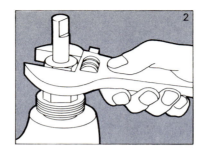

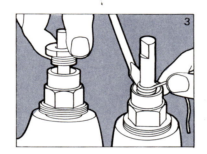

Taps – replacement

Tools and materials needed
New tap
Washers (see below)
Spanner
PTFE tape

Method
1 Having drained the water supply (see page 19) remove the old tap by undoing the pipe and the nut below the basin. (If these are so awkwardly situated that an ordinary spanner will not reach, obtain a special basin wrench as shown in the diagram.)
2 If the new tap is to go on a ceramic basin, place the washers above and below the ceramic before securing the tail of the tap with a nut.
3 If it is to go on an enamel or steel sink or bath, it will need one ordinary and one 'top hat' washer, the latter to be fitted below the enamel rim as shown; secure tail with nut.
4 Before securing the nut which joins the pipe to the tail of the tap, wind PTFE tape clockwise round the screw-thread of the tail.

Note You can get extra-long tap connectors, which are easier to install. These plastic connectors need no sealing round the thread.

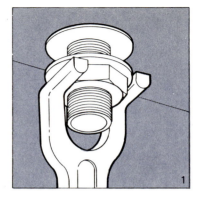

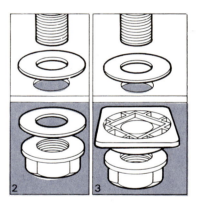

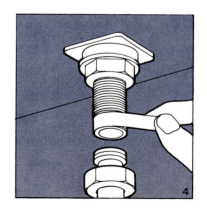

Water-pipes – leaking

Cause
Crack, insecure joint

Tools and materials needed for cracks
Hammer (for lead pipe)
File or abrasive paper
Special tape or filler: see below
Spanners (for insecure joints)

Methods for cracks
The following are a choice of temporary measures, to use after draining the system (see page 19). Usually a cracked pipe will need to be replaced in due course.

1 **First aid** A small crack can be sealed for a short period by rubbing soap into it and tying a rag round; or by tying with a rag saturated in paint, Vaseline or something greasy; or by securing with plastic sticky-tape or a waterproof sticking plaster. Many of the fillers and tapes mentioned on page 21 will seal a crack. If the split is in a lead pipe, it can be hammered together. Restore water supply gently and at low pressure.

2 **Epoxy resin** This type of adhesive filler gives a more durable repair. Rub the surface with a file or abrasive paper, mix the resin in accordance with the maker's instructions, and smear over and round the crack. Bind a glassfibre or other bandage round and smear more resin over this. Leave to set before restoring water supply.

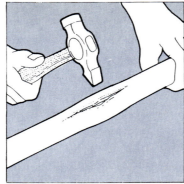

first aid: hammering a lead pipe

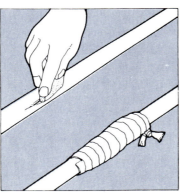

first aid: filling with soap, bandaging

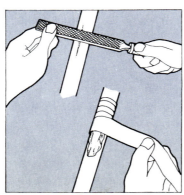

epoxy resin repair

Water-pipes – leaking

3 **Epoxy putty** is an even simpler alternative. This comes in two parts which need to be blended together by repeatedly rolling, breaking up and kneading before it is applied. It can then be smoothed down by wiping with a damp cloth smeared with soap. A very shiny surface is left if the putty is covered with polythene (from a plastic bag) while setting.

4 **Plastic steel** is specifically for pipes: epoxy plus steel particles.

5 **Pipe seal** is a special two-part tape, giving a permanent seal. Wind the impregnated tape round the pipe (or hose), then the reinforcing tape, and then more of the impregnated tape.

Notes
1 Neglected leaks can start rot in woodwork.
2 If water leaks into electrical fittings, there is a danger of shock: turn off electricity main switch.

Method for joints
Compression joints (those assembled with nuts). Using spanner, tighten nut from which water is leaking. Grip the body of the fitting or the pipe very firmly (with spanner, vicegrip, etc.) to avoid loosening other nuts.

Soldered joints Treat like leaking pipe, or call in plumber to replace joint.

Water-pipes – frozen

Tools and materials needed
Boiling kettle and cloths; or hair drier, fan heater, blow-lamp (not on plastic pipes) etc.; or hot water bottles; or candles. Salt (for waste-pipes)

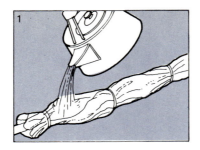

Methods
1 Apply warmth to the frozen pipe wherever it is accessible; the heat will travel along the pipe to other parts. Start near tap, turned fully on, or near other outlet from which melting ice can escape. (If in doubt which part of the pipe is frozen, turn each tap on in turn and observe which ones run dry.)
2 In the case of waste-pipes and WC, put salt in to thaw the ice, followed by boiling water.
  Watch out for possible leaks as the ice thaws.

Water-pipes – noise – poor flow

Symptoms
Hammering or other noise
Poor flow

Cause
Faulty gland packing in a tap (see page 24); or faulty ball-float (see page 27). In the case of poor flow, a stop-cock may not be fully turned on. Some noises are due to pipes being inadequately secured to joists or walls.

Water-pipes – air-lock

Symptom
Erratic flow from tap, often with hissing and spluttering

Cause
Air-lock (trapped bubbles)

Tools and materials needed
Hosepipe and tap-connectors or clips

Methods
1 Connect one end of the hose to a cold tap served direct from the rising main (usually, only the kitchen tap) and the other to the affected tap. If the kitchen cold tap is inconvenient, connect to any other tap. Turn both full on, and the pressure of the water should blow the bubble out. It helps to turn on other taps that are on the pipe-run that has the blockage. If it is a hot pipe, it helps to stop up the overflow pipe that goes from the hot system into the cold tank. (If air-locks occur often, a plumber can fit an air-release lock.)

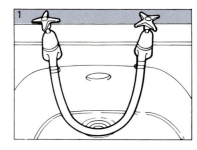

2 Alternatively (unless the air-lock is in a hot pipe), push a piece of hosepipe into the outlet of the cold tank and, with all cold taps turned on (except the kitchen one), blow down the hose.
3 If neither of these methods will do, drain the water system (see page 19). Then close each tap two-thirds before turning the water-supply on again. When all are flowing gently and equally, turn each tap on a little more (lowest ones first), then a little more again. Turn off equally gradually and in the same order.

Water tanks – rust

Symptom
Rust traces (in the water supply or in the tank)

Cause
Corrosion of the galvanized steel tank

Tools and materials needed
Wire brush or abrasive paper
Goggles (or eye protectors, sold by opticians, to clip on spectacles) if using wire brush
Rust-killer and steel wool
Possibly epoxy filler or plastic steel
Odourless bituminous paint or zinc paint (these are suitable only for cold-water tanks, not hot)
Paintbrush (or soft broom)
File (if zinc paint is used)
Brush cleaner or white spirit

Method
1 Drain tank (see page 19).
2 Dry it, and remove all loose rust with a wire brush or abrasive paper (wear goggles if you use a wire brush).
3 Coat with rust-killer, rubbed on with a steel wool pad and left to soak for 10 minutes.
4 If the tank is deeply pitted, apply epoxy resin (see page 25).
5 Apply two coats of bituminous paint. Alternatively, use zinc paint. The latter involves filing bare some patches of the steel, dabbing the paint on and, after 10 minutes, painting it liberally everywhere. After $\frac{3}{4}$ hour, splash water lightly all over. Restore the water supply when the paint is dry, about 1 to 2 days.
An alternative is to line the tank with a flexible plastic liner.

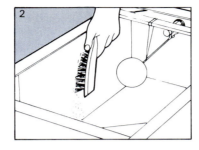

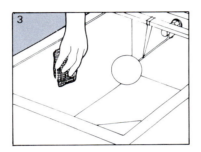

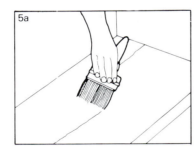

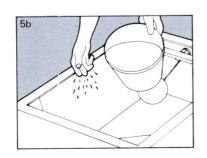

Water tanks – overflowing

Cause
Faulty ball-float; or deteriorated ball-valve washer

Tools and materials needed
Possibly new ball float (plastic)
Pliers
Possibly new washer, screwdriver, Vaseline, and steel wool for cleaning

Method
1 Unscrew the float and shake it: if you hear water inside, it is leaking and needs replacement. To keep water from entering the tank or cistern until the new float is screwed on to the arm, tie the arm to a piece of wood lying across the top of the tank as shown left. Alternatively, enlarge the hole, shake the water out and – after screwing the float back – tie a plastic bag round it. If there is no leak, adjust the float arm: bending it down (gently) will shut off the water supply at a lower level. (A few have an adjustable nut on them.)
2 If overflow continues, cut off water supply (see page 19) and use pliers to remove the split pin holding the arm. If the pin looks worn, replace it. In the case of a WC cistern, you may have to remove the flush-handle first in order to get at it. Coax the arm out of the slot in the valve.
3 Unscrew the cap at the end, if there is one, and slide the plug out with the help of a screwdriver if necessary (there is a slot in it for this purpose). Tapping gently round the end with a hammer may help.
4 Unscrew the two halves (you may need to apply hot water or a release lubricant) and put a new washer in. (Rather than damage the plug while forcing it apart, it may be better to pick out the old washer with a penknife and squeeze the new one in.)
5 Clean and grease the plug and the inside of the valve, before re-assembly.

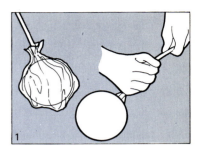

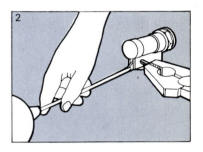

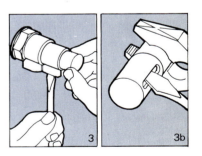

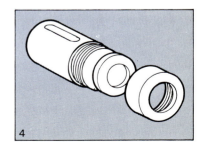

Water tanks – slow refilling

Cause
Possibly, scale or grit in ball valve

Tools and materials needed
Pliers
Screwdriver
Vaseline

Method
As for rewashering ball-valve (see page 27).
If this is ineffective, a plumber may need to
put in a different type of valve. Some old-
fashioned ball valves can be replaced
completely with diaphragm valves, less
likely to go wrong.

Cisterns – noisy refilling

Materials needed
Silencer pipe (a short tube with a screw
end)
Vaseline

Method
1 Tie up the arm of the ball-float (see page
  27) and flush the WC to empty the cistern.
2 Grease the screw-thread and screw it into
  the hole that is beneath the ball-valve.
3 Release the arm.

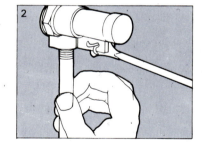

Cisterns – noisy flushing

Cause
Old valve

Tools and materials needed
Float valve
Spanner
Scissors

Method
1 Having drained off the water (see page 19)
  and unscrewed the old valve, pass the
  connector of the new valve through the
  hole in the cistern, in order to hand-screw
  it to the inlet pipe (with washer between
  pipe and cistern). Check that the polythene
  tube of the valve is hanging straight down,
  then tighten the nut with a spanner.
2 Snap the rod of the float on to the float-
  arm. (The rod length can be adjusted after
  the water is restored, and any surplus cut
  off.)
3 Restore the water supply and check
  whether the valve operates properly when
  the WC is flushed. (If, after repeated
  operation, it fails to close properly, the
  cause is likely to be debris from the cold-
  water system. Open up the valve and clean
  it out.)

Other noise-reduction methods
Put rubber sleeves round screws fixing WC
cistern to wall. Put resilient draught strips
round and under WC door, and panel both
sides of it.
Box in waste-pipes with thick chipboard,
sealing all gaps, but leave space between
boards and pipes. Pipes should not fit too
tight in clips or holes; nor be so loose that
they vibrate against hard surfaces (use
resilient padding, polyurethane foam, or
something similar to cushion them).

Cisterns – failure to flush

Cause
Water level too low; or deteriorated valve in the siphon

Tools and materials needed
Spanner
Siphon flap-valve

Method
1 If the water level is more than 10mm below the overflow pipe, detach and bend the arm of the ball-float up a little.
2 If the water level is correct, tie up the float arm (see page 27) and flush the cistern to empty it.
3 Disconnect the flush pipe, unscrew the nut below the cistern, and lift out the siphon.
4 Replace old valve as shown.
5 Reassemble and release float arm.

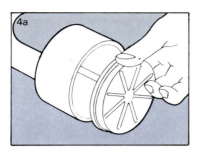

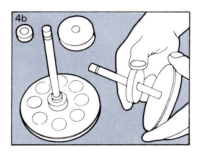

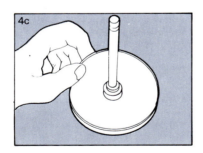

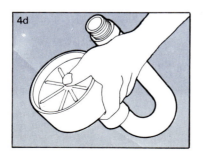

Cisterns – condensation

Symptom
Drips from exterior of cistern

Cause
Condensation due to inadequate ventilation in the room

Tools and materials needed
Anti-condensation paint, paintbrush and brush cleaner (or white spirit)
Or foam strips (as sold for condensation that runs down windows and on to sills)
Or polystyrene (as sold for lining walls)
Sandpaper, scissors and waterproof adhesive

Method
1 **Anti-condensation paint** (This is suitable only for iron cisterns, not ceramic ones. It is often sold by ship's chandlers.) Paint on in the usual way, then finish with a stippling action. It has a textured look because it contains cork granules. After a day, it can be painted (its natural colour is off-white).
2 **Foam strips** Stick round bottom of cistern to catch the drips.
3 **Polystyrene** Drain cistern (see page 28) and after glasspapering inside it, glue polystyrene on. Dry overnight.

Symptom
Overflowing – see Water tanks, page 27
Slow refilling see Water tanks, page 28

WCs – uneven flush

Cause
Obstruction; or tilting of pan

Tools and materials needed
Spirit level
Screwdriver
Dryish mortar made with 1 part cement to
3 of sand (or buy ready-mixed mortar)
Grommets

Method
1 Check that nothing is obstructing water
inlet or rim (a mirror will help you see
under this).
2 If the spirit level shows the pan is not level,
loosen the screws fixing it to the floor.
Remove those on the side that is to be
raised.
3 Raise this side with scraps of board until
the spirit level shows the pan is straight.
4 Pack mortar below. Replace screws loosely,
with grommets (sleeves) round them, and
screw tight three hours later.
Warning Do not attempt this if pan is
rigidly fixed to an iron waste-pipe; you
might crack the joint.

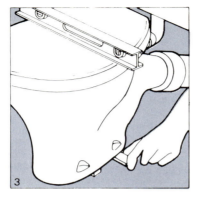
3

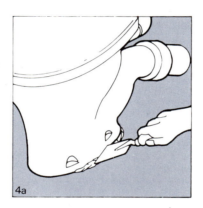
4a

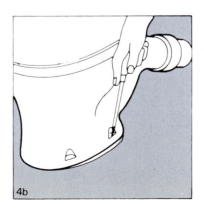
4b

WCs – seat and lid replacement

Tools and materials needed
New seat and lid set (tell retailer the size of
the bolt holes in the WC, and their distance
apart)
Pliers
Screwdriver

Method
Undo nuts fastening old seat to WC, and
remove it. Follow manufacturer's
instructions for assembling and fixing new
set. Do not over-tighten wing nuts.

Note A break in a plastic seat or its hinge
can be repaired with epoxy putty (see page
21).

Bathroom fitments

Cracks, chips
(in basins, baths, sinks, WCs)

Temporary repairs can be made with
waterproof sticky tape on the underside of
cracks; or cracks and chips can be
permanently filled with epoxy putty (see
page 21). Allow time for drying before
running any water on. Use bath enamel to
paint the repair (several coats). Some bath
manufacturers supply their own filler for
repairs.

Gaps at wall
(round basins, baths and sinks)

As a hard-setting filler would probably
crack, use a flexible and waterproof bath
sealant, preferably made of silicone rubber.
Clean off all soap traces first, and squeeze
the sealant well inside the gap.
Alternatively, to fix outside the gap, use
special plastic tape supplied with contact
adhesive, or press-in sealing strip (see page
21).

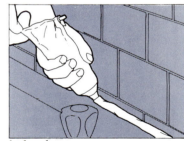
bath sealant

press-in sealant strip

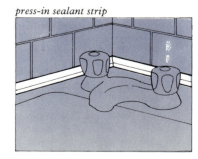

Showers

Symptom
Continual dripping

Cause
Deteriorated O-ring (a kind of washer)

Tools and materials needed
Screwdriver
O-ring

Method
1 Having turned the water supply off (see page 19) unscrew the flexible hose.
2 Unscrew the shower-diverter.
3 Beneath this is a connector with a slot: holding screwdriver in this slot as shown, push the connector off.
4 Pull out the mechanism from the body of the tap, slide off the old O-ring, and put a new one on.

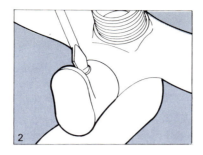

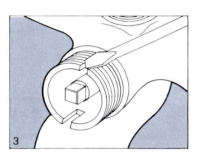

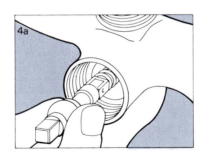

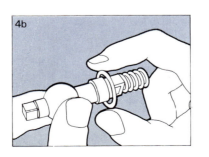

Water heaters – electric immersion

Symptom
Water too hot or cold; slow reheating

Cause
Thermostat wrongly set
Possibly, scale from hard water

Tool needed
Screwdriver

Method
1 Turn off electricity.
2 Undo screw holding the cover.
3 Prise off cap covering the regulator.
4 Use screwdriver to turn screw that regulates the setting; 60°C (140°F) is normal in hard water areas, 70°C (160°F) in soft water areas.

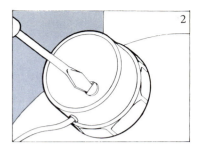

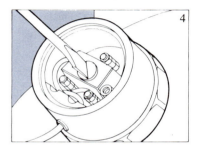

Showers

Symptom
Reduced flow

Cause
Scale in shower-head or mixing valve

Tools and materials needed
Descaling powder or liquid
Or vinegar

Method
Unscrew affected parts and soak for an hour in 2¼ litres (4pt) of nearly boiling water to which the powder has been slowly added, or in descaling liquid or vinegar.

Water heaters – gas

Symptom
Pilot flame inadequate

Cause
Wrongly adjusted, or clogged

Tools and materials needed
Small screwdriver
Primus pricker

Method
1 Remove front of casing (pull off control knobs first if necessary).
2 Use screwdriver to adjust the screw on the pilot while it is alight.
3 If the jet is blocked, turn pilot off and use the pricker to clear it.
4 Reassemble and, after lighting pilot again, wait 5 minutes before using the water heater.

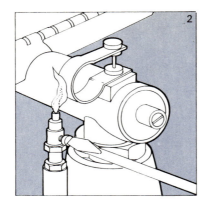

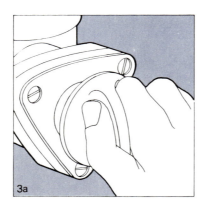

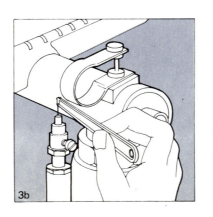

Water heaters – gas

Symptoms
Poor flow or not hot enough; drips from spout

Cause
Possibly, scale from hard water (removing this in a *large* heater is a job for a gas serviceman)

Tools and materials needed
Rubber tube
Plastic funnel
Descaling fluid

Method
1 Turn off water and gas supplies.
2 Disconnect water inlet, and in its place attach about a metre of rubber tube.
3 With end of tube held above top of heater, pour fluid into it through the funnel – very slowly to prevent it foaming back.

Symptom
Burners fail to light when water is turned on, or light feebly

Cause
Possibly, metal strip by pilot light is not functioning; or gas filter needs cleaning; or gas pressure needs increasing
(see also Pilot flame, left)

Tools and materials needed
Screwdriver
Possibly new bimetallic strip

Methods
Check that control knob or lever is fully in 'on' position; and that gas main tap is fully on.
Metal strip
1 Press strip down with screwdriver tip (with pilot light on). If burners now light, this means strip is at fault. Turn off gas and put

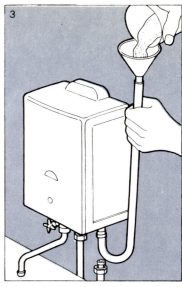

pouring descaling fluid into heater

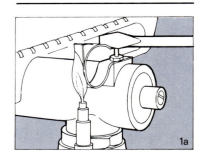

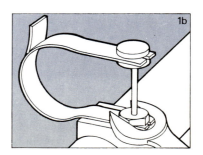

in a replacement (loosen the nut to free the old one from the pin).

2 Alternatively, if strip is not at fault, press pilot fitment gently nearer to the strip so that its flame can make contact.

3 If the pin holding the metal strip is too tight, turn off gas and work it up and down repeatedly to loosen it.

Filter

4 Look for this on gas inlet pipe. Undo cover; take out and clean filter; reassemble.

Pressure

5 Look for governor on gas inlet pipe. Remove cover and adjust screw till pressure increases. One cause of low pressure can be rust flakes in old pipes: the gas authority can vacuum these out (no charge).

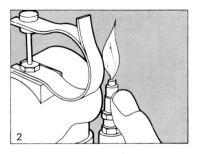

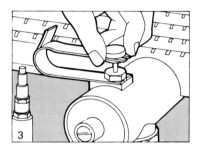

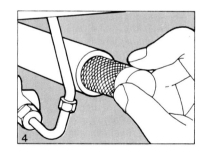

Symptom
Lights with sudden roar

Cause
Build-up of gas before pilot lights the burners

Tool needed
Screwdriver

Method
With gas off, gently bend pilot fitment nearer to burners.

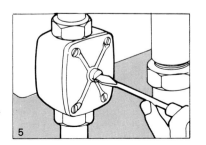

Water-heaters – gas

Symptom
Smell of burnt gas when in use (this is dangerous)

Cause
Blockage in ventilation duct (or running a small unflued heater for more than 10 minutes)

Method
1 Hold a match under the cowl while the water heater is on. If this goes out, it may be because the burnt gas is coming back into the room.

2 Check from inside and outdoors whether duct is blocked by, for instance, a bird's nest which you can remove. If this is not the cause, call gas service.

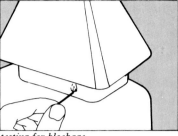

testing for blockage

Symptom
Leaks from joints

Cause
Loose nuts

Tools and materials needed
Spanner
Vaseline
Possibly washers

Method
Grease and then tighten (but not too much), replacing any worn washer.

Note Any room containing a small unflued heater should be well ventilated. One simple method is to drill a row of holes through both a window-frame and a door to ensure a current of air, but window-ventilators or airbricks are neater.

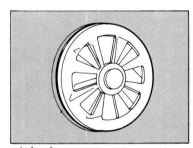

window fan

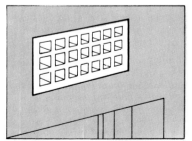

air brick

Boilers – descaling

Symptom
Poor flow of hot water; sometimes with gurgling, hissing and knocking sounds

Cause
Scale from hard water (you can check whether this is the cause by seeing whether your kettle, too, has scale in it)
Descaling pipes or a hot water cylinder is a job for a plumber; descaling a boiler can be done by an amateur

Tools and materials needed
Method A
Boiler descaler (6kg for an average boiler)
Hired descaling unit
Hose and clips
Method B
Boiler and central heating kit
Method C
Liquid descaler for central heating systems

Method A
1 Turn off or rake boiler out. Drain hot water system (see page 19)
2 Check that the drain cock on the boiler has no leak (if it has, the washer must be renewed before proceeding further) and connect tube of descaling unit to it.
3 Pour into the unit 1kg (2¼lb) of the descaling powder and add 1 litre (2pt) of nearly boiling water; shake to mix.
4 With the unit standing 2 metres (6ft) above the floor, turn its tap on so that the fluid flows into the boiler via the drain cock.
5 Repeat this operation until 3kg (6½lb) of the descaling powder has been used and then wait 3 hours or until the liquid is motionless and silent (it gurgles while it is active).
6 Repeat steps 3 to 5 with the remainder of the powder.
7 Restore the water supply and flush the system clean for fifteen minutes by means of a hose connected to the drain cock and leading to an outdoor gulley.

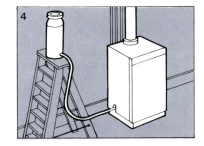

Boilers – descaling

8 Turn off the drain cock and disconnect the hose. After refilling and lighting the boiler, run hot water from all taps until the water is free of all colour.

Method B
1 Switch off boiler and turn off water supply to boiler tank. Drain the boiler, wearing rubber gloves.
2 Pour descaling liquid into the tank, then turn the water supply on again.
3 Switch boiler on again and run at low temperature for 3 hours.
4 Turn off water supply, drain boiler.
5 Dissolve neutralising crystals in hot water and add to tank.
6 Turn on boiler for 15 minutes, drain, flush with clean water.
7 Close drain cock, fill with water.

Method C (central heating system)
1 Drain the hot water system.
2 Fully open radiator valves and vents.
3 Add the acid to the header tank while it refills with water (allow 4½ litres [1 gallon] of special descaler for every 90 litres [20 gallons] of water in system and for every 5 years of its age).
4 With temperature control at 65°C (150°F) leave to circulate for 2 days. (Repeat steps 3–4 if system needs more than 4½ litres (1 gallon) acid per 90 litres (20 gallons) water.) Alternatively, in summer, circulate cold for a week, then turn heat on for 6 hours only.
5 Drain and rinse three times as follows: tie-up ball-valve in header tank and drain the hot solution out with radiator vents closed, release ball-valve and refill with cold water, then re-open vents. Drain, then bail out any water left at the bottom of the tank.
6 Refill.

Note When the system is clean, corrosion inhibitor can be put in to prevent future trouble.

Waste-pipes – blockage

Symptom
Water unable to flow away, or flowing sluggishly

Cause
Blockage from solid matter and/or grease. Avoidable causes include: flushing disposable paper goods down WC; allowing hairs from shampooing to go into washbasin drain; pouring fat or cooking oil down sink drain; failing to add a sink-strainer to drain-hole or to use sink-tidy for food scraps.
For frozen waste-pipes, see Waterpipes, page 26.
For main drains, see page 38.

Tools and materials needed
Alternatives, depending on method chosen, include: washing soda, caustic soda, spirits of salts, flex or steel-tape drain-clearer; plunger: large spanner and bucket; hosepipe and clip or connector. Some waste-hole grids can be removed with a screwdriver.

Alternative methods
1 **Boiling water and washing soda** may clear minor blockages.
2 **Caustic soda** (sodium hydroxide) can be used in jelly form to dissolve material blocking WCs. First, bail out as much of the trapped water as you can. Empty the tin into a gallon of cold water, stir well, and pour slowly in. Leave for an hour before flushing it away. Repeat if the first application was ineffective. Caustic soda crystals are less powerful but adequate for many sink and basin blockages (and to clean overflows made smelly by a build-up of soap–alternatively, use a wire-handled bottle brush). Having bailed out what water you can, put 3 tablespoons of crystals in the wastepipe, followed by a cup of hot water. Flush away after half an hour. Be careful not to splash: caustic can damage textiles, paintwork or aluminium and will injure skin or eyes. If an accident occurs,

Waste-pipes – blockage

flush the injury with plain or (better still) salt water. Any eye injury should be reported to a doctor immediately. Store the tin out of children's reach. Other chemical solutions for this problem are fluid sold for caravan WCs; or a product sold for cleaning masonry.

3 **A flex drain-cleaner** is similar to curtain flex (from which a drain-clearer can in fact by improvised). It consists of about a metre of spiral wire with one end opened up like a corkscrew. This end is gently inserted into the blocked wastepipe or overflow of a basin or sink, while turning the handle at the other end in a clockwise direction. When the obstruction has been shifted, by pulling more than pushing, continue turning while withdrawing the wire. It may help to use the flex from the other end of the waste-pipe if this is accessible nearby outside the house.

4 **A steel-tape drain-clearer**, also for use in sink or basin waste-pipes, is much longer and can usually penetrate right through to the outside end of the waste-pipe. By pushing and then pulling, while at the same time twisting the tape by means of a grip provided at the other end, the conical front of the tape can be worked past the blockage and then used to free it. Finally, wind it back. A more powerful flexible drain-clearer is obtainable from hire shops.

5 **A plunger** consists of a rubber or flexible plastic cup on a handle. Larger sizes have a disc above to spread the pressure on the cup and to prevent it from turning inside out. More expensive pump-type plungers are also sold. A plunger can also be improvised: tie a plastic bag round the head of a mop, or round a sponge tied to a stick; or screw the rubber disc from a power sander to a stick. When using a plunger in a sink, bath or basin, first stop up the overflow with a wet cloth so that air cannot escape this way. Fill the basin, and place the plunger over the waste hole. Pump vigorously up and down. When the pool of water disappears, the blockage has

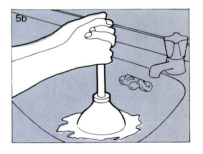

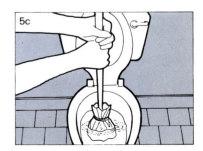

Waste-pipes – blockage

been shifted. In the case of a WC, a long-handled plunger is needed and the action needs to be swift and energetic, but not so vigorous as to crack the pan.

6 **A large spanner** may be needed if it proves necessary to open up the trap in the waste-pipe below the sink, basin or bath. (See advice about spanners and release-lubricants on page 20.) Before starting, place a bucket below the trap to catch water (or a tray in the case of a bath trap) and put the plug in the waste-hole.

U-traps

a Undo the screw-plug at the bottom of the trap using a screwdriver between the lugs, or else using a spanner. Hold the trap steady with the other hand, otherwise you may pull it out of shape. In the case of a bath, you may need an angled bath wrench to reach it.

b If the obstruction does not then clear itself unaided, use a flex drain-clearer inserted from below, directing it into first one half then the other half of the U.

c When screwing the plug back, grease the screw-thread first and do not over-tighten. If its washer is worn, replace it.

Alternatively (where there is no plug at the bottom):

a Use a spanner, if necessary, to undo the two nuts that join the tops of the U to the pipes.

b Use flex to clear the U and the ends of the pipes.

c Screw back carefully – forcing can ruin the screw-thread.

undoing U-trap

clearing U-trap

Waste-pipes – blockage

Bottle-traps

Unscrew the bottom half by hand and poke a flex up into the waste-pipe in both directions.

7 **A short piece of hose-pipe** fastened to a tap can be used to force water into a sink, basin or bath waste-pipe in the hope of clearing the obstruction, but it will be necessary to plug the waste-hole and the overflow with wet cloths as previously described.

A device which may help when all else fails contains a cartridge of liquid gas which gives a burst of pressure. It can be hired.

Note Do not leave cleared waste-pipes unflushed, for it is necessary to keep their traps filled with water in order to seal off smells from the drains outside. Occasionally, siphonage keeps on emptying a trap: remedying this is a job for a plumber.

If the blockage is beyond the WC or wastepipe, see Drains, page 38.

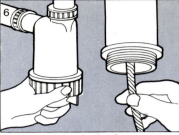

undoing and clearing bottle trap

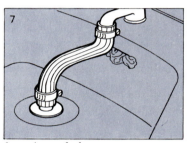

hose-pipe method

Waste-pipes – leaks

Cause
Crack
Or non-watertight joint

Tools and materials needed
Cracks: see Water pipes
Joints:
Large spanner,
New washer(s),
Vaseline
Or waterproof building tape and non-hardening sealant

Method
1 **Cracks** See water pipes.
2 **Joints** Disconnect (see page 20) and replace old washer(s) with new. Grease screw-threads before reconnecting.
3 **WC joint** Rake out old filling, bind tape round outlet from WC and thrust hard into socket, push sealant in, cover with more tape.

Typical drainage system

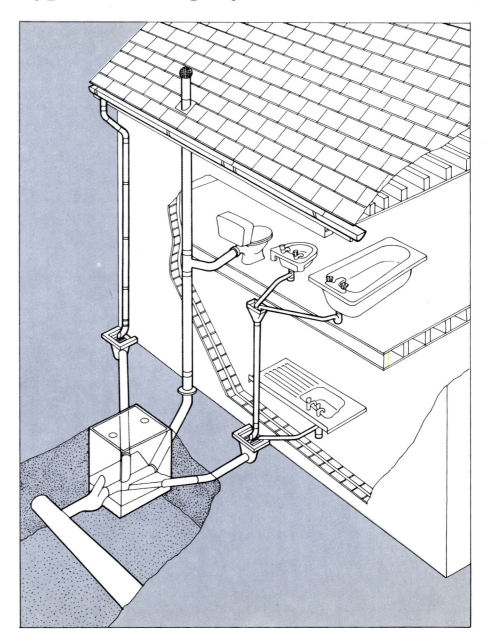

Gulleys and drains

Symptom
Overflowing gulleys

Cause
Blockage

Tools and materials needed
Trowel
Washing or caustic soda
Possibly a new grid
Rubber gloves

Method
1 If the blockage is in the gulley itself, remove and clean the grid, and dig any leaves or debris out. Use washing or caustic soda as described on page 35, probing with a stick to help loosen the blockage. Silt at the bottom is best removed by hand.
2 If the blockage is in the drainpipe below the gulley, use hired drain-clearing rods (see right).
3 If iron grid is broken, replace with new plastic one.

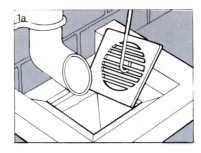

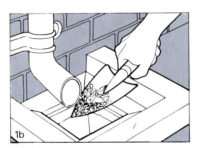

Gulleys and drains

Symptom
Water in drains unable to flow away, or flowing sluggishly. Inspection pit in garden overflowing.

Cause
Blockage

Tools and materials needed
Drain-clearing rods and attachments (from hire shops)

Method
1 Remove cover from pit nearest house. If it has water in it, blockage is further on. Remove cover from next pit if there is one; if this has water, blockage is still further.
   If pits are dry, blockage is within one of the waste pipes coming from the house to the first pit. To identify which one, send water down each in turn and observe which lot fails to reach the pit. (Some houses have only one waste-pipe.)
2 Working from an empty pit, screw the flexible rods together one at a time while pushing them up the pipe that has the blockage. Turn clockwise only, otherwise you will unscrew the rods. The first rod should have the corkscrew attachment on it to loosen the blockage; the rubber plunger is attached instead when pulling is needed.
3 If you have to work from a full pit, bail this out to locate the outgoing pipe (centre bottom of the side nearest the road) and try to clear this with the plunger. Failing that you will have to take the stopper out of the 'rodding eye' (a small opening above the outgoing pipe) and rod through this. Sometimes it is this stopper that has fallen and is causing the blockage.

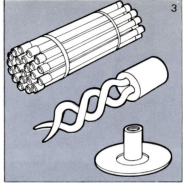

drain rods and attachments

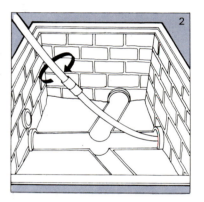

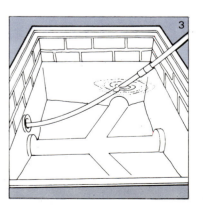

Gulleys and drains

Note Specialized drain-clearing firms using powered rods or pressure jets can be located through the Yellow Pages: ask for a quotation before going ahead, and a guarantee. Alternatively, ask the environmental health department of the local council whether they will clear the drain or recommend a firm. A few councils provide this service free. Jet-operated drain clearers can be hired.

Where a drain serves more than one home its clearance will, if it was laid before October 1937, be treated as a public responsibility though the council may bill the householders concerned for doing it. Shared drains laid since then are the responsibility of the householders concerned. If you call in a drain-clearing firm without prior agreement with others, you will be liable to pay the bill.

Gutters and rainwater pipes

Symptom
Overflows and leaks, stains on wall

Cause
Blockage in gutter; cracks or holes due to rust

Tools and materials needed
Ladder
Stiff brush
Long stick
For cracks: waterproof building tape and scissors
Or waterproof filler

Method
Choose a dry day, without frost.
1 Brush leaves and debris out of gutters.
2 If possible, remove any angled pieces joining gutters to downpipes and clear these out; clear any hopper heads.
3 Thrust a long stick (with rag tied to its end), or a hose, down pipes. Have a pan ready at the bottom to catch debris.
4 Many cracks can be mended by binding waterproof tape round the pipe or along a gutter (buy an adequate width for the cracks, keep the tape in a fairly warm place, and do not stretch it as you apply it). Clean the suface well first, and overlap the strips of tape (which should extend beyond the actual crack.) Or use a waterproof filler (see page 25) or else a non-hardening mastic.
5 If a small part of a gutter has broken off, tie cardboard over the gap, grease the inside and coat thickly with waterproof epoxy filler (let it overlap the gutter by 50mm or more). When it is hard, remove the cardboard.
6 If mesh guards are missing from tops of downpipes, these should be put on. Gutters can be kept free of leaves by clipping on a special gutter grid made of rotproof mesh.

Note There may be gutters not visible from below: between two pitched roofs, or around flat roofs.

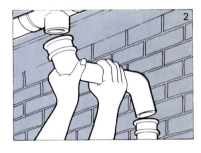

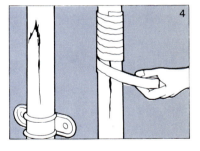

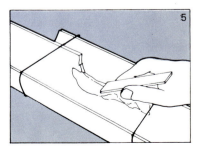

Gutters and rainwater pipes

Symptom
Gutters leaking at joints

Cause
Deteriorated sealing material

Tools and materials needed
Ladder
For plastic gutters:
Petrol
New rubber seal
For iron gutters:
Spanner
Screwdriver
Putty
Putty knife
Possibly, hacksaw, bolt, washer and nut

Method
For plastic gutters
(Long sections are usually connected by a short one, called a union, which is lined with sponge rubber seal.)
1 To replace the seal, unclip the union and take it to the retailer to get a new seal of the right size.
2 Use petrol or lighter fluid to clear off all remains of the old seal.
3 Insert the new one and squeeze the gutter ends in order to slip the union back on again.
For iron gutters
(Long sections usually overlap one another and are fastened with a bolt and sealed with putty.)
1 Using a spanner and screwdriver (and possibly dismantling lubricant), remove the bolt.
2 If it is immovable, saw the nut off.
3 Prise the two sections apart and scrape out old putty.
4 Spread new putty in, press the two sections together.
5 Secure with bolt, washer and nut. Alternatively, treat as for cracks, see page 25.

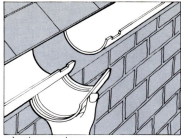
plastic guttering

iron guttering

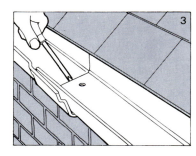

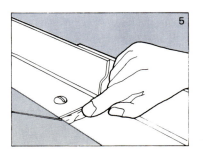

Gutters and rainwater pipes

Symptom
Gutters dripping from middle

Cause
Sagging

Tools and materials needed
Ladder
Bradawl
Screwdriver
Hammer
Large nails

Method
1 Clear out debris that has accumulated in the sag.
2 Lift the sagging section to the correct level again. The gutter should slope slightly but steadily down to the downpipe at one end.
3 It may be necessary to refasten its brackets again in a new position: no problem if they are simply screwed to the fascia board behind the gutter but many are secured to the ends of rafters, inaccessible behind the tiles. Very long nails hammered into the fascia board may give sufficient extra support to prevent the sag recurring, or wedges between gutter and brackets.

Note If the sag is more than about 2cm (1in), rectifying it may break the seal between sections, which will then need renewing as described left.

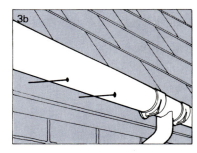

Gutters and rainwater pipes

Symptom
Rainwater pipes leaking from cracks

Cause
Pipe not held securely; or pressure of debris that has entered through unsealed joints

Tools and materials needed
Ladder
Claw hammer
Punch
Epoxy putty
Waterproof mastic filler

Method
1 To secure a wall bracket that has loosened, remove each section of pipe below the bracket. This is done by unfastening the brackets holding them, using a claw hammer and a piece of wood to lever their nails out as shown. Repair any cracks as on page 21, or buy new section if necessary.
2 To fasten the wall brackets anew, use a hammer and punch to make large holes in the mortar, fill with wedges of wood and hammer in the nails through the brackets.
3 Clean any debris out of the pipes before replacing each section, fill the joints with mastic. Do not seal the joints with hard filler – you may want to disconnect them in the future.

Replacement
Because of their light weight and easily clipped on fastenings, plastic rainwater goods are easy to install. Lifting down the heavy old iron ones is the effortful part of the job.

75mm (3in) gutter is usual for sheds, porches and garages; 100mm (4in) for houses. Pipes are 50 or 65mm (2 or 2½in). Only the larger ones are available in black or white as well as grey.

Assemble all the parts on the ground first. Then mark where the gutter brackets are to go on the fascia board (which runs along the top of the wall) and screw these on.

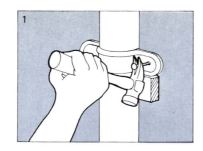

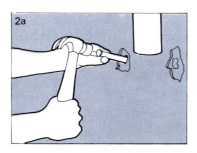

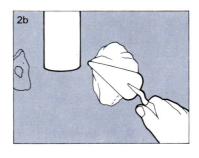

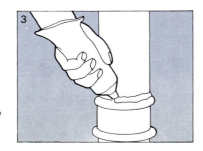

Gutters and rainwater pipes

They should be not more than 1m (3ft) apart; leave no join in the gutter unsupported by a nearby bracket. Some houses have no fascia boards, so special brackets are needed to screw to the ends of rafters under the tiles. The gutter should slope slightly towards its outlet, so nail on a piece of string as a guide before fastening the brackets.

To attach the end outlet to a length of gutter Clip the notched end of the gutter inside the outlet, secured by a gutter strap.
To join two lengths of gutter Clip the end of one inside the other, secured by a gutter strap.
To shorten a length of gutter Use a fine-tooth saw to cut, and a file to make new notches at the sawn end if necessary.
To close the end of a gutter Clip on a stop, secured by a gutter-strap.
To attach a pipe to a gutter outlet An angled pipe, called an offset, is usually needed, pushed on to the end of the outlet. The pipe is then pushed into the offset. If more than one length of pipe is needed to reach the ground, the lengths are simply pushed together.
To secure a pipe to wall Clips encircling the pipe are screwed to plates behind it and these are nailed to the wall. Usually each 3 m (3yd) pipe needs 3 clips.
To terminate the pipe Unless connected to an underground drain, the pipe needs a 'shoe' at the bottom, directing the rainwater into a gulley or water butt.

In addition to these components, there are various clip-on bends and angles for special situations. Downpipe adaptors and waterbutts can be used to conserve rainwater.

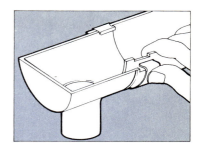

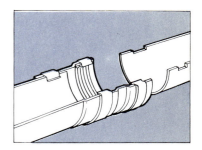

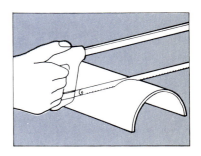

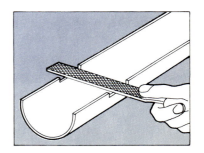

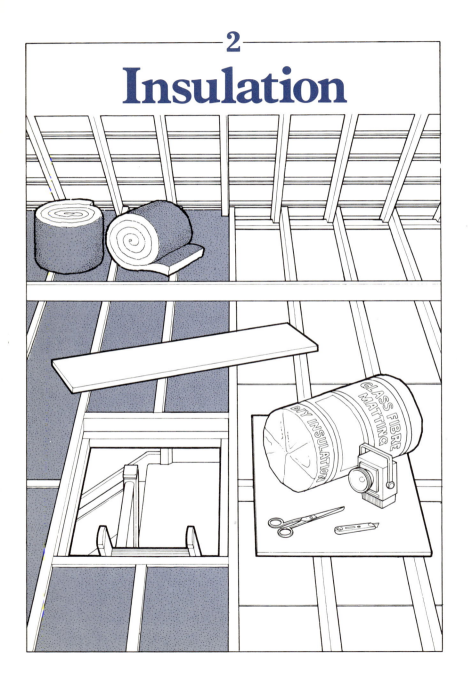

2
Insulation

Why insulate?

Home insulation is meant to serve three purposes.

Economy To reduce fuel consumption while letting you enjoy as warm a house and as much hot water as you are used to, or to increase temperatures while using no more fuel. At a time of rising fuel prices, the object may be to avoid ever-increasing bills rather than actually to save money.

Comfort To make the house a pleasanter place to live in by, for example, eliminating chilly spots near sitting-room windows or making a bedroom tolerable for homework or sewing in the winter.

Frost protection By preventing cold-water pipes and tanks from freezing, damage and inconvenience can be forestalled.

Insulation for economy and comfort consists of keeping heat in and cold air out. The latter is first a matter of common sense: not leaving windows open for longer than the short period necessary for ventilation, for example. But keeping heat in calls for special measures. These all depend on the facts that, as long as the house is warmer than the surrounding air, it will lose heat, but that the rate at which it does so can be slowed down.

Walls	35%
Roof	25%
Floor	15%
Draughts	15%
Windows	10%

Lagging the hot-water tank
Draughtproofing
Insulating the roofspace
Cavity-wall insulation
Double glazing

Losses and savings

This is the way in which the heat losses from an ordinary house are often shown as percentages of the total. The figures are very rough, and they are affected by the

Why insulate?

type of house: a bungalow will lose a greater proportion of its heat through its roof than will a three-storey house, for example, and a mid-terrace house will lose less through its walls than will a detached one.

The figures might make it look as though the first area to insulate is that where the most heat is lost – the walls. This is where the cost of insulation comes in. While some measures are quite cheap and simple, wall insulation can be the reverse. But draughts, by which much less heat is lost, are controlled easily and economically.

A common way of showing the value of a particular type of insulation is to work out how soon its cost will be paid for by fuel savings. This list shows the order. The range is from weeks to many years, but figures would be misleading. For example, unless your heating is thermostatically controlled, and you adjust it with care, you may find that you live in greater comfort when your intention was to make the insulation pay for itself in fuel savings. Similarly, if you have heating downstairs only and you insulate the roof, the bedrooms will become warmer, the rooms below will remain at the same temperature, and the total reduction of heat loss will not be as much as you expected because the warmer bedrooms will lose heat more quickly than they used to. The house will have been improved, but you may not get the economies you planned.

So when insulating with economy and comfort in mind, start by taking the simplest and cheapest steps first for maximum return on your money; do not count on getting exactly the benefits you hoped for; and take into consideration the type of house you live in and the way in which you use it. And realise also that doubling the amount of insulation does not make it twice as effective.

Before starting any major work, enquire of your local authority about the availability of grants for insulation. Find

Why insulate?

out too whether heat-saving measures, such as double glazing, may be incorporated into other home improvements for which you are applying for grant aid.

Simple measures

Draughts Begin by ensuring that all doors and windows fit well (pages 97, 110), draught-stripping them where necessary (page 97). Block all gaps round windows and door-frames, and below skirtings, etc. (page 107). If there are gaps between floorboards, either fill them (page 162) or cover the boards with building paper, brown paper, or several layers of newspaper, or, if the boards are very uneven, with hardboard (page 163).

Sash windows are difficult to draughtproof. Consider sealing them up for the winter with masking tape, but leaving some means of ventilating the room. In the spring, the tape can be removed and the paintwork should be undamaged. Use masking tape also for little-used doors, windows, etc.

Much cold air can enter through the letterbox. Fit a purpose-made draught excluder (either an inner flap or one made of bristles) or improve the fit (page 101).

Block unused keyholes with flexible filler, screwed-up paper, or sticky tape. (Tape on only one side allows the key to be used from the other.)

Windows Curtains and blinds can be almost as effective as double glazing – during the hours they are closed, that is. So think about installing pleated-paper or roller blinds in addition to curtains.

Improve the effectiveness of curtains in the following ways. Ensure that they fit closely at the top of the reveal, moving the curtain rail up if necessary or adjusting the position of the tape.

The bottoms should touch the cill but not sag. If the curtains are not inside a reveal and there is not a box-pelmet, rest a well-

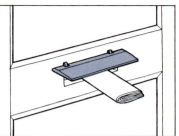

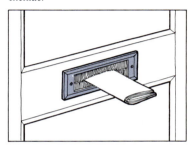

two types of purpose-made draught-excluder

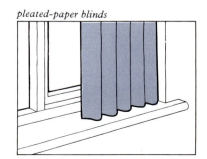

pleated-paper blinds

Why insulate?

fitted strip of card or hardboard on the curtain-rail brackets to hinder the flow of air behind them.

Heavy curtains are more effective than thin ones, and lined ones than unlined ones. With some curtain tapes and rail systems, it is easy to add a loose lining.

Radiators Some of the heat from a radiator (up to a quarter) is lost into the wall behind it. Reduce this by as much as half by fitting a reflector – most worth doing for a single-panel radiator on an outside wall. There are proprietary materials for the purpose, most consisting of foil with an adhesive or foam backing. Application may involve detaching the radiator from the wall temporarily – not to be lightly undertaken. Much cheaper though less durable (and harder to fit unless first stuck to cardboard, etc.) is aluminium cooking foil. Any foil should be kept clean.

Heat which rises straight to the ceiling from a radiator is largely wasted, though it helps to heat a room above. A radiator shelf will throw more of it into the room. Either by a purpose-made shelf or fit a home-made one. It should touch the wall at the back and be at least 4cm (2in) above the top of the radiator.

If curtains overhang a radiator, much of its heat will be lost through the window. Adjust the position of the curtain rail or fit a shelf.

Doors When covering a panelled or ledge-and-brace door with hardboard, fill the space between with insulating material such as foam polystyrene or leftovers from insulating the roofspace. This will improve a chilly corner in the kitchen or hall.

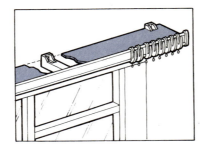

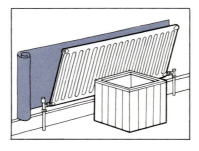

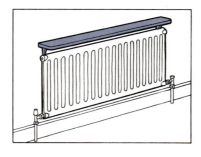

Insulation – the roofspace

Before insulating the roofspace
Fill any gaps between the roofspace and the room below, even small ones, and repair any leaks in the roof itself.

Measure the distance between the joists so that you will know if there is a width of material to fit them.

Measure the total area to estimate how much material to buy.

Old wiring should be replaced – and certainly not covered with insulation in case it overheats. Any junction boxes, etc., should be secure.

Check that the insulation material you are considering comes in packages which will go through the opening to the roofspace.

If there is a cold-water tank, or any pipes which will not be covered by the insulation, they are easier to deal with beforehand if you plan to use insulation which will cover the joists (see pages 46–7).

Just before starting work
Provide a good light in the roofspace. An inspection lamp, or even a reading-lamp on an extension lead, is much better than a torch. Do not use candles.

On no account tread on the ceiling between the joints. If you are reasonably agile, it is easier to stand on two joists than to work from a short board between them. But if the ceiling is springy (get someone in the room below to look for signs of movement while you are above), a board across the joints will help to distribute your weight and avoid the risk of damage to the plaster.

Which material?
To give the degree of insulation which is now regarded as minimum, a thickness of 10cm (4in) is needed for most materials (more for some loose fill). You can have more if you want – and you may have to have more if you are adding to existing but inadequate insulation and cannot buy thin mat. (In this case, there is no objection to mixing materials.)

Insulation – the roofspace

Mat Mineral or glass-fibre mat is easy to lay, usually needing only to be unrolled. The commonest width fits between the joists of a modern house. If joists are more or less than 40cm (16in) apart, and you cannot get material in a suitable width, you can lay mat across them (which will require more material) or use loose fill.

These fibres can be slightly irritating to the skin – more to some people than to most. If you think you may be affected, wear loose rubber or plastic gloves, overalls, and perhaps a dust mask, and avoid working when your skin is sweaty. Do not wear woolly clothes, to which fibres may cling, and rinse exposed skin before you wash with soap after work.

Loose fill This is of two types: mineral or cellulose fibre, which is usually professionally applied by blowing it into place; and particles, most commonly of expanded vermiculite (a mineral) for laying yourself. They are particularly useful for insulating irregular areas or where the joists are not at a standard spacing, and for 'topping up'. Some loose fill has to be laid to a depth which will bury most joists.

Sheet materials, such as fibreboard and foam plastics, can be laid between or over joists. They will need cutting and tailoring, and whole boards may not go through the trapdoor.

Insulation – the roofspace

Whatever insulation you use
Open the packages only inside the roofspace.

Do not put any insulation underneath the cold-water tank, as doing so will make it more likely to freeze.

As the roofspace will be colder after insulation, the tank and any uncovered pipes must be lagged (page 47).

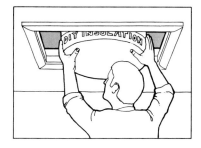

If you have to cover the tops of the joists, it will be more difficult to see where to tread when getting around afterwards – perhaps in an emergency – and to use the roofspace for storage.

Insulate the top of the trapdoor: nail, glue, or tie a piece of mat or rigid material to it. Draught-strip the trap-door if it is not a tight fit.

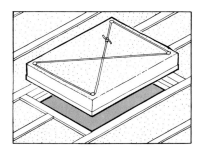

The roofspace must not be left unventilated. There are probably slits or holes in the eaves: these should not be blocked with insulation. If there are not, check for other means of ventilation – in darkness, look for chinks of light. If there is none, some means of ventilation will have to be provided by a builder.

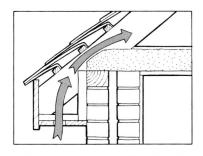

Tools and materials needed
Insulating material
Knife or large scissors
Board at least 30cm (2ft) long

Method – mat
1 Unroll the mat between the joists, starting at the eaves. Push it over the top of the outside wall (using a piece of wood if necessary) but do not block any ventilation openings.
2 Cut the mat to length at the opposite side of the roofspace. Cut at a slant if necessary to allow ventilation.

Insulation – the roofspace

3 When a length falls short, start again at the opposite side and cut the new length square to fit against the end of the previous one.
4 If you have to lay the mat at right angles to the joists, ensure that the edges of the lengths are close together. Slit the outermost ones where necessary to fit them round the ends of the rafters, etc. With mineral-fibre mat, when laying is completed, cut the mat along the centres of the joists and tuck it down between them.

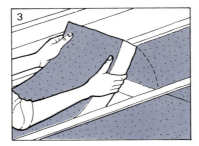

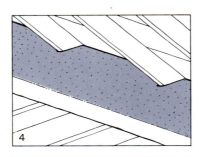

Method – loose fill

1 Check that material will not block (or be lost in) ventilation spaces at the eaves.
2 Pour out the material to an even depth. As most joists are 10cm (4in) deep, and this is a common thickness for insulation, the material can be levelled by pulling a board across the tops of pairs of joists.

Insulation – tanks and pipes

Cold-water tanks

Fibre mat A cold-water tank can be insulated with the mat you are using for the roofspace. Turn it up the sides, then tie offcuts in position with string or wire. If the tank has no lid, make one of hardboard, etc., and tie insulation to it, making holes for any pipes. If an overflow pipe overhangs the tank, fit a cheap plastic funnel into a hole in the lid to catch drips.
Sheet insulation A box and loose lid can be made of foam polystyrene sheet at least 2cm (1in) thick, held in place with a wire, string, or adhesive tape. Ready-cut kits are available in this and other materials.

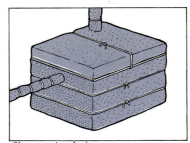

fibre mat insulation

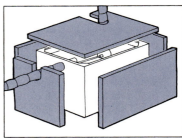

sheet insulation

Insulation – tanks and pipes

Pipes – hot and cold

All exposed pipes in the roofspace should be insulated, including overflows. So should any other cold-water pipes in danger of freezing or on which you want to stop condensation.

   As far as possible, all hot-water pipes should be insulated; this includes central-heating pipes where you do not want them to give off heat.

Bandage Special felt or fibre pipe-wrapping or strips of leftover roofspace mat are wound diagonally round the piping. Secure the ends with string or tape, and avoid flattening the material. Wrap taps, etc., as far as the handle, too.

Plastic foam Slit tubes of several types of foam are manufactured in sizes to fit the commonest diameters of pipe. Some makes have to be tied or taped in place, others are made with adhesive-tape or 'zip-fastener' seams. Tailor the insulation at joints, etc., using the manufacturers' adhesive or tape as recommended.

Hot-water cylinders

Insulation-filled jackets are made for standard sizes of hot-water cylinder. Measure the diameter of the tank and the height to the top of the dome.

   When fitting, avoid crushing the material, make sure there are no gaps between the sections, and leave the cap and cable of the immersion heater uncovered.

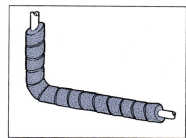
bandage insulation

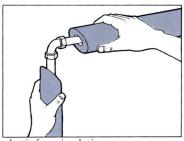
plastic foam insulation

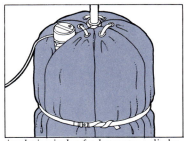
insulating jacket for hot water cylinder

Insulation – double glazing

There is a bewildering choice of ways of double glazing – *Handyman Which?* identified about 15 – apart from those which are professionally made and installed. (The last include complete replacement windows – which are advisable if the existing window frames are in poor condition – and, usually, 'sealed units', which are factory-made glass sandwiches for fitting into ordinary frames.)

Fixed systems cannot be opened once they are in place. Some can be taken down (during the summer, for example) with greater or lesser difficulty; others cannot be removed without spoiling them and probably the appearance of the window frame.

Hinged and **sliding systems** can be opened for ventilation, etc.; most can be taken down and replaced as well.

   There is also a choice of glazing materials, though some systems have to be used with one or another.

Glass weathers well and is clear, but it is breakable, heavy, and not cheap.

Rigid plastics are generally cheaper, lighter, and less fragile. But, depending on the particular plastic, they are less clear and become worse with age, are more easily scratched, may attract dust, and some can burn.

Insulation – double glazing

Plastic films – stiff but flexible – are the cheapest of all. They have the characteristics of rigid plastics in greater or lesser measure. Unless they are very successfully put up, reflective ripples can be unsightly.

Provided that you will get the best air-gap for insulation – about 2cm ($\frac{3}{4}$in) – choosing among the various systems and materials and the brands of each depends on the following.

Cost, taking into account both glazing and framing or fixing materials. The range is from plastic film applied with adhesive tape up to complete units assembled (even measured for) by the manufacturer for you to put up yourself.

Convenience of ventilation, removal, and replacement.

Appearance including neatness and compatibility with the window frame.

Ease of assembly: the simplest systems tend to be the easiest to install, but study the literature carefully. The type of window frame may limit your choice, as do metal frames.

Availability: as well as those sold over the counter, many systems and materials are obtainable by mail order.

In spite of its limitations, flexible plastic film is relatively so cheap that you could use it to try the effect of double glazing before going in for a more elaborate system. For maximum cheapness, use it with double-sided adhesive tape; there is a dearer, foam-based tape which may be better for less even surfaces. Other fixing methods include self-adhesive touch-and-close tape, and plastic channels which snap together to grip the film: these are dearer still but allow the film to be removed and replaced.

Insulation – double glazing

Tools and materials needed
Plastic film
Double-sided adhesive tape
Rule
Scissors
Craft knife
Length of broomstick
Scrap cardboard

Method
1 Clean glass and frame thoroughly. Remove loose paint; if repainting, leave for a week to harden.
2 Cut film 3cm (2½in) larger than the inside measurement of the frame.
3 Lightly fit tape round frame, leaving 2cm (1in) between edge of tape and edge of frame. When position is correct, rub backing paper firmly.
4 Roll film on length of broomstick.
5 Pull backing off top strip of tape. Apply end of film.
6 Gradually pull off backing paper at sides, applying film as you go and stretching it sideways as well as possible. When film is satisfactorily positioned, rub it down firmly on to the tape.
7 With craft knife, trim edge of film up to the tape, using cardboard under the film to protect paintwork.

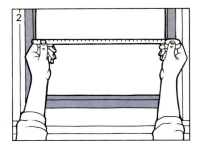

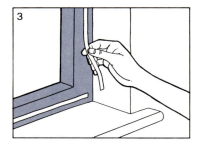

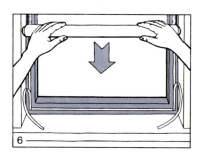

Insulation – further measures

The following measures are very unlikely to be quickly repaid in fuel savings, though they should give increased comfort. They are well worth bearing in mind when you are planning redecoration, refurnishing, or alterations to the house.

Floors
Wall-to-wall floor coverings help to conserve heat, especially if they consist of carpet with thick underlay. Some vinyl floor coverings are better insulators than others (study makers' literature), and cork is also an insulator.

A very cold floor can be improved by laying insulation board topped by chipboard, but expert advice is needed about precautions against condensation if the floor is of stone or concrete and about laying the chipboard. Inward-opening doors will have to be trimmed and possibly some fittings repositioned.

An alternative way of insulating a wooden floor is to take up the boards and either rest rigid insulating material on battens nailed to the joists, or drape fibre mat across the joists.

Walls
Where walls have got to be resurfaced, they can be covered with insulating material, fixed between rotproofed battens and with plasterboard over all. An elaborate job which involves removing and replacing joinery, etc., this is an answer where professionally-applied cavity-wall insulation cannot be used. Again, expert advice should be taken.

Be aware that damp walls, over and above all the other problems they cause, are worse insulators of heat than dry ones. Remedial measures, which may be simple (see pages 104–6) or may have to be applied by a specialist firm, should result in a warmer as well as a dryer house. Dealing with damp walls may make more elaborate measures unnecessary, and it should certainly be done before, for example, having cavity

Insulation – further measures

walls insulated or lining walls on the inside.

Extensions
A porch on an outside door will not only cut down draughts: it will serve as an airlock and reduce the amount of heat lost every time the door is opened. A conservatory or large lean-to greenhouse will positively help to warm a house by means of solar radiation.

Shutters
Indoor shutters can be used to cut the heat lost through windows. They can be made from rigid foam plastic framed in wood and hinged to the window frame concertina-fashion, or held in channels or by magnetic catches. Paint or curtain fabric can be used to decorate them.

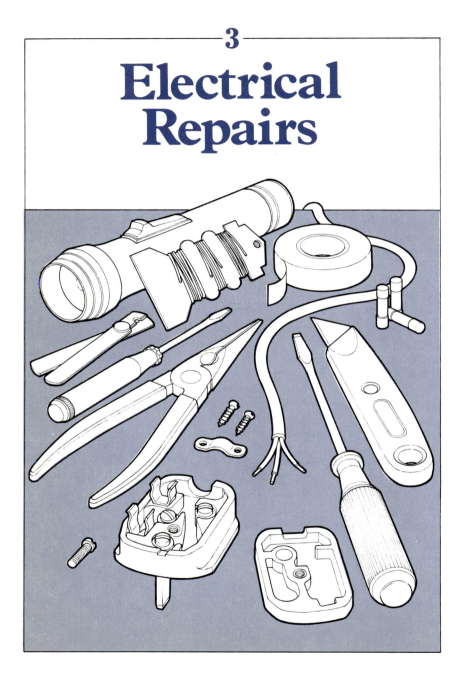

3
Electrical Repairs

Volts, amps and watts

Voltage This means the degree of force behind the supply of electricity: 240V (volts) is the normal average in Britain, slightly less in most of Northern Ireland. If you buy appliances in Europe or Amercia you need a transformer to adjust the voltage when using them here. In very cold weather when demand is high, the voltage may be slightly lowered: lights and TV become dimmer, kettles and cookers take longer to boil water. If voltage is higher than it should be, light bulbs will have short lives (tell the electricity board if this is happening: as boards have a responsibility to keep voltage steady, a fault should be only temporary).

Amperage This is the amount of electricity flowing through a circuit. Every home is likely to have several circuits of differing amperages (and therefore with cables of differing thickness), each intended for different appliances and protected by different fuses (see pages 57–8).

Wattage This is the amount of electricity consumed by an appliance per hour. If, for example, an appliance uses 5A of electricity at 240V, its wattage is 5×240 – that is, 1200W. One thousand watts is one kilowatt (kW).

A 30A circuit is capable of serving any number of sockets, but a total of more than 7200W switched on simultaneously would overload it, eventually causing the 30A main fuse to blow.

Each appliance usually carries a rating-plate which states the voltage for which it is designed and its wattage. Divide the watts by the volts and you will know its amperage (for example, $1200W \div 240V = 5A$), useful information if you are uncertain what kind of flex or plug fuse it needs.

5A (amp)	for lighting (ceiling or wall)
30A	for sockets to serve most appliances
15A or 20A	for immersion heater
45A or 60A	for cooker
probably 20A	for electric central heating system

The electricity supply

Whose responsibility?

Electricity is supplied to each home via cable ending in a sealed fusebox which only the electricity board may open: this is usually near the front door, under the stairs, or in a cellar. Near this is a meter and then a fusebox containing several circuit fuses (sometimes called a consumer unit), and from here the householder's responsibility begins.

The circuits

At the fusebox, the supply is divided among several different circuits – separate cables serve the sockets (sometimes called power points or outlets) and the ceiling or wall lights. There is likely to be more than one circuit for the sockets – for instance, one upstairs and one down, or even more in an old house. In addition, there may be a separate circuit for the cooker and another for the immersion heater (it is possible to run the latter on one of the power circuits, but because it is capable of consuming so much electricity, it normally has a cable of its own).

New and old systems in use

In modern systems, all power sockets have square holes and are 13A; anything from a small lamp to a large heater can be plugged into any of them. The main difference between 13A circuits and older installations is that 13A plugs each contain a cartridge fuse. If an appliance is faulty, this fuse will blow without affecting the rest of the circuit. An installation of this kind is called a ring circuit or ring main. But in pre-1947 systems, identifiable by the round holes of the sockets, sockets may be 2A, 5A or 15A – intended for lights,

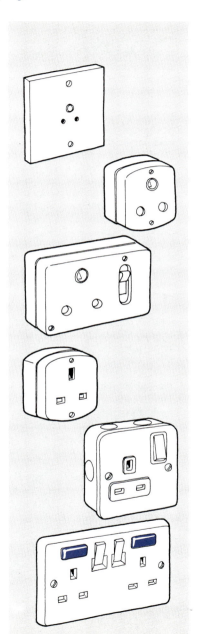

Sockets: top three will be found only in out-of-date installations. Bottom three are 13A type for fused plugs. Those available include single and double, switched and unswitched, with or without pilot lights.

The electricity supply

Simplified diagram showing main fuse box serving two 13A ring circuits (with sockets) and circuits to water heater and cooker.

The electricity supply

Simplified diagram showing main fuse
box serving two lighting circuits,
upstairs and downstairs.

The electricity supply

appliances up to 1000W, and larger
appliances, respectively. Not only is such
diversity inconvenient but any system as
old as this is likely to be a fire risk by now
and should be replaced (by an electrician).

In fact, the safety of all circuits should be
tested every ten years or so by an
electrician because the insulation on cables
can deteriorate with time.

Additional sockets can be put into any of
these circuits but this, too, is a job for an
electrician, not least because it can be
difficult for an amateur to determine
exactly what load any circuit is already
carrying, and to add another socket might
create an overload and a risk of fire.
Further, a survey carried out by
Consumers Association in 1971 showed
that one house in six had at least one socket
inadequately earthed – a potential danger
to life. In houses where there have been
many changes over the years, entire
circuits may be unsafe. For example, at one
time metal waterpipes were used as a
means of earthing: where these have been
partly replaced by plastic pipes the
earthing may have been made ineffective.

Overloading circuits

No power circuit with 13A sockets is
designed to supply more than about 7kW at
a time (see page 50 for explanation) and so
if a number of large appliances are used
simultaneously on its sockets, it may
become overloaded. The appliances that
consume most electricity are those that
produce a lot of heat (any that produce
power, refrigerate, or give light consume
very little).

Where pre-1947 systems are concerned,
each 15A socket has its own circuit and fuse
in the fusebox; although the total supply
available will probably be 12kW, each
circuit is limited to about $3\frac{1}{2}$kW. Therefore,
any attempt to run, say, two 2kW heaters
simultaneously from one socket (using an
adaptor) would create an overload and fire-
risk.

The electricity supply

Lighting circuits, new or old, cater for about $1\frac{1}{4}$kW, the equivalent of a dozen 100W bulbs. They are rarely earthed.

Turning off

The main switch, to turn off the entire supply to the house when doing repairs or leaving it empty, will be found on or near the fusebox. (Older systems which have separate fuseboxes for power, light etc. will have several main switches, one to each fusebox.)

When turning off for any length of time, or if a prolonged power cut occurs, remember that this will lead to defrosting of the refrigerator and freezer unless you keep these closed, it will inactivate any electric burglar or fire alarm as well as doorbells, it will stop the pump of the central-heating system, and it may affect greenhouse controls. Electric clocks and auto-timers will need re-setting later. Be sure also to turn off any fire, iron or kettle that is in use, because when the electricity supply is restored its heating-up may go unnoticed.

If you want to turn off the supply to one circuit only (for instance, you may want to keep the lighting circuit on while changing the fuse on a power circuit), turn off the main switch, remove the fuse of the circuit you want to work on, and turn the main switch on again. Repeat this procedure when you want to put the fuse back.

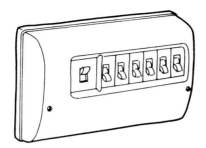

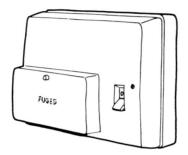

Consumer units with (top) circuit breakers and (bottom) fuses.

Tools

Pliers Although 177mm (7in) pliers are a popular size, smaller ones will be more convenient for many electrical jobs.

Although handles may be covered in insulating material, this is not an absolute protection against shock.

Wire-cutter Pliers will cut wires, but nippers specially designed for the purpose are even better, particularly if lever-assisted so that little pressure is needed; but they are not essential.

Wire-stripper This makes the stripping of insulation from wires very easy indeed.

Screwdrivers Plastic-handled ones, although safer, are not an absolute protection against shock. Those with a neon light in the handle can be used to test whether a wire or terminal is 'live' (see below) but always remember to turn off at the main switch when working. Some electrical screwdrivers have a wire-stripper in the handle. An offset (angled) screwdriver may be useful for awkwardly placed screws.

If you are prepared to pay more, you can get screwdrivers that will hold the screw securely while it is being positioned; but you can improvise a screwholder yourself by slipping a bit of rubber tube, or even Plasticine, over the tip of the screwdriver.

There are angled screwdrivers designed to get into awkward corners.

Easier to operate are ratchet screwdrivers, available in the larger sizes.

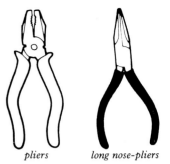

pliers   *long nose-pliers*

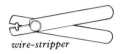

wire-stripper

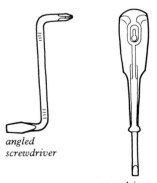

angled screwdriver   *screwdriver with wire-stripper handle*

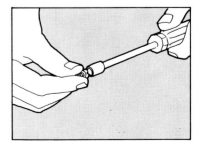

Right: *screwdriver with device to hold screw*

Tools

Ordinary screws call for a plain-tipped screwdriver, but you may come across some screwheads that need a screwdriver with a cross shaped tip. (There is a screwdriver that has a reversible tip – one end of it plain, the other with a cross.)

Where plain screwdrivers are concerned, the width of the tip should correspond with the slot of the screw. There are some screwdrivers on sale which come with a set of interchangeable tips.

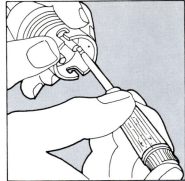

mains tester screwdriver in use

Testing tools

You may want to test whether current is flowing, whether the flex or the wiring of an appliance is intact, or whether a cartridge fuse is functioning or dead.

To test whether current is flowing, you can buy a special screwdriver with a small neon tube in the handle. Push its tip into the live section of a socket (switched on) while keeping one finger on the handle end. The bulb will glow if the current is flowing.

To test whether the fuse in a plug is working or not, you put it into the hole at the top of this screwdriver and press it down. If the light glows, the fuse is all right. (Another way to test a fuse, using a metal torch, is described on page 62.)

A circuit-tester, containing a battery, is used for testing whether there is anything wrong with the flex or the appliance. This has a clip at one end and a sharp probe at the other. When anything metallic is between the clip and the probe, the circuit is completed and the bulb glows. A circuit-tester can also be used to check fuses.

mains tester screwdriver　　*circuit tester*

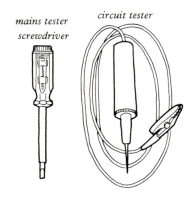

circuit tester in use

Flexes – appliances

Symptom
Worn or damaged flex, or hot spot

Tools and materials needed
Plastic-sheathed flex
Screwdriver
Knife
Wire stripper
Buy the right kind of flex (if in doubt, the bigger the better):

25A	3-core	For some cookers and central heating units up to 6000W
15A	3-core	For appliances up to 3000W
10A	3-core	For appliances up to 2400W
6A	3-core	For appliances up to 1400W if earthed
6A	2-core	For lights; or for appliances up to 1400W if not earthed
3A	2-core	For lights or hi-fi up to 700W

Unearthed appliances may include some power-tools, lawn mowers, shavers, small food mixers, etc. Such appliances are double-insulated, a fact indicated on them by this symbol ▣; or they may be fully insulated by being completely enclosed in plastic. Use 3-core flex for table or standard lamps made of metal: the earth wire attaches to the metal frame. For things like kettles and irons ask for non-kinking flex (it has a braided rubber sheath). There is a 3A 2-core flex for lights or unearthed appliances up to 750W which coils up into a few cm when at rest but stretches to nearly 2m (6ft) when required.

Method
1 Unplug the appliance. To locate the connection of the old flex, unscrew the appropriate part of the appliance; or detach its connector if it has one and unscrew it.
2 Release the screws that hold the flex.
3 Loosen terminals enough to remove the old flex (if there is a rubber or plastic collar on it, slide this on to the new flex). Note which wires went to which terminal – live, neutral and earth. The terminals may be colour-

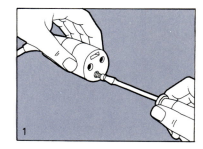

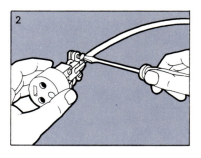

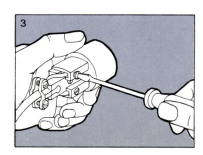

Flexes – appliances

coded (for explanation of this, see page 56 – Plugs).

4 Measure amount of sheath to cut off the new flex.

5 Strip about 1½cm of insulation from each of its wires.

6 Twist their ends. Double the wires back on themselves if they are thin before connecting them to the appropriate terminals in place of the old wires and then reassemble.

7 Remove the plug from the old flex and attach it to the new one (see page 56).

Note Insulating tape can be used to repair the damaged outer sheath of flex provided the inner wires are intact. An alternative is silicone rubber adhesive, flexible and a non-conductor of electricity.

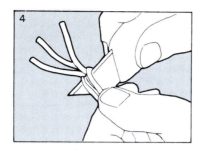

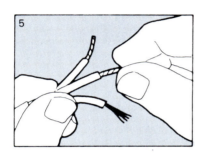

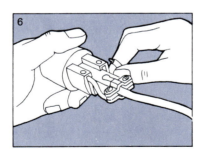

Flexes – ceiling lights

Symptom
Brittleness or browning at lower end (do not wait till it short-circuits or breaks and lets the light fitting crash)

Cause
Possibly heat from high-wattage bulb in too narrow a shade; or undue load caused by connecting an appliance to a lamp-holder

Tools and materials needed
Heat-resistant 2-core 6A flex (or stronger flex if light fitting weighs more than 3kg (6½lb)
Screwdriver
Knife
Wire stripper
Step ladder

Method
1 Attach lampholder to new flex (see page 63).

2 Turn off main electricity switch. Unscrew cover of ceiling rose. (Dismantling fluid may be needed.)

3 Unfasten the two wires of the old flex, noting their position.

4 Cut sheath away from new flex, and strip insulation from its wires, using the old flex as a guide to lengths. Thread rose cover over flex (right way up).

5 Twist the wires before attaching them very securely to the correct terminals.

6 Replace cover of rose. Turn on electricity.

Notes
1 'Plug-in' ceiling roses consist of a 3-pin socket and plug, wired up just like other plugs. They are only found on very modern, earthed lighting circuits.

2 You can buy a flex with a 'rise and fall' fitting, enabling you to lower a light over, for example, a desk or table, and raise it when not in use.

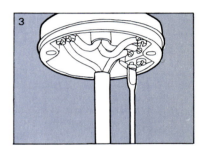

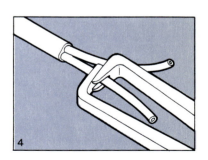

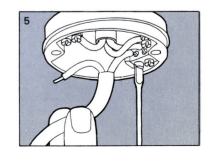

Flexes – lengthening

It is often better to put a new, longer flex on an appliance: see below.
Do not use insulating tape instead of a connector: it can pull apart and create a fire risk.

Tools and materials needed
Screw-down or push-on connector of appropriate amperage (2-pin or 2-core flex, 3-pin for 3-core; fused if your plug has no fuse in it; rubber if for use in a damp place such as a kitchen)
Flex (for type, see page 54)
Screwdriver
Wire-stripper
Knife

Method
1 Detach the plug from the present flex and in its place fix half the connector (the pronged part in the case of a push-on connector), wired on like a plug (see right). You will need to thread the connector cover on to the flex before securing the wires.
2 At one end of the new flex fit the other half of the connector; and at the other end fix the plug. (It is vital not to have the pronged part of a push-on connector on the flex that goes to the socket.)
3 Push or screw the two halves of the connector together.

Note A lengthy flex can be a danger by causing falls, or running under a carpet where treading may chafe it: be sure to get thick-sheathed flex in a bright colour. Flex can often be kept from trailing by fastening it to a wall, using only insulated staples or other devices designed for the purpose (illustrated).

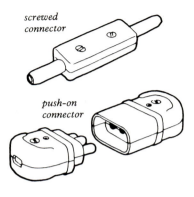

screwed connector

push-on connector

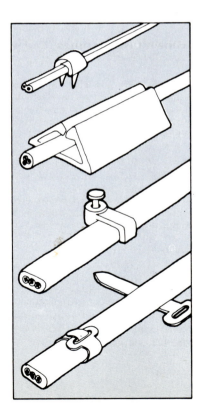

Plugs – attaching

Tools and materials needed
Plug
Screwdriver
Wirestripper
Knife

Method
1 Take cover off plug (its screws are on the underside of the plug).
2 Free the flex-grip by removing one screw and loosening the other. Remove the cartridge fuse.
3 Strip about 5cm of sheath away from the flex.
4 Secure the sheathed end of the flex under the flex-grip.
5 If necessary, shorten the brown (or red) and blue (or black) wires.
6 Use the wire-strippers to pull the insulation off the wires: if the terminal screws have holes, remove about 5mm ($\frac{1}{4}$in); if they do not, 1.5cm ($\frac{2}{3}$in).
7 Either pass the bared wires through the holes, or loop round each screw clockwise, as follows (it helps to twist the wires together first):
   Green/yellow (or green) Earth terminal, marked E or ⏚
   Brown (or red) Live terminal, marked L
   Blue (or black) Neutral terminal, marked N
   When using flex that has only two wires (for lights, or for double-insulated appliances: see page 54), connect these to L and N only as there is no E wire.
8 Before reassembling, check that the cartridge fuse is of the right amperage for the appliance: see page 57.

Warning If wires are wrongly connected, an appliance may remain 'live' even when turned off.
   Never pull plugs out by their flexes – this may loosen connections.

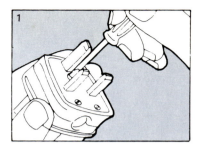

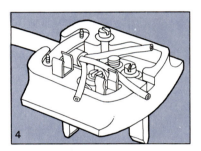

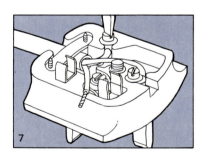

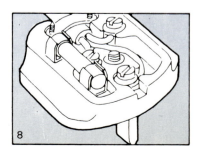

Types of plugs

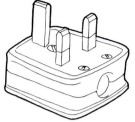

plug with insulated pins

unbreakable rubber plug

plug with pilot light

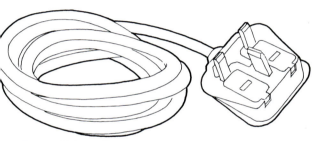

plug moulded onto flex, with spare fuse

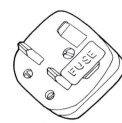

plug with easily accessible fuse

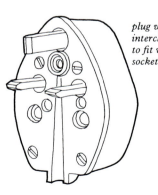

plug with interchangeable pins to fit various sockets

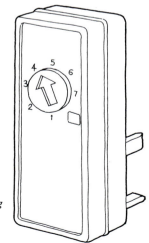

plug incorporating heat control

Plugs – fuses

Fuses for plugs (and for wall connections of fixed appliances)

3A red (previously blue) for appliances up to 720W
13A brown for appliances of 720–3000W

Some low-wattage appliances start with an initial high surge of electricity and therefore need a 13A fuse: these are colour TV sets and motor-driven appliances such as spin-driers and vacuum-cleaners. Plugs are commonly sold with a 13A fuse already in, which may need changing to 3A. Fixed appliances (clocks, immersion heaters, cookers, wall fires, storage heaters, etc.) which have no plugs have wall units instead, each containing its own fuse. Sizes range from 2A to 45A.

Blown fuses in plugs (and wall connections)

Symptom
Appliance 'dead'

Possible cause
Short-circuit in appliance, its flex or plug (sometimes this makes a bang); or overheating of one of them; or overload of a motor

Tools and materials needed
Fuse of correct amperage (see above)
Screwdriver

Method
1 Disconnect plug and remove its cover. (Or turn electricity off and unscrew cover of wall connection if necessary.)
2 Remove old cartridge fuse to test whether it has blown (see page 54) and if so press new one in. Check that wires inside plug are well connected.
3 Replace cover.

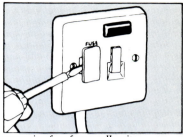

removing fuse from wall units

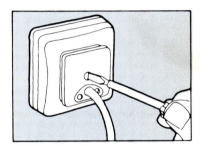

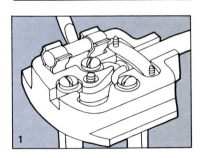

1

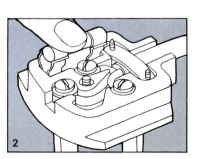

2

Plugs – fuses

Before putting the plug in the socket, try to determine the cause of the trouble (for instance, check that the flex is still well connected to the terminals in the appliance and in the plug, that it does not feel broken or hot at any point, that there are no scorch marks on the plug). If you cannot rectify what is wrong, do not put the appliance in use until an electrician has examined it.

Plugs – Overheated

Symptoms
Hot to touch, scorch marks, smell of hot plastic

Causes
Cartridge fuse not firmly in; or some strands of wires inside not firmly held by screws; or deterioration due to age

Method
Disconnect, trace cause, and rectify

If a plug is stiff to remove from its socket, smear its prongs with a little Vaseline, then replace.

Sockets and switches – damaged

Symptoms (A)
Cracked or chipped; gaping from wall

Materials needed
Epoxy putty
Alternatively, replacement to screw on (see below).

Method
1 Blend the two parts of the putty together, fill the hole, and smooth. If rejoining two broken pieces, place the putty on one piece and press the other on to it, wiping off any surplus with a cloth dipped in suds.
2 Leave under a weight or sticky-taped together until set (about a day; less if put in front of a heater). If a piece of polythene from a plastic bag is placed over the putty while it sets, a shiny surface will be left when the polythene is taken off.
3 If a gap has developed between a socket or switch and the wall, this too can be filled with a thin roll of the putty pressed into the gap and smoothed off with a knife dipped into suds.

Note An alternative is silicone rubber adhesive in a tube. This gives a flexible filling which does not conduct electricity.

Symptoms (B)
Hot to touch, scorch marks, smell of hot plastic (indicating a fault that is causing overheating)

Method
Turn off electricity, unscrew cover and check for any loose connections inside. If this is not the cause, call an electrician.

Sockets and switches – replacement

Tools and materials
Switch or socket
Surface box if necessary
Screwdriver
Screws

Method
1 Turn off at mains, then unscrew and remove the old fitting.
2 Thread the cable that is in the wall through into the new box if a new one is being fitted
3 Screw the box to the wall.
4 Connect the wires from the cable to the terminals in the new fitting and screw it in place.

In the case of a flush fitting, only the old cover will be unscrewed and the wires reconnected to the new one.

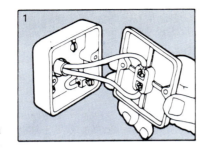

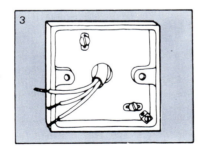

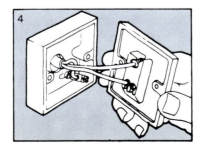

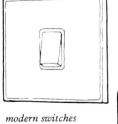

modern switches to replace old ones

Sockets – adaptors

An adaptor is merely plugged into a socket, and the plug or plugs are then put into the adaptor. There is a wide variety of adaptors, shown here, performing different functions.

Some contain their own fuses. It is important not to overload an adaptor for if, say, two 2kW heaters were used on a 13A adaptor, it and the socket could overheat and possibly start a fire. Even the presence of a fuse is not an absolute protection against this. (About fuses, see page 57.)

Circuit units
These can provide for as many as six plugs to be used from one socket. They are safer than adaptors because they incorporate a circuit breaker that will switch the whole thing off if there is an overload or fault (some have a fuse instead). In addition, pilot lights indicate when current is connected. It is possible to get models with an on/off switch for each plug. Some models stand on the floor, others are for screwing to the wall. The only wiring needed is the attachment of a plug to the flex of the unit, which is then plugged into the socket.

Foot-switch
It can be useful to have a foot-switch operating an appliance such as an electric drill at times when both your hands are occupied with the work in progress. This calls for a special adaptor to be used at the socket: from the bottom of it a flex is permanently connected to the foot-switch, and at the top the plug on the flex of the drill, saw, lathe, sander, etc. is pushed in. The use of a foot-switch is not only often convenient but always safer because current flows only when the switch is pressed down by foot. A hand or treadle sewing machine can have a motor and foot-switch attached, but this needs to be done by a sewing-machine technician.

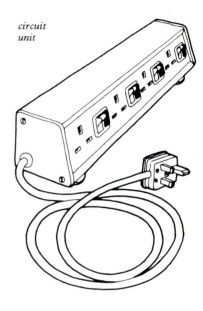

circuit unit

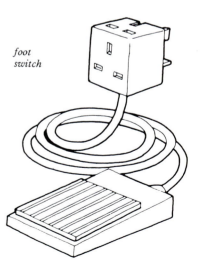

foot switch

Types of adaptors

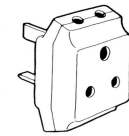

adaptors enabling 2 or 3 plugs to be used at one socket

to adapt a 3-hole socket to take a 2-pin plug

to adapt a square-holed socket to take round-pinned plugs

to adapt a socket to take 5A plugs

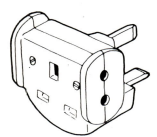

to adapt a square-holed socket to take both square and round-pin plugs

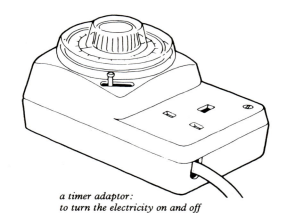

a timer adaptor: to turn the electricity on and off

Sockets – conversions

To convert a single 13A socket (for instance, to a double or triple one) is simple provided that you use a surface-mounted socket: flush ones have complications.

Tools and materials needed
Surface-mounted socket and mounting box
Screwdriver and bradawl
Or drill and wallplugs if socket is on plaster not on woodwork

Method
1 Turn electricity off at main switch.
2 Unscrew the socket plate.
3 Undo the screws holding the cables (probably in pairs).
4 Screw the new box on.
5 Ease the cables out far enough to connect to the new surface plate (red to live, black to neutral, green to earth).
6 Screw plate to box, and switch electricity on again.

Choose sockets with switches on them. One with a red neon light will warn whether the appliance is on or off (useful with a freezer or with a convector that has no pilot light of its own).

Installing a shaver socket in a bathroom is a job for an electrician, but an amateur can fit a shaver socket (surface mounted) in place of an ordinary socket in, say, a bedroom.

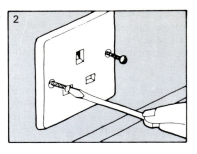

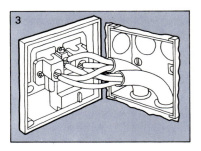

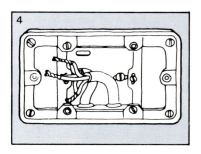

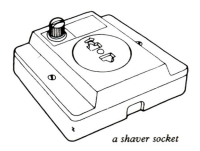

a shaver socket

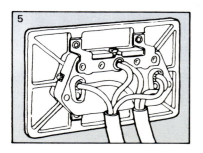

The consumer unit – main fuses

Blown main fuse

Symptom
Not only one appliance but all on the same circuit go 'dead'.

Causes
Too many appliances in use at once; fault in cable or socket; fault in appliance, its flex or its plug (if no plug fuse, or if plug fuse does not operate)

Tools and materials needed
Fuse wire or cartridge of appropriate amperage
Possibly: screwdriver, wire cutter, metal-cased torch

Method
1 Turn off main switch, and the appliances on the affected circuit. If necessary, unscrew front of fusebox.
2 Unless each fuse is already labelled to show which circuit it serves, you may need to pull out one fuse at a time in order to identify the blown fuse. Some fuses have a colour to indicate their amperage, which may narrow the search (usually the largest is nearest the main switch; and differing sizes are also an indication of amperage):

    5A   white   lighting
    15A blue   immersion heater
    20A yellow   immersion heater
    30A red   power sockets or cooker
    45A green   cooker
    60A purple   large cooker

Wire fuse (running across or through ceramic holder) will be broken if blown.
Cartridge fuse will show no change. Either use the torch test (see page 62) to check each one; or put a new fuse of correct amperage into each holder in turn, checking as you go to see whether the supply has been restored or not.

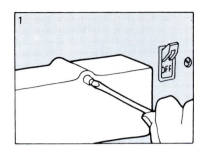

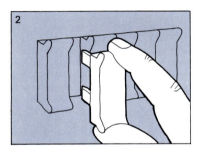

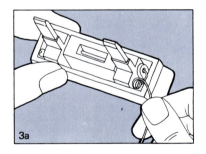

3 To renew a wire fuse, cut a length of fuse wire of the correct amperage (this is vital) and, positioning it where you have removed the remains of the old wire, wind its ends clockwise round the two screws and tighten them (the wire should not be taut). Turn the main switch on.
4 Identify the cause of the trouble or else it will recur. For instance, if a fuse blew when you turned on a light, either the bulb or the light flex may have a fault. If a fuse wire merely has a gap in the middle, this suggests that the circuit was overloaded★; but one that has vanished completely indicates a fault. To find out which appliance has this, switch on one at a time and when the fuse blows again you will know what is responsible. Disconnect it and take it to an electrician. If the affected circuit is still not working, call an electrician.

Note Some houses still have very old cast-iron fuseboxes containing an obsolete type of fuse ('double pole') which can in some circumstances give a shock to anyone handling it. If yours is of this type, get it replaced.

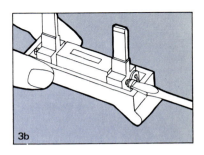

★ An overload has to be more than double the rating of the cable, and to continue for some time, before a main fuse will blow – so this is not an absolute protection against fire risk from overloading by using too many watts at one time.

The consumer unit – main fuses

Circuit breakers
Some homes have circuit breakers (illustrated) instead of fuses: a switch clicks automatically into the off position when there is trouble and can be pushed back when it has been rectified. In some fuse-boxes, it is possible to replace fuses with such circuit-breakers: take one of your fuses to the electricity showroom when enquiring.

Testing a cartridge fuse
Remove the end of a metal-cased torch and hold the suspect fuse firmly between the battery and the torch case. If the torch fails to light when the switch is turned on, the fuse has blown. Alternatively buy a gadget for testing fuses.

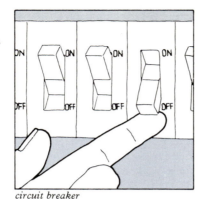

circuit breaker

Lighting – fluorescent tubes

Symptom
Flickering, failure to start, buzzing, blackening at tube ends

Cause
New tube needed or starter faulty or loose connections

Tools and materials needed
New tube or new starter of same type and wattage as old one
Screwdriver

Method
1 Turn off electricity and push starter in (this is a metal canister in a socket on the fitting). If tube still does not work buy a new starter to put in: the old one will come out when turned, like a lightbulb. If a failing tube has affected the starter, put in a new tube too.
2 A common cause of buzzing may be loose connections. Tighten any parts that seem loose, especially the lampholder, and if this does not work call an electrician.

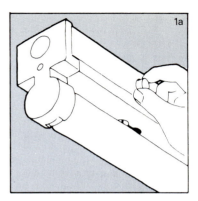

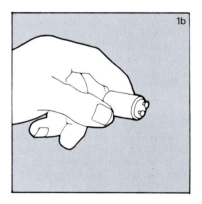

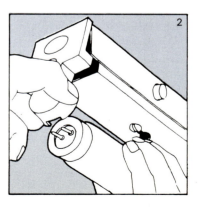

Lighting – replacing lamp-holders

Symptom
Chipped or scorched plastic lamp-holder, or weak contact (pins in the cap no longer springy when pressed)

Cause
Possibly, high wattage light bulb in too small a lampshade; or connecting an appliance of more than 200W to the lamp-holder

Tools and materials needed
New lamp-holder (switched or unswitched)
Screwdriver
Knife
Wire stripper
Vaseline

Note An unswitched lamp-holder can be replaced by one with a switch on it

Method
1 Turn off main switch if working on a pendant or wall fitting. Unplug if working on a standard or table lamp. Remove shade and light bulb. (If lamp-holder has jammed, see page 77 – stiff screw-threads.)
2 Unscrew and remove the old lamp-holder, and trim the flex, to expose an equal length of both the inner wires.
3 Take the new lamp-holder apart by unscrewing, and thread the flex through as shown.
4 Strip 5mm (¼in) insulation off the two wires, twist and secure to the terminal screws. (The flex in metal lamps also has an earth wire, screwed to the metal case.) Loop ends of flex round projections in lamp-holder.
5 Reassemble, smearing screw-thread with Vaseline; put light bulb in; and reconnect electricity.

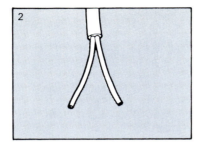

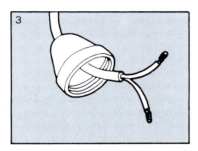

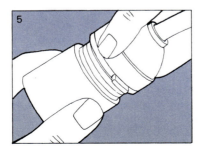

Lighting – Christmas tree lights

Symptom
No light

Cause
One bulb 'dead'

Materials needed
Bulb

Method
1 Turn electricity off.
2 First, screw all bulbs in firmly: it may be that one has worked loose and when it is tightened the whole lot will light up.
3 If this does not work, put a new bulb in place of the first one, then the first in place of the second, and so on — turning electricity on and off each time – until the whole lot light up.

Note Some sets continue to light even if one bulb has failed, but replace the failed bulb soon otherwise overheating may occur. Sets made to British Standard specifications have one special lamp with a fuse to prevent overheating: it is dangerous to replace this lamp (distinguishable by being partly white) with any but another fused lamp.

Repairs to appliances

If an appliance does not work, it is not necessarily faulty. Start by checking *fuses* (in plug or wall unit; or in fuse box if appliance has a circuit to itself); *flexes*; and also all *connections* to appliance terminals or connector, and to the plug. (Fuses, see pages 54 and 62. Appliance terminals, page 54. Plugs, pages 57–8.) Some appliances have neon lights; if one is still glowing, you can be sure there is no fault in the connections, flex or fuse.

Do not repair any appliance that is still under guarantee, if the guarantee terms forbid this. When buying any replacement part, take the old one to the shop to ensure that you get the right size and design.

It is possible to tackle more ambitious repairs only if the manufacturer will supply both spare parts and a service manual (likely to cost a few pounds). Only simple repairs are dealt with in the next pages.

Some repairs common to many appliances are:
   renewal of *gaskets* round doors or lids
   cleaning of *filters*
   lubrication of *motors* and of *wheels*
   replacement of *control-knobs, switches* and *pilot lamps*
   repair of damaged *plastic parts*;
   and *leaks*
These are dealt with on page 77.

About *electric blankets*: on no account attempt repairs to these. They are the only electric appliance which needs annual maintenance by the manufacturer and should be sent back for this.

Repairs – to cookers

Symptom
Boiling ring 'dead' or heating unevenly

Cause
Worn out or defective

Tools and materials needed
Radiant boiling ring (6in or 7in, 152mm or 177mm, single or dual circuit)
Screwdriver
Spanner
Hacksaw
Pliers.
Note Most cookers of 1945–1960 have plug-in rings, requiring no wiring

Method
1 Turn off main cooker switch. Lift up the cooker hob.
2 Remove cover (if any) from boiling-ring connection.
3 Unscrew plate fixing element to cooker.
4 Disconnect the flex and remove the plate.
5 The new ring will have *both* screw *and* tab terminals on it: remove whichever is not required (using hacksaw and pliers). Straighten the support rod if it has got bent.
6 Connect the new plate like the old one. Check carefully that there is a gap of at least 13mm (½in) between the terminals and the cooker.

Symptom
Oven hums

Cause
Metal parts vibrating

Method
Check that cooker is level and oven racks straight.

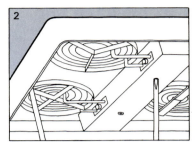
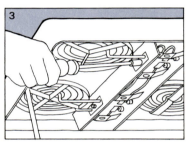
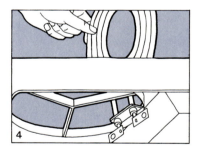
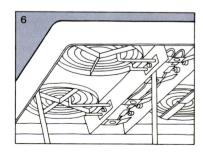

Repairs – to cookers

Symptom
Fluorescent light 'dead'

Cause
Tube or starter worn out

Tools and materials needed
Screwdriver
Tube or starter

Method
1 Turn off main cooker switch. Unscrew case round the light. Slide glass out and wash.
2 Prise ends of tube out, and fit new one in.
3 If light is still 'dead', find starter unit at back by following wires. Unplug and replace.

Symptom
Oven light 'dead'

Cause
Bulb worn out or switch faulty

Tools and materials needed
Screwdriver
Bulb

Method
Unscrew back panel of cooker to gain access and replace bulb. If this does not work, a new switch is needed (a job for an electrician).

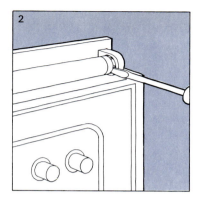

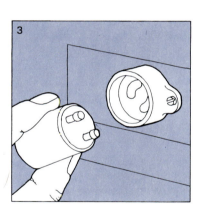

removing oven light

Repairs – to kettles

Symptom
Slow to boil, or stops heating before boiling point is reached

Cause
Scale on element from hard water

Materials needed
Descaling fluid 150ml ($\frac{1}{4}$pt) or powder

Method
1 Fill kettle two-thirds with lukewarm water, add half the descaler, wait till frothing ends, empty.
2 Repeat if necessary.
3 Boil fresh water with a teaspoon of soda, wait 5 minutes, and rinse out.
Warning Descaler can harm some enamels.

Symptom
Connector ejected

Cause
Kettle has boiled dry

Method
Press ejector back (using, for instance, the handle of a wooden spoon).

re-setting ejector

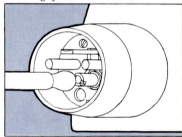

Repairs – to kettles

Symptom
No heat

Cause
Element worn out

Tools and materials needed
New element of same size and shape but higher wattage if preferred (provided flex is of high amperage too). Ordinary elements can be replaced by automatic ones. Screwdriver.

Note Russell Hobbs automatic elements should be replaced by an electrician.

Method
1 Unscrew connector shroud by hand; use screwdriver to release element. It may be necessary to descale in order to shift it.
2 Insert new element via top of the kettle: be sure it is right way up, parallel to the bottom of the kettle and not touching it.
3 With the rubber washer inside the kettle body (unless maker's instructions state otherwise) and the fibre one outside, screw the element in place and replace the shroud.

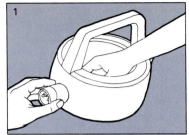
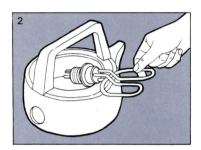
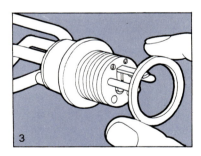

replacing element

Repairs – to kettles

Symptom
Leak near connector

Cause
Worn washer

Tools and materials needed
Washer
Screwdriver
Abrasive paper

Method
Disconnect element (see above) and replace washer. Screw shroud well down. (If there is scale around the hole, use abrasive paper to get it off.)

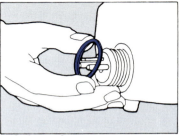

replacing washer

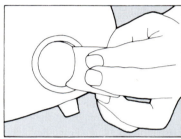

removing scale

66

Repairs – to waste disposers

Symptom
Jammed

Cause
Obstruction in grinder

Tools needed
Special release tool
Screwdriver

Method
1 Check that safety cutout has not stopped the machine.
2 Use reversing control if there is one, or release-tool supplied with the machine (fit it to nut visible through sink outlet and twist to and fro).

Symptom
Flooding from plug

Cause
Blockage in pipe or drain

Method
Clean from drain end.

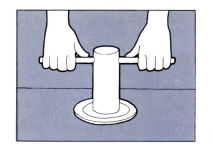

Repairs – to dishwashers

Symptom
Water emptying slowly

Cause
Blockage in inlet filter

Tool needed
Screwdriver

Method
Disconnect inlet hose at back, prise out filter and rinse it.

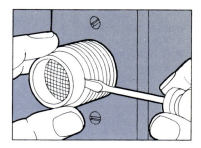

Symptom
Leak from hose

Cause
Loose clip

Tool needed
Screwdriver

Method
Tighten clip. (If hose itself is leaking, see page 77.)

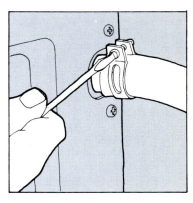

Repairs – to dishwashers

Symptom
Dishes not clean

Cause
Blockage in spray-arm

Method
Unscrew hub-cab of arm (by hand) and rinse it out.

Symptom
Hard-water scale on the heater

Method
Write to manufacturer for advice on the correct application of descaling acid for your own machine.

Repairs – to toasters

Symptom
Bread jams

Likely cause
Failure of pop-up mechanism

Tool needed
Screwdriver

Method
1 Take plug out.
2 Open base, clean out crumbs, and pull bread out with fingers, not a knife.
3 Adjust spring mechanism carefully with the screwdriver.

Symptom
No heat

Possible cause
Worn-out element (non-automatic)

Tool and materials needed
Screwdriver
New element of same type

Method
Undo screws holding old element and insert new one in its place. (The repair of pop-up toasters is a professional job.)

Repairs – to vacuum cleaners

Symptom
Poor cleaning

Cause
Hose split or badly connected; or dust-bag needs emptying; or worn roller brushes; or clogged or damaged filter; or blockage in hose

Materials needed
Alternatives:
Plasticised-fabric sticky tape
New roller
New filter
New dust bag

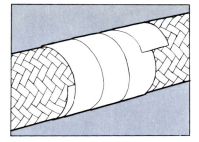

Method
1 Bind tape round hose where it is split or gaping.
2 If necessary, replace roller (on upright machines) or filter (on cylinders: its whereabouts differs from model to model – see maker's instruction book). Unplug the machine first.
3 If a dust bag has a hole (or is more than half full), it should be replaced (or emptied).
4 Any blockage in a hose should be poked out.

Symptom
Hard to push (uprights)

Cause
Wrongly adjusted; or stiff wheels

Material needed
Lubricating oil

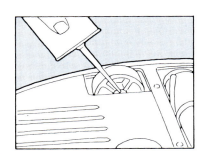

Method
1 A foot-control adjusts the machine for low-, medium- or deep-pile carpets.
2 Wheels need a drop or two of lubricant every few months

Repairs – to vacuum cleaners

Symptom
Burning smell (uprights)

Possible cause
Worn belt, or string, etc. round impeller

Tools and materials needed
New belt
Possibly a screwdriver

Method
1 Unplug. Remove roller, discard old belt, place new one on.
2 Replace roller, twist belt clockwise and stretch over pulley of impeller.
3 Or unplug, release belt and cut away any objects caught round the pulley.

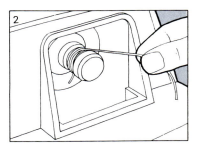

Repairs – to floor polishers

Symptom
Abnormal noises

Possible cause
Loose screw(s)

Tool needed
Screwdriver

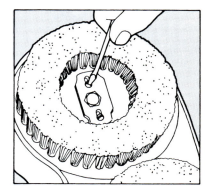

Method
Unplug and turn the machine upside down. Tighten the screws on the driving shafts (see diagram) and brush fastening clips.

Repairs – to refrigerator/freezers

Symptom
Motor runs but unit does not refrigerate properly

Possible cause
Condenser not being cooled properly; blocked tube in refrigerating coil

Method
1 Check that the air inlet grille is not blocked.
2 Switch unit off for half an hour; blockage may clear itself. If not, call serviceman.

Symptom
Motor runs continuously regardless of thermostat setting

Possible cause
Door seal damaged or worn; door warped or damaged; condenser not getting enough air

Method
1 Check door gasket by testing with a piece of paper, which should give a slight resistance to being pulled out when door is closed. The door may need new hinges. (If thermostat is at fault, this is a job for an electrician.)
2 Check that the air inlet grille is not blocked.

Symptom
Cabinet sweats

Possible cause
Fluctuation in air temperature

Method
Improve ventilation in room.

Repairs – to cooker hoods

Symptoms
Cooking smells, grease on nearby walls

Possible cause
Unclean filters or ducts

Method
Replace filter. Clean filter trays and check any ducting for breaks or leaks.

Symptom
Motor working intermittently

Possible cause
Motor chamber blocked with grease

Method
Clean motor chamber.

Symptom
Steam and grease escaping hood

Possible cause
Hood at wrong height

Method
Resite 90cm (3ft) above hob. Re-mount hood 12.5cm (5in) out from wall above eye-level grill.

Repairs – to washing machines

Symptom
Water leaking

Possible cause
Door seal faulty
Hose or hose connections faulty
Blocked outlet or faulty pump

Method
1 Check seal on automatics; see if clothes are caught in door gasket.
2 Check hose and connections for leaks – temporary repair may be possible (see page 77).
3 Switch off, remove laundry and check filter. Check outlet hose. Test pump by using small quantity of water and switching on rinse cycle (see advice in instruction book).

Symptom
Drum not turning

Possible cause
Broken belt

Method
Fit new belt (see instruction book first).

Repairs – to dryers

Symptom
Motor runs but drum will not revolve

Possible cause
Belt slack or broken

Method
Check instruction book – on some models belt replacement is simple.

Symptom
Squeaky

Possible cause
Lack of lubrication

Method
Check instruction book for advice on oiling.

Symptom
Poor drying (tumbler)

Possible cause
Lint filter blocked; thermostat failure

Method
Remove and clean filter. Check heat control with drum empty – but usually needs serviceman.

Repairs – to irons

Symptom
No steam coming from steam iron

Cause
Scale from hard water

Materials needed
Descaling liquid or powder.

Method
Use descaling liquid or powder according to makers' instructions.

To prevent scale forming, use only distilled water (from a chemist) or water saved from defrosting a refrigerator.

Symptom
No heat

Possible cause
Worn-out element (non-thermostatic)

Tools and materials needed
Pliers or small spanner
Screwdriver
New element of same type

Method
1 Remove the nuts and take off the handle.
2 Lift up the cover and undo the screw holding the contact strips of the element.
3 Undo the nuts holding the cast iron plate, asbestos pad and element above the sole plate.
4 Replace the old element with the new one and reassemble, screwing the nuts on hard.

Note The repair of thermostatic irons is a professional job.

Repairs – to immersion heaters

Symptom
Water too hot or cold; slow reheating

Cause
Thermostat wrongly set; or scale

Tools needed
Screwdriver

Methods
Resetting thermostat
1 Turn off electricity.
2 Undo screw holding the cover on the element.
3 Prise off cap covering the regulator.
4 Use screwdriver to turn screw that regulates the setting. 60°C (140°F) is normal in hard-water areas, 70°C (160°F) in soft-water areas.

Scale from hard water
Methods vary with different makes. Write for instructions to the maker of the water heater or of descaling powder.

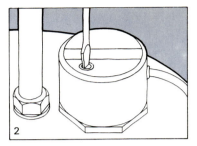

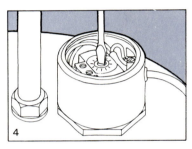

Repairs – to electric fires

Repairs – to electric fires

Symptom
No glow

Possible cause
Broken element

Tools and materials needed
Possibly, screwdriver
Element (or coil) of same size and design as before

Method
Unplug fire.
Fire with rod or glass element Unscrew or press guard inwards to release it. Unscrew terminals at end of element to remove it. Screw new element in and replace guard. (If a glass sheath is intact, it can be rewired to save buying a new one.)
Bowl fire Undo 2 screws near coil, remove the cover at back of fire and release the screws connecting wires to coil. Replace coil with new one and reassemble as before.

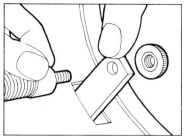

replacing rod element

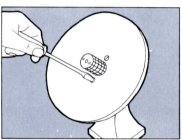

bowl fire element: front

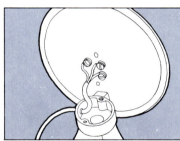

bowl fire element: back

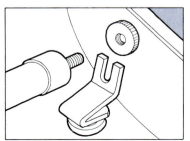

glass element

Fire with 'brick' elements If the brick is intact, a new spiral can be fitted to it after removal. If cracked it should be mended with fireclay; or else replaced. (To do this, unscrew back of fire and connecting wires first; if flex inside is brittle, renew it with new heatproof flex.)

Note Polish the reflector before reassembling the fire.

Symptom
Flame effect ceased

Possible cause
Spinner not revolving

Tools and materials needed
Screwdriver
Possibly, new spinner

Method
1 Unplug fire.
2 Remove spinner (it will be found below the elements), clean and if necessary straighten the bearing.

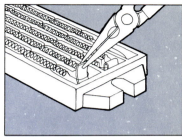

replacing spiral in brick element

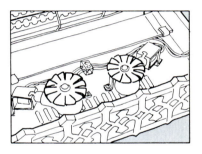

Repairs – to convector heaters

Symptom
Smell when heating up

Possible cause
Dust inside

Tool needed
Screwdriver

Method
1 Unplug heater.
2 Detach grid at bottom of heater. Lightly brush, or use vacuum-cleaner attachment.

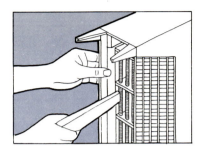

Repairs – to fan heaters

Symptom
Glow visible inside

Cause
Fan sluggish

Tools and materials needed
Oil can
Screwdriver
Small soft brush

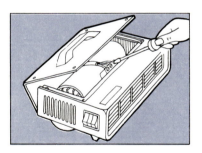

Method
1 Make sure nothing is obscuring the vents.
2 Unplug heater, unscrew back or bottom. (If fan cover hides the motor, detach connections and unscrew this.)
3 Brush motor clean and put two drops of oil on its bearings.

Note Fan heaters should be regularly cleared of dust and fluff by blowing through the side or bottom with a vacuum nozzle (unplug the heater first).

Repairs – to extractor fans

Symptom
Switch-pull broken

Tools and materials needed
Screwdriver
Needle
New cord

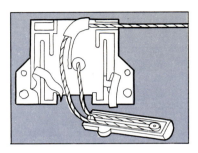

Method
1 Disconnect electricity. Remove grille and unscrew switch unit (at top).
2 Slide switch selector out gently.
3 Remove remains of old cord and guide new one into position with the help of a needle. Secure with a knot at the hole.

Symptom
Fan noisy

Cause
Damaged louvres or unit loose in its mounting

Tool needed
Screwdriver

Method
Tighten screws holding the fan, and check the louvres.

Repairs – to extractor fans

Symptom
Fan sluggish

Cause
Dirt and grease

Tools and materials needed
Screwdriver
Small soft brush
Detergent suds

Method
1 Disconnect electricity
2 Take flex connector out and remove grille; undo screws holding fan and motor unit in place; unscrew fan and lift off motor.
3 Wash grille and fan, brush motor.
4 Reassemble.

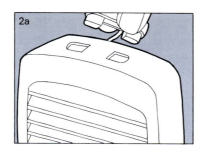

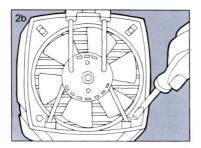

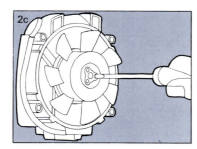

Repairs – to hair dryer

Symptom
Buzzing, flashing or intermittent running

Possible cause
Dirt on contacts

Tools and materials needed
Screwdriver
Fine abrasive paper
Small soft brush

Method
1 Unplug the dryer.
2 Unscrew the case.
3 Clean the contacts with abrasive paper (they are the two metal strips with wires attached). Clean interior with brush and remove all loose hair.
4 Reassemble.

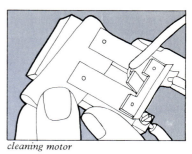

cleaning motor

Symptom
No heat

Possible cause
Broken element

Tools and materials needed
Screwdriver
New element of same type

Method
1 First check that safety cut-out button does not need resetting.
2 Unplug drier, unscrew case and detach element from wires.
3 Replace with new one; reassemble.

Note Each screw and its sheath must go back in the hole they came from.

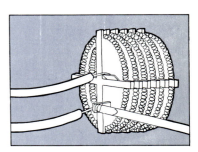

Repairs – to power tools

Symptom
Sluggish action

Possible cause
Dirt or lack of lubrication

Tools and materials needed
Screwdriver
Lubricant grease

Method
1 Unplug tool.
2 Unscrew case, wipe motor clean, lubricate bearings (unless they are sealed) and pack grease around fan and gear wheel.

Note Dust can be regularly sucked out by holding a vacuum cleaner attachment to vents at rear. Unplug drill first.

Repairs – to electric sewing machines

Symptom
Sluggish or noisy motor

Cause
Fluff in mechanism, or lack of lubrication

Tools and materials needed
Oil
Gear-lubricant
Screwdriver

Method
1 Unplug the machine.
2 Clean away any lint or fluff, particularly around bobbin case.
3 Unscrew the cover from the top.
4 Apply oil as described in the instruction book.
5 Apply gear lubricant to the gears.
6 Unscrew the cover on the underside.
7 Apply oil as described in the instruction book.
8 Screw the cover back. Plug in.

Note The exposed mechanism needs oiling even more frequently: see your instruction book.

General maintenance of appliances

Gaskets are put on doors or lids to provide a good seal. To check whether a gasket is effective at any point, test whether it grips a postcard when the door is closed. Many gaskets are replaceable by lifting up the edge to reveal screws that can be undone. When putting a replacement on, screw the top edge first. A tube of silicone rubber can be used for repairs; mould it to shape with a damp finger. If an oven or refrigerator door is not airtight, there will be an excessive consumption of electricity or loss of efficiency.

Filters are to be found on many appliances that pump water or fan air out (such as washing machines, tumble driers, cooker hoods, etc). Apart from any that are in the main body of the appliance, look for them by the inlet or outlet. Sluggish operation may mean a filter needs to be cleaned or renewed.

Lubrication of any wheels or other parts that get stiff (eg, lamp-holders) is likely to be needed occasionally. Where motors are concerned, study instruction books. Lubricants in aerosols are ideal for penetrating switches and motors. Use them also for cleaning plated parts, as they have a damp-proofing and rust-inhibiting effect as well as shifting dirt and grease. They help when dismantling stiff components. Use Vaseline when screwing things together again, to keep them from seizing up.

Control knobs, switches and pilot lamps often unscrew or unclip easily for replacement when damaged or worn out. Reconnect any wires exactly as before. In a few switches, soldering may be needed.

Thermostats may become inaccurate with time. If possible, check with thermometer of appropriate temperature-range. Any repair should be done by an electrician.

Electric clocks may become slow if the voltage is deliberately reduced during a period of excess demand. This is known as 'load shedding'. Power stations speed up, after the crisis, until the correct time has

been restored, so there is no need to make any adjustments.

Plastic parts, such as handles, can be repaired with epoxy putty.

Leaks in tubes and hoses can often be repaired with hose seal tape or silicone rubber adhesive; leaks in, for example, washing-machine tubs can be repaired with epoxy putty.

Electrical emergencies

Safety habits
Electric shock (sometimes fatal) and fires would rarely occur if everyone observed sensible rules of behaviour, of which the most important are:

Bathrooms Water increases the risk of shock. Never use an extended flex to bring an appliance into the bathroom – and, of course, it is out of the question to have a socket installed in a bathroom (shaver socket excepted). Lampholders should be of the skirted kind so that no one with wet hands can touch the live pins.

Flexes Worn ones, those with old insulation and non plastic-sheathed, long and trailing ones, short and taut ones, or flexes of the wrong amperage (see page 50) are all causes of shock, fire or other accidents. So are flexes run under carpets or stapled all round the room, or any carelessly connected to plugs or appliances – for which reason, never yank plugs out by their flexes. Be careful that appliances like drills, mowers and irons do not cut or burn their own flexes.

Lighting Bulbs give off a good deal of heat, so wide non-flammable shades are best, with heat-resistant flex and lampholder, not too close to the ceiling or any flammable surface.

Electrical emergencies

Heated appliances (fires, blankets, cookers, irons, kettles etc.) Leaving these unattended can be the cause of fires. It is best to switch off whenever leaving the house or even, in the case of irons, kettles, boiling-rings and grills, when answering the door or a telephone: you cannot be sure how long you will be and even safety cut-outs do not always work.

Metal objects Cooking foil, knives, screwdrivers, etc., can convey a current from an appliance into your body, so do not let these make contact with elements or live parts – for instance, to dislodge bread from a toaster. Unplug first. Children can poke metal objects into empty lampholders, empty contacts for fire elements and so on; so it is better to leave even dead lamps or elements in place until renewed.

If anyone gets a bad electric shock

1 Do not touch him if he is still in contact with electricity (his fingers may be unable to release their grip). Turn off first, at the main switch.
   Note If you are the victim and cannot release your grip, JUMP: this will break your contact with the ground and thus enable you to free your hand. Or pull out the appliance's plug if you can.
2 If for any reason you cannot turn the electricity off, put on dry rubber gloves before pulling the victim away; or hold him with something else that does not conduct electricity (plastic, paper, woollen clothes, wood).
3 Phone your doctor or dial 999 for an ambulance: electric burns and the effect of shock on the heart may be greater than appears.
4 Keep the patient lying down covered with a blanket and with clothes loosened, legs slightly up. Offer a hot sweet drink (not a lot) and ensure as much quiet and calm as possible. Dress any minor burn.
5 If breathing is affected, give the 'kiss of life'. Lay the patient on his back. Tilt the head back, to open windpipe. Open the

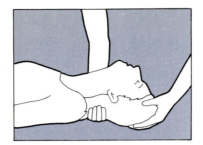

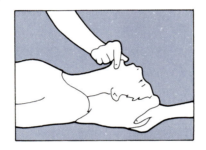

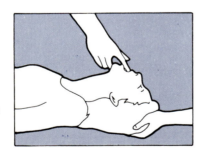

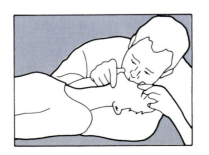

Electrical emergencies

mouth, and make sure nothing is obstructing the windpipe (dentures, tongue, etc.). Pinch the patient's nose and breathe gently into the patient's mouth until the chest rises. Allow the patient to exhale, and repeat until normal breathing resumes.

If a fire starts in an electrical appliance or in wiring

1 Pull plug out or turn off electricity at main switch.
2 Dial 999 for fire brigade and close the door of the room concerned, unless the fire is so small that you can deal with it by one of the following means:
   Smother with a wool blanket.
   Extinguish with bicarbonate of soda.
   Only if the electricity is disconnected, use water or a wet cloth.
3 Before using the electric appliance or wiring again, call an electrician to rectify whatever fault started the fire.

4

General Repairs

Tools and materials

Your basic needs

The fewer tools you have, the more important it is that each should be of the right type and size, and of good quality.

To do most of the jobs in this chapter, it is desirable to have the following tools and materials at the outset . . . getting others that are mentioned only if and when a job needing them turns up. Fuller descriptions are given later. Large specialised tools, such as creosote-spray, ladder or post-borer, need never be bought – they can be hired on the rare occasion when they are needed. When you want specialised materials (glass, fencing, etc.), look for local suppliers in the yellow pages of the telephone directory.

When a repair amounts to a replacement, a kit may make the job easier. But spend time reading the instruction sheet before you buy. How complex is the work? What extra tools (or materials) will you have to get? Could you buy the components more cheaply if they were not in a kit?

2 hammers
Pliers
3 screwdrivers
Drill with set of bits
and a masonry bit
Tenon saw
Cold chisel
Craft knife
Abrading tool
Filling knife and/or
putty knife

Sticking things together

Most sticking jobs around the house could be dealt with by a polyvinyl acetate (PVA) or an epoxy adhesive (both keep well after opening, if not exposed to air; it's worth buying PVA in a large size which costs less in the end). Others will be needed for special jobs only.

PVA
This is a fairly strong adhesive, widely used for sticking wood and hardboard, and it will also do for many other jobs (see chart on page 81) but not for sticking plastics. Setting time varies: $\frac{1}{2}$ hour is average. Water will remove any spills. It can be added to the water when mixing cement or plaster fillers to strengthen them when filling holes. Only moderately water-resistant.

Epoxy adhesives
These (particularly the 'super' grades) are strong, heat-resistant – and dear. They come in two parts that need to be mixed together. Usable on any rigid material except a few plastics. Most epoxies fill small gaps well, and to bridge larger ones a bandage of any loose-woven material (such as glassfibre, hessian or wire mesh) can be laid and then coated with the epoxy. Epoxy putty is both gap-filler and adhesive in one. Another version is plastic steel: 80% steel particles and 20% epoxy. Setting time is usually short but can vary a lot, from minutes to hours; it can be speeded up by warmth. Spills can be removed with soapy water (until they have set).

Contact adhesives
These are the ones that give a pretty strong bond immediately the two surfaces touch. The adhesive, spread on both surfaces, is left to dry for half an hour before the two parts are brought together. Once they touch, they cannot be moved, which limits their usefulness (an exception is a thixotropic version which allows a little time for adjusting position).
They are useful on wood and hardboard, metal, hard plaster, rubber flooring (not vinyl) and such rigid plastics as Formica.

Sticking things together

Because there have been some fatal tragedies with solvent-based makes, choose a non-flammable one. Spills of these can be removed with water.

Urea
A good choice for woodwork exposed to damp, and will fill gaps up to 1mm. Setting time, about 3 hours. Fresh spills can be removed with a damp cloth.

Elastomeric
Though very flammable, this may be worth getting for situations where continual movement makes it important to have an adhesive that will stay resilient. It may take nearly two days to set, and weeks to reach full strength. Although it is pricey, not much is needed (pea-size dabs 30cm (1ft) apart suffice for most jobs). Can be removed with paraffin.

More specialised adhesives
For certain jobs, specially formulated adhesives are best: wallpaper, ceiling tiles, flooring, wall tiles and other wall coverings, rubber, acrylics such as Perspex, and most other plastics. For minor repairs, any water-based adhesive will do for wallpaper; a water-based paste for ceiling tiles; and a tube of ordinary clear glue may suffice for others – with the exception of plastics and rubber, which usually need specialised adhesives no matter how small the repair.

Opposite is a guide to the most appropriate adhesive for minor repairs to various surfaces about the house.

Sticking things together

Material to be applied	Brick	Concrete	Plaster	Stone	Wood
Same as sub-surface	epoxy	epoxy	—	epoxy	PVA or urea
Hardboard	elastomeric or contact adhesive	elastomeric or contact adhesive	contact adhesive	contact adhesive	PVA or contact adhesive
Metal	epoxy	epoxy	epoxy or contact adhesive	epoxy	epoxy or contact adhesive
Wood	elastomeric or epoxy	contact adhesive or elastomeric	contact adhesive	contact adhesive or elastomeric	PVA or urea

Adhesive tapes and pads

These may have adhesive coating on one or on both sides. The former are good for spanning cracks or (in the case of the more flexible ones) wrapping round split pipes or bars; the latter for these purposes or for bonding one surface to another. The secrets of success are a freshly cleaned surface, generous overlaps and edges pressed well down. Do not stretch tapes, and use them slightly warm if possible.

Tapes sticky on one side (top surface may be paintable) may be made of: flexible plastic (like insulating tape); plastic-coated fabric (strong and often wider); reinforced foil (wide); reinforced foil, bitumen backed (wide and extra waterproof); transparent plastic (for windows, Perspex, etc).

Tapes sticky on both sides may be made of impregnated fabric (various widths and strengths); plastic (various widths and strengths).

Plaster- and cement-impregnated tapes (wide) are wetted before use and quickly set hard. The cement ones give a waterproof seal.

Pipe- and hose-sealing tapes come in two parts: bituminous cloth tape is wrapped round, followed by plastic tape, and then by more cloth tape.

Sticking things together

There are repair tapes for PVC pools, etc.

Lighter weight tapes are sold in a variety of shops – stationers, furnishing, etc.; the strong, wide, waterproof ones are stocked by builders' merchants.

Finally, there are sticky foam pads (sold by stationers), useful when you want a space filled as well as two things stuck together – for instance, when replacing a loose wall tile.

Methods

The success of an adhesive depends upon having a clean, solid, grease-free and (usually) dry surface. Abrasive paper or an abrasive tool is often useful (see page 119), not only to remove rough or loose bits but to get off old glue or paint so that the adhesive can make contact with the surface of the base material. Very shiny surfaces often need to be abraded to give the adhesive a better grip. Occasionally, very porous or powdery surfaces may first need sealing by painting or primer, diluted PVA or wallpaper paste – let this dry before attempting to stick the parts together.

Do not use too much adhesive. Often a thin coat is stronger than a thick one: read the instructions.

When an adhesive takes hours to set, the parts it is joining may need to be weighted down or held together meantime – a matter for improvisation if the job does not warrant buying clamps designed for the purpose. Here are some ideas. If none suits the job you are doing, use – if appropriate – a high speed adhesive, while you stand and hold the pieces together. (Do not fasten too tightly, otherwise you will squeeze out all the adhesive.)

Sticky tape may hold two parts together temporarily: do not pull it off until the join has set really hard. Masking tape is particularly easy to pull off. Brown paper and flour-and-water paste may be useful because the paper shrinks as it dries, pulling the stuck parts together, but it is slow to dry.

Sticking things together

If wire, string or buckled webbing can go round the object and be well tightened, twisted or wedged, this will pull the parts together. For small jobs, clothes pegs, paperclips (the bulldog type) or elastic bands have their uses.

Fine nails may be driven in to hold one piece of wood to another while the adhesive sets. If necessary, filler and stain can be used later to conceal their holes (or their heads, if they are not removed).

Wedges hammered temporarily between doors or windows and their frames will force them square while joints or splits are setting in place.

Plasticine or any doughy substance can be useful as a temporary support for small parts while being glued together. Kitchen foil is sometimes an alternative, moulded to shape, or a box of sand.

Weighting things down with something like a brick or stone is not always feasible, but a bag of sand will weight down things that have a curved or uneven surface.

A vicegrip can be locked to grip things while adhesive is setting.

An overhead or overhanging join (for instance, in a window sill) may be given support if a stick with a board on top can be wedged below it, or a board clamped as shown on page 110.

Smaller items that can be moved to a drawer can be clamped together in it.

In many situations where support is difficult (for instance, when sticking something to a vertical or overhead surface) the solution may be to use contact adhesive or double-sided sticky tape.

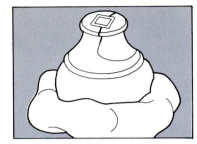

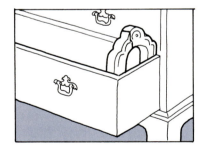

Nailing things together

Hammers
The two most useful types to have are:
A claw hammer, as heavy as is comfortable for you. Its curved claw is for pulling out old nails and levering up boards.
A Warrington hammer, half the weight of the claw hammer. Its narrow face is for starting small nails.

Nails
For jobs described in this book, the following nails will prove best:

Wire nails, for many purposes. Though round-headed ones are easier to hammer in (and to get out), ovals are less likely to split wood and their small heads can be punched below the surface. Place the heads longways to the grain of the wood.

Masonry nails Specially hard, to penetrate concrete (if not very hard) or brick. Tap in with quick, light blows (mind your eyes: hammer through a piece of card as a shield against pieces of flying masonry). Take care to use the right length, for over-long ones may split hard bricks (2cm [1in] should be the maximum penetrated except in softer surfaces). Never use many in one brick; and do not hammer into the mortar between the bricks.

Panel pins Small, slender and with a tiny head that can be punched below the surface. A spring pin-pusher is ideal for them. Used on thin wood such as beadings.

Clout nails Large heads on short bodies, serrated for maximum grip. Used for things that smaller heads might pull through: roofing felt, qmates, sash cords, fencing. Galvanized.

Floor brads Big, flat and square, with a strong grip that doesn't split.

Some nails are available rustproofed for outdoor use.

Nails are cheaper bought in quantity than in tiny packets.

About sizes: the fatter the nail the better it will hold in wood (but not in hard bricks). When nailing a piece of wood on to

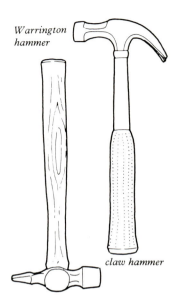

Warrington hammer

claw hammer

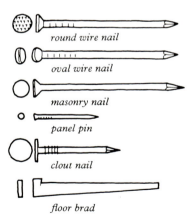

round wire nail

oval wire nail

masonry nail

panel pin

clout nail

floor brad

Nailing things together

another, the nail should normally be 2½–3 times longer than the first piece of wood is thick.

Using a hammer

Holding it right at the end of the handle, rest it on the nail head, then raise it and hit the nail. Let the weight of the hammer head to the work, not your arm and shoulder.

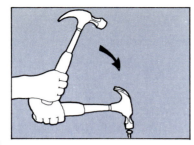

When using a large nail where it may split, first make a small starting hole for it with a drill. A dip in paraffin will help the nail to go in smoothly.

A nail-punch is used when you want to hammer a nail-head below the surface of the wood. Tip-sizes vary, and dimpled tips are better than flat ones.

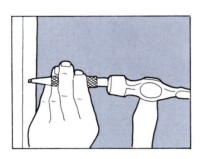

To hold fine nails, or any nails used in confined spaces, when your fingers would be in the way of the hammer, use a slip of card with the nail through it – or use a dab of Plasticine or anything doughy – or a wire paperclip.

Nails hold better in wood if hammered in at a slight angle.

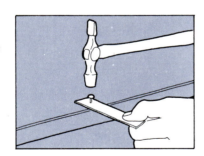

When hammering in several nails along the length of the grain, stagger them a little to reduce the risk of a split. (Do not nail into end grain, nor near edges if you can avoid doing so.

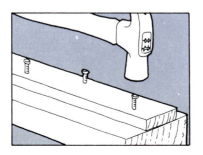

Nailing things together

To remove a nail, place the claw of a hammer under the nail-head and lever it up (in the direction of the grain) until the hammer handle is vertical, no further. Use card to protect the wood from the hammer head.

Put a piece of wood under the hammer head and lever again. To pull smaller nails out, pliers can be used or, better still, pincers. After each pull, shift the jaws a little lower down the nail.

Particularly when hammering extra-hard masonry nails, be sure the hammer face is clear and smooth: slivers of metal flying off are very dangerous.

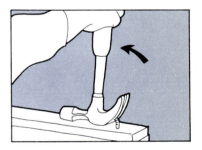

If an ill-aimed blow dents wood, apply steam and this may restore it (an iron over a wet cloth will do).

Screwing things together

Although nailing is quicker, screwing is stronger – and screws are easier to get out later, if need arises. The longer the screwdriver, the more effective it is – a 15cm (6in) shaft would suit most jobs in this book. (Extra-short and extra-long screwdrivers are for use in confined spaces or narrow ones into which your hand cannot reach. Offset screwdrivers enable you to screw from the side.)

You will need at least three screwdrivers with different widths of tip, because it is of the greatest importance that the tip should exactly match the slot of each screw being used (a handle with interchangeable blades is an alternative). For the repairs in this chapter, tips 5–8mm ($\frac{7}{32}$–$\frac{5}{16}$in) wide would suit screws of gauges 6, 8 and 10.

The best handle is whatever you find most comfortable: the fatter and smoother the better, as a rule. Some people like a pistol-grip, shown here. A good choice is ratchet screwdrivers because they are easier to manipulate. Some shafts are square, or have a squared area at the top, so that pliers can grip when you need to exert extra force. Look for a thick strong shaft, and a really square tip.

Increasingly, domestic appliances are sold with Pozidriv screws in them, so a screwdriver to match will be needed for jobs on these, too. A no. 2 Pozidriv screwdriver will drive screws in gauges 6, 8 and 10. Another type of cross head, Philips, can be used with a Posidriv screwdriver.

Screw heads may be rounded (usually for fixing metal to wood), or 'countersunk', to fit flush with the surface of the wood or metal. Raised-head screws are a cross between the two. Plated or brass ones are preferable out of doors or wherever damp may cause rust.

The length of screw is normally determined by the thickness of the fitment being fixed: the screw should be at least three times as long as this. The thicker it is the better, if you are screwing into a soft material. The 'gauge' of a screw is its

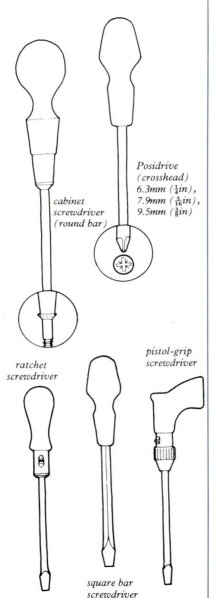

cabinet
screwdriver
(round bar)

Posidrive
(crosshead)
6.3mm ($\frac{1}{4}$in),
7.9mm ($\frac{5}{16}$in),
9.5mm ($\frac{3}{8}$in)

ratchet
screwdriver

pistol-grip
screwdriver

square bar
screwdriver

Screwing things together

thickness: commonest are nos. 6, 8, and 10. Screws are much cheaper if bought in quantity, not small packets.

Screwing into woodwork

1 Hold the screwdriver shaft precisely in line with the screw, curling the left forefinger round to steady it. The right hand should have the handle in its palm while thumb and forefinger grasp the ferrule.
2 A starting hole may be made by several means. A small screw or nail can make one for a larger screw. Lightly hammering a screw will sometimes do. It is better to use (in order of size of screw) a bradawl, which is pushed in with its blade at right angles to the grain; a gimlet, which is twisted in and then untwisted; or a drill. Starting holes should be smaller than the screw thread but never force a screw to get it started.
3 Screws turn more easily if grease or wax is put on the tip, and this will discourage rust too.
4 Screwing into end grain or near edges is likely to cause a split. Splits also result from a close row of screws along the grain of wood, so try to stagger them.
5 Except in soft materials, do not try to drive the wide (smooth) part of the shank in the narrow hole made by the screwthread (see pages 86–7).

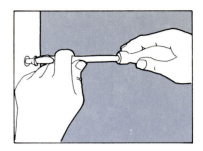

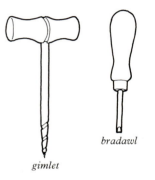

gimlet

bradawl

84

Screwing things together

6 To hold a small screw when starting it off, slip a small piece of tube (even a drinking-straw) over it and the screwdriver tip; or use something doughy, like Plasticine, to hold it; or push it through a bit of card or a wire paperclip which you can hold.

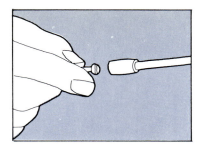

7 Plywood, chipboard, veneered board, hardboard and softboard should be drilled before inserting a screw. There are special screws for chipboard and softboards, because these do not hold ordinary screws well; or chipboard plugs can be put in before using ordinary screws.

8 Have screwdriver tips reground when they loose their squareness. Do not use them for prising and chipping jobs – buy a cheap one just for this.

Using round-headed screws

1 Drill hole in fitment, of same width as the smooth part of the screw's shank.
2 Make starting-hole for screw in the woodwork.
3 Put screw through fitment and drive into woodwork.

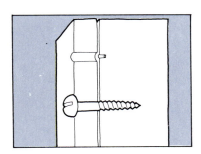

Using countersunk screws

1 As 1 above.
2 Use countersink bit to widen the top of the hole in the fitment, to fit head of the screw. (With soft wood this may be unnecessary.)
3 As 2 above.
4 As 3 above.

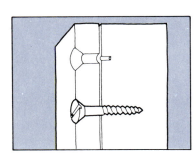

Screwing a thin metal fitting on to woodwork

1 Drill hole in woodwork of same width and length as the smooth part of the screw's shank. (With soft wood this may be unnecessary.)
2 At the end of this, make a starting hole for the point of the screw.
3 Drive screw through fitting into woodwork.

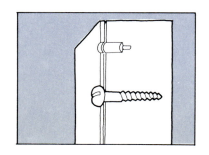

Screwing things together

Screwing a thick fitment to woodwork (unless its weight demands a very long screw)

1 Drill hole in fitment wide enough to receive the screw-head and screwdriver tip, followed by a narrower hole to fit the smooth part of the screw's shank.
2 Make starting hole for screw in woodwork.
3 Put screw in through fitment, and drive into woodwork.

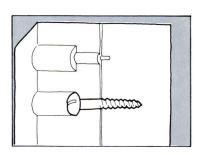

Screwing into walls (brick or concrete)

A hole has to be bored then lined with a resilient wallplug of the same width as the hole, or with hard-setting filler, before a screw can be driven in.

Hole, plug and screw must be related in both width and length (if the wall is plastered, allow at least 2cm [1in] more length for getting through this: the plaster will not give the screw any support). A no. 8 screw does for most things, except very heavy loads.

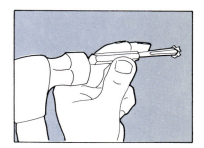

To make the hole, a drill may be used (drilling is dealt with on page 88) but often a simple wall-plugging tool will do. Tap lightly with a hammer, turn it a little, tap, turn, tap – and so on. Choose a size to match the plug and screw. These tools are not suitable for use on tiled walls, which should always be drilled.

Wallplugs are little tubes which may be of a wood-like fibre or (better) of nylon or other plastic, often with elaborate ridges or slits designed to grip the sides of the hole when the screw is driven in. Plastic ones can be bought in strips that can be cut into whatever length is required.

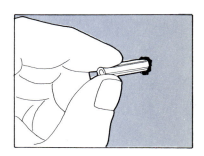

An alternative is to use wall-filler, which will suit any length or width of hole – handy if re-using an old hole that has widened. The type sold for the job is a mix of cement and asbestos fibres, but other fillers can be used if strong enough (epoxy putty, for instance). The filler takes a few minutes to set. Drive the screw in while the filler is still soft.

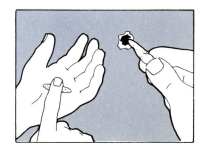

Screwing things together

If a screw will not go right in, or is loose when it is in, start again with a different size of hole and plug. Or try dipping the screw in adhesive, if it is loose, or inserting a matchstick inside the plug.

Instead of plugging a hole and driving a screw into it, an expanding bolt can be used (this costs more). It does not grip by means of a screwthread but has a flexible sleeve which expands to grip the hole when the bolt is driven in with a screwdriver. Various sizes are available.

Using a wall plug
1 Drill a hole in the masonry, of the gauge of the plug to be used and slightly deeper than its length. Blow out the dust (mind your eyes).
2 Insert screw half-way into plug, push plug into hole and drive screw in (the wide part of the shank should be partly in the plaster or tile – if any – not in the masonry, and partly protruding).
3 Drill a hole in the fitment of the same size as the smooth part of the screw's shank. (If using a countersunk screw, see page 85).
4 Withdraw the screw, put the fitment in place, and drive the screw through it and into the wall.

Note Some plastic or nylon plugs differ from this in that they are shaped to accept part of the wide shank as well as the screw thread.

Screwing things together

Using wall filler
1 Drill a hole longer than the thread of the screw – try to make the end wider than the opening. Pack with damp filler and make a starting hole in it.
2 Drill a hole in the fitment of the same size as the smooth part of the screw's shank. (If using a countersunk screw, see page 85).
3 Put the fitment in place and insert the screw through it and into the wall.

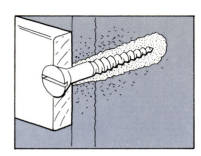

Screwing into other surfaces
Very hard, very soft and hollow surfaces present problems. Either screws go in with difficulty or they fail to stay in. So first consider alternatives: powerful adhesives or even double-sided adhesive tape (heavy-duty grade) may suffice for purposes not involving support of loads, provided wallpaper or paint are removed first. Self-adhesive hooks and other fitments have their uses. Surprisingly heavy fitments can be hung quite safely from hooks in picture-rails. Sticking on lengths of wood with extra-strong adhesive, to which fitments may then be screwed, is another expedient. But for some fitments there may be no alternative to screwing into the wall. Here are some methods that help.

Lath-and-plaster, plasterboard, hollow hardboard doors: try to locate, with a sharp point, one of the wood uprights which, in walls, are usually about 40cm (15in) apart or, in doors, run down the middle; then screw into this, as for woodwork. Otherwise, drill a hole and use a toggle or other expanding screw, see below, provided the load is not too heavy for the wall.

Hollow concrete blocks (internal walls only): Drill a hole and use a toggle screw, see below.

Aerated cement blocks (internal walls): Alternatives are: extra-big screws and more of them than usual; ribbed plastic wallplugs; expanding bolts; cut nails. First smearing cement filler on the screw or plug will help to hold in this soft material.

Screwing things together

Toggle screws, when driven through a hole drilled in a board, spread out a device behind them which spreads the load on the back of the board. To get the right type, tell the shop the thickness of the board and of the fitment to be fastened to it, and also how much space there is behind in which the device can operate. With some, after the anchor has expanded, the screw is withdrawn then re-inserted through the fitment that is being hung. With other types, the job has to be done in one, as the holding device falls off and is lost if the screw is withdrawn.

Where no great strain is involved, use plastic wallpugs that, when pushed through the hole, expand behind the board and anchor themselves to the back of it. A screw is then driven into the plug. There are coathooks for doors which operate like these plugs. These are suitable only for 2cm (1in) board.

There are also special nuts with rubber sleeves which, after passing through a hole in a board, spread out to anchor the bolt to the back of the board, and these have a wide variety of uses.

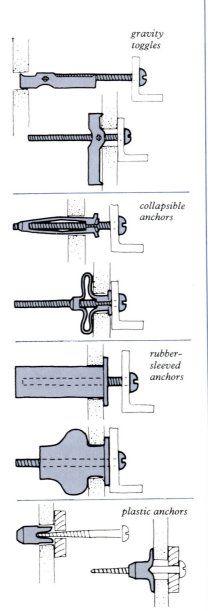

gravity toggles

collapsible anchors

rubber-sleeved anchors

plastic anchors

Screwing things together

Undoing stiff screws
(Many of these methods also apply to nuts and bolts, hinges, window fastenings, etc.)
If stuck by paint or rust, apply paint- or rust-stripper.
Use dismantling lubricant: the best type has exceptional penetration, and also releases rust.
Tighten screw before undoing it – this may break rust inside.
To exert more force, hammer the screwdriver; or use pliers or a vicegrip on the shaft of the screwdriver.
Apply the top of a hot poker to the head of the screw, to expand the metal.
Use hammer and cold chisel at an angle to the slot in the head, to exert force on its outer edge.

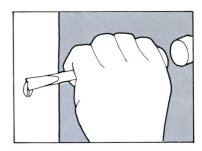

87

Making holes

Drills

Holes may need to be drilled in walls for screws; to make a starting point from which to saw a slot in wood; or in order to pour preservative or damp-proofing fluid into woodwork or walls. For big jobs like this last one, it may be best to hire an electric drill equipped for the particular job in hand, but the others can be done with a simple hand-drill.

Hand-drills take drills up to $\frac{5}{16}$in as a rule. A set consisting of sizes from $\frac{1}{16}$in to $\frac{1}{4}$in would be a good start, together with a countersink (see diagram) and at least one masonry drill, gauge 8, for walls. Good drills are worth resharpening, and some manufacturers offer this service free.

Masonry drills soon blunt, so it is worth getting the most durable – tipped with tungsten carbide as a rule. On concrete it is better not to use a drill but a wallplug tool (see page 86).

An alternative for wood is a push drill, if all you want to do is make screwholes: merely pump up and down with one hand – very easy.

Keep drills lubricated, clean and rust-free.

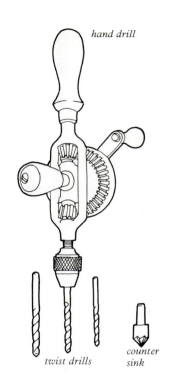

hand drill

twist drills

counter sink

| Screw gauge | Screwdriver tip | Twist drill | | Masonry drill (and plugs) |
		For thread of screw	For shank of screw	
6	6mm ($\frac{1}{4}$in)	2.5mm ($\frac{3}{32}$in)	3.5mm ($\frac{9}{64}$in)	6
8	8mm ($\frac{5}{16}$in)	2.7mm ($\frac{7}{64}$in)	4.3mm ($\frac{11}{64}$in)	8
10	9.5mm ($\frac{3}{8}$in)	3mm ($\frac{1}{8}$in)	4.7mm ($\frac{3}{16}$in)	10

Making holes

Using a drill

1 To insert a drill, hold the crank-handle to lock the gear wheel. Unscrew the chuck a little and put in the drill. Holding the chuck with one hand, turn the crank handle with the other to screw it up again, and tighten by turning the chuck.

2 Before starting, make a small dent with anything sharp in which to locate the drill tip. If the surface is slippery or likely to crumble (tiles or plaster, for instance), first put a bit of sticky tape on.

3 Drilling a wide hole is sometimes easier if you first drill a narrow one.

4 To ensure that you drill to the right depth, mark it on the drill with a piece of sticky tape.

5 Exert pressure on the handle, not on the wheel. Pressure and turning should both be steady. The harder the wood or wall, the slower should be the speed.

6 Keep the drill accurately in line with the intended direction of the hole. Vertical drilling: try to keep your eyes above the drill shaft.

7 If the drill tip needs lubricating while you work, put white spirit in the hole, not oil, which may stain the surface.

8 When drilling walls, frequently withdraw the drill to let the brick dust out. Go deep enough to get well beyond the plaster (or tiles). You can drill into the joins between tiles but not into the joins between bricks.

9 When withdrawing a drill from a hole, continue turning it clockwise unless it has jammed.

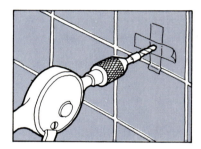

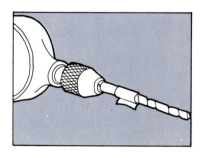

Cutting things

Saws

A tenon saw is the most useful type for the jobs in this chapter. An alternative is a multi-purpose saw which will do other work too (such as cutting metal pipes).

When buying a tenon saw, choose one that is about 25cm (10in) long: 12 to 14 teeth per inch is about right for most house repair work. It will have a strip of brass or steel along the top to give it rigidity. Some are sold with blade-guards; some with a non-stick coating to help the blade pass easily through the wood.

Multi-purpose saws either have changeable blades or one blade with specially shaped teeth of tungsten carbide, in order to cope with any material, thin or thick, soft or hard, smooth or coarse. The former are replaceable when worn out. The angle of the blade can be adjusted, making it easier to keep it at the correct angle to work that is awkwardly situated, like a stair nosing or a floorboard.

For work in small spaces where neither of these saws could penetrate, a craft knife that can take a narrow saw blade will do (see page 00). A junior hacksaw, for cutting metal, costs very little.

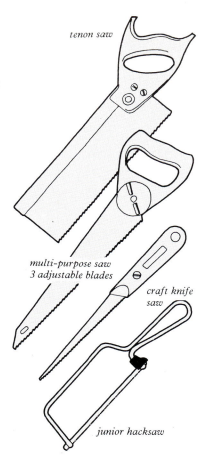

tenon saw

multi-purpose saw 3 adjustable blades

craft knife saw

junior hacksaw

Using a saw

1 The best way to mark wood is by scoring with a craft knife. Allow 1mm for the thickness of the sawcut, which should be on the 'waste' side of the line.
2 Start by pulling the teeth slowly backwards, using the thumb of your other hand to keep the side of the blade in position.

Cutting things

3 When cutting across the grain of wood, start at a slight angle then keep the edge of the saw horizontal. (Or at a very slight angle if the board is thin or wide.)
4 When cutting along the grain, tilt the saw to 45°. (Because of the thickness of the back of a tenon saw, it is not very suitable for long cuts.)
5 If a cut has to go deep, first saw a down-slanting cut from middle to front, then another from middle to back. Keep repeating this, gradually straightening the blade.
6 Sawing should be steady, with your wrist stiff but exerting only light pressure. Use the whole length of the blade at each cut. (The cutting is normally done on the pushing stroke only.)
7 On long cuts, watch the blade near the handle to check whether you are still sawing straight. Support the end towards which you are sawing so that it does not break off before you get there, go slowly, and shorten your cutting strokes.
8 If you have many 45° angles to cut (sometimes needed at corners where two pieces of wood join), buy a mitre block to guide the saw. Otherwise cut the corner of a postcard in half and drawing-pin it to the wood as a guide.
9 When sawing painted wood, remove the paint first to reveal hidden nails. Both paint and nails will blunt the saw.
10 Here are some ways to hold a board steady while sawing it.
   a. Use a stool or box and kneel one leg on it;
   b. Make a bench hook from 3 scraps of wood to use as shown;
   c. Either buy G-cramps to hold the board to the table, or improvise with, e.g., vice-grip, kitchen mincer clamp. Cramp work as near as possible to a table leg, for stability.

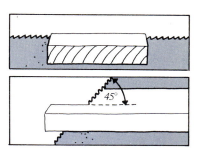

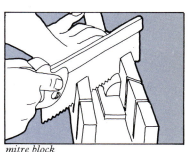

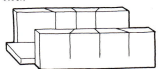

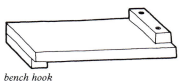

mitre block

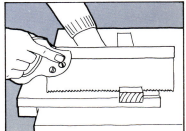

bench hook

Cutting things

Cold chisels

Cold chisels are heavy steel tools used with a weighty hammer to break up defective concrete, plaster, tiles, etc. (A squat, heavy club hammer is best, but an ordinary one will do.) Choose one with a flat tip about 2cm wide; very wide ones, called bolsters, are mainly for grooving plaster, concrete, etc., and for prising up floorboards. Take chisels back for regrinding when the blade, or the top, loses its proper shape, or file them. When chipping concrete with one, wear goggles.

Wood chisels

Wood chisels are precision-made tools with a razor-sharp edge that should never be used on any surface except wood – some makers provide blade covers to protect them when not in use. Those that have bevelled sides are easier to use, provided that, for the sort of jobs in this book, they are of really sturdy quality. Plastic-handled ones stand up well to use with a hammer (or ideally, a wooden mallet). For most jobs in this book a width of 2cm or ¾in would be suitable. Take chisels back for sharpening and regrinding occasionally.

Knives

Apart from a sturdy pair of scissors (like the 'snips' shown here, which will cut almost any material), you will need a craft knife with a razor-sharp blade, strong and about 2cm (1in) wide. Blades can be replaced when worn out and are interchangeable with others for special purposes like cutting floor coverings, cutting round fitments, a saw blade for wood and so on.

   The safe way to direct a knife (or chisel) is away from or at the side of your body in case it slips. Never press excessively hard lest it slips or snaps; if you need to do so, it probably means the blade is blunt and should be changed. Keep your hands behind the cutting edge.

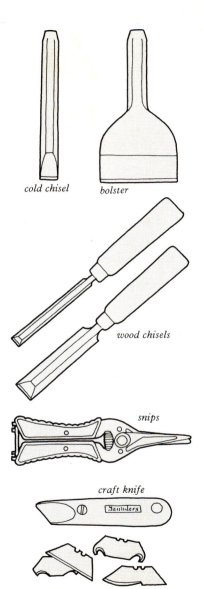

cold chisel   *bolster*

wood chisels

snips

craft knife

Cutting things

Abrading tools

These tools have thousands of tiny blades on their face, which rasp away the surface of wood or other materials – either to reduce its thickness (for instance, a sticking door) or to smooth out irregularities (for instance, uneven plaster). The cutting is usually done on the forward stroke. Their blades vary in coarseness to suit different materials, and in shape. They are replaceable.

   If the resultant dust irritates you, wear a gauze mask, sold by chemists

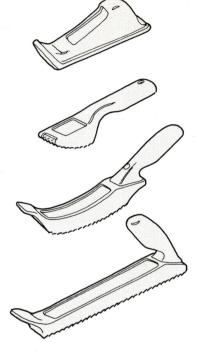

abrading tools

Filling things

For every kind of hole, gap or crack there is an appropriate filler – coarse or fine, rough or smooth, hard or resilient. There are waterproof grades for out of doors and bathrooms. Most fillers can be painted over; or else can have colouring matter mixed in. A standby kit of just two fillers, one hard and one resilient, would be adequate for most small jobs about the house.

Some adhesives and adhesive tapes, already described on pages 80–1, fill as well as stick – PVA can be combined with (for example) sawdust, sand, plaster, shredded newspaper, string or any other absorbent material suited to the gap or crack in question, provided it is not exposed to damp.

Cement-based products
When water is added (the less of this the better) these rapidly start to set and will become waterproof. They soon harden once the bag is open, so buy minimum quantities. A strong mix of mortar (3 or more parts sand to 1 cement) is used for cracks in bricks, concrete and pools; a weaker one to fix loose paving-stones, tiles or bricks and to repair rendering on walls. Bought ready-mixed, nothing else is required except water, though PVA adhesive can be added for extra strength. Cement alone can be used to repair metalwork – pipes and gutters, for instance. Quick-setting cement is firm in 10 minutes, hard in half an hour. Where great strength is needed (like drives, steps or the foundation of a fence post), ask for concrete mix. For a fine surface effect, there is a cement-resin powder usable on all kinds of materials.

The white cement filler used between ceramic tiles is called grouting.

The fillers sold as an alternative to wallplugs are a cement-fibre compound.

Wash trowels, and clean off any splashes, before cement sets.

mixing cement

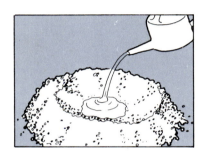

Filling things

Plaster and its alternatives
Plaster is itself a fast-setting filler, very smooth; but alternatives based on hard-setting cellulose compounds or resins are now much used instead because they are easier to handle. Most are for indoors only, where they can be used not only on walls but woodwork and metalwork too. The majority are in powder form, and water has to be added; easier but dearer are ready-mixed pastes.

Epoxy putty
This is worth its extra cost when an extremely hard, strong, waterproof filling is needed. It comes in two parts, of doughy consistency, which are kneaded together before use. This is similar in nature to the glassfibre kits sold by car accessory shops: epoxy adhesive with glassfibre reinforcement, setting rock-hard. Another variant has resilience.

Resilient fillers
Usually described as sealants or mastics, these are needed wherever movement takes place (around door and window frames, floorboards and skirting boards, and where baths and sinks join the wall). There are many brands of mastic in varying degrees of water-resistance. They are gummy substances, usually squeezed out of a tube or a cartridge, which set with a rubbery surface and remain flexible indefinitely. An alternative is silicone rubber (white or coloured, in tubes), which has a particularly smooth and shiny surface and a strong grip. It takes a few hours to set.

Leak-sealer
A rubbery paste usable even under water, this fills cracks or holes not only in metal but glass, rubber, most plastics, wood, or fabrics such as awnings. It can be reinforced with fabric to span wider gaps.

Plastic sealing strips
To push into or glue over cracks between,

carrying plaster, etc., on a home-made hawk or board

picking it up on trowel

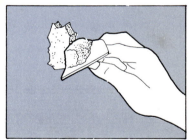
applying it

Filling things

for example, baths and walls. Plastic foam strips can be used inside wide cracks, with sealant on top.

Other specialised fillers

On some occasions it may be worth getting a product specifically formulated for filling a particular surface – wood, metal, plastic.

Methods

Detailed instructions are on packets, but cracks and holes always need to be cleaned out first (then sometimes wetted, sometimes dried – depending upon the type of product) and the filler pressed in. It is important to squeeze or press fillers down well, and not leave them spanning a hollow space. In wide areas, fillers often need a 'key' to hold them: smooth surfaces can be roughened with abrasive paper; sometimes hammering in a few nails helps.

Deep holes can sometimes be packed with paper, chicken wire, kitchen foil or other suitable material. Large gaps can often be bridged, or curved shapes created, by using perforated metal sold by hardware shops for the purpose. Two thin layers of filler are normally better than one deep one, the first being left to set (after roughening its surface) before the second goes in. Some fillers can be reinforced with a bandage or patch of open-weaved fabric, metal mesh, etc.

When building up a broken edge on anything, a support of wood, stiff card or some other straight material needs to be secured, to hold the filler while it is setting. (See pages 81–2 for suggestions about supports.)

If there is an adjoining surface to which it is important that straying filler (or adhesive) should *not* stick, either cover it with Vaseline or sheets of polythene (plastic bag) because almost nothing will stick to these materials; or else use masking-tape and paper which can be peeled off later.

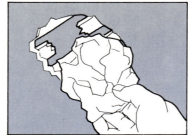

filling a deep hole

Filling things

Hard fillers usually need finishing off with abrasive paper after they have set if a smooth finish is wanted; others may be smoothed with a wet finger or trowel; polythene film (plastic bag) can be used over a filler while it sets, to leave a shiny surface.

Warning Don't wash filling knives and trowels at the sink – cement or plaster can clog a U-bend.

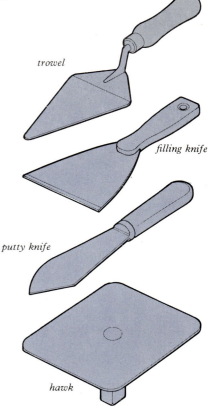

trowel

filling knife

putty knife

hawk

Woodwork in general

Wet rot
Signs are: strands of fungus fanning out; soft, darkened wood; splits; flaking paint.

Method
Locate the source of damp and deal with it. The woodwork will then dry out.

After scraping out rotted wood and applying fungicide to the rest, filler can be used.

If a vertical post bearing weight is affected, use epoxy filler for strength. Hammer some nails in to provide reinforcement for the filler.

Prevention
Damp-proofing preservatives for wood exposed to rain are of two types. Creosote (which should be labelled as conforming to British Standard 144) is the cheapest and most effective material. As it will not penetrate damp wood, use it in dry weather. Plants nearby need to be covered until the creosote is dry. To get it into inaccessible timber (such as the buried parts of fence posts), drill down-sloping holes and fill these, using a funnel. Plug the holes with a filler or corks that you can remove when another application is needed. The other alternative is to use oil- or spirit-based preservative. This needs more frequent renewal, and may harm birds or pets as well as plants while it is still wet. For fences with creeper on them, get a preservative that will not harm plants. There are preservatives that will restore its natural colour to cedar that has gone grey. Fences, etc., should be repainted with preservative every few years.

Woodwork in general

Dry rot
Signs are: crumbling of softened wood (probe with a sharp knife), wood breaking up into cubes, a smell of mushrooms, reddish dust, fungus, white strands or 'wool', warping or cracking, bulging plaster.

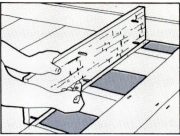

evidence of dry rot

Method
Despite its name, dry rot too is caused by damp, so locate the source of this and deal with it.

Dry rot is more serious than wet rot because it can spread rapidly and far, even through masonry: everything affected must be cut out (when joists or roof timbers are affected they must be replaced in their entirety by a professional, because they will no longer bear much weight). Replacement timber should be bought impregnated with preservative.

1 Affected material (together with adjoining good material in every direction, to a distance of ½m or more) must be cut out from its surroundings and burned lest the spores of the fungus spread.

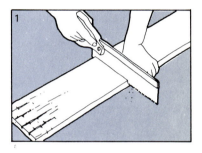

2 Fungicide is then applied liberally to every surface within 1½m of the outbreak (masonry and plaster as well as wood) and to the replacement wood. The fluid can be brushed on or, if large areas are involved, it is worth hiring a spray. Masonry can be sterilized with a blow-lamp.

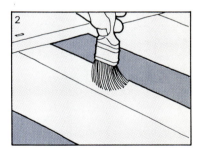

3 In addition 1.5cm (¾in) down-sloping holes should be drilled all round the area and the fluid poured into them through a funnel.

4 Where appearance is unimportant, a coat of black bitumen paint on walls will help to prevent new growth (apply it after the use of the fungicide and when the walls have dried).

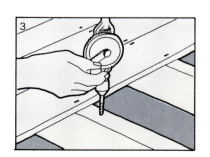

Woodwork in general

Woodworm (furniture beetle)
Signs are: tiny holes with powdered wood nearby. (Holes alone may mean the woodworm is no longer active.) In Surrey, the far more serious longhorn beetle makes holes nearly 1cm ($\frac{1}{2}$in) across.

Tools and materials
Woodworm fluid. (An aerosol with fine nozzle may be useful. If appearances do not matter, choose a tinted fluid so that you can see what area you have covered.)

Method
1 Cover any carpets, plastics, etc., that might get fluid on them, including electric flexes. Dust the surfaces to be treated. Read instructions very carefully.
2 Inject the fluid into the woodwork at 10cm (4in) intervals (using the woodworm holes for this purpose) if it is made of hardwood: for instance, oak beams. This is not essential for softwoods, such as roof timbers.
3 Then cover the whole surface with fluid. It is important to do undersides, insides and backs of any affected woodwork, including stairs. Furniture as well as structural timber should be treated if necessary; and every fifth floorboard raised so that you can spray the joists underneath if they have been affected. (The holes you see are merely exit holes. Other woodworms are still inside: the insect can live up to 10 years inside the wood before emerging.)

Woodwork in general

If large areas, such as roof timbers or floors and joists, need treating, buy 5 litres for every 20sq m to be done and use a spray – with a long extension to reach into attic apex and eaves (wear non-rubber gloves, face mask and headscarf or cap). If there are spaces between attic joists, take planks to stand on and be careful not to spill fluid where it may stain ceilings below. Water tanks, insulation materials and cables must be covered and the attic cleared of things being stored. In fact, insulation ought to be lifted to expose joists fully. The fluid is explosive, so only a dim light is safe (and no smoking). It is simpler to use a paste insecticide to spread on woodwork, if you can reach it.

A much easier alternative, provided the attic is not draughty, is to place in it every April insect killers which release a vapour which will kill the insects throughout the summer (their emergent period). They will need renewal every year and are not a cure for a really bad infestation.

Doors

Splits, gaping joints, sagging

Where strength matters more than appearance (e.g., garden gate), screw on a metal brace, or nail a piece of plywood across the crack. Before fastening a brace the gate, etc., will have to be either removed or wedged to get it square.

Large, sagging doors can be braced with a bar fixed diagonally as shown (or by a wire tautened by a special device at the end – as sold for tensioning wire fences).

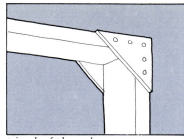

triangle of plywood

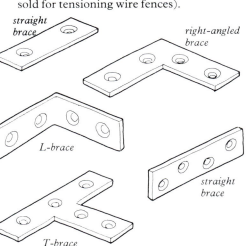

straight brace

right-angled brace

L-brace

straight brace

T-brace

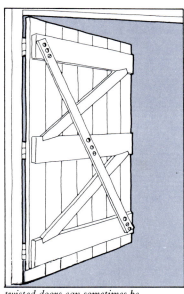

twisted doors can sometimes be corrected like this

Doors

Difficulty in closing

Possible causes
(a) tenons protruding slightly – see diagram
(b) hinges loosened
(c) wood swollen
(d) joint loosened
(e) frame (or threshold) distorted
(f) multiple layers of paint

Methods
(a) protruding tenons
1 Wedge the door open firmly with scrap wood between it and the floor.
2 Level the tenon ends with an abrading tool.
3 Repaint.

(b) loosened hinge
1 If the screws will not tighten, wedge the door open at right-angles to the frame, and undo the screws.
2 If the screw holes have become enlarged, fill them with plastic wood or epoxy putty and re-insert the screws after it has hardened. Even better, it may be possible to use larger screws in the holes, but keep the screws in their original position – do not move the hinge.
3 If the hinges seem too deeply recessed, unscrew one at a time on the deeper side and slip a piece of card underneath. If the recesses are too shallow, deepen them in turn with a wood chisel. Doing this to one hinge may cure a door that is sticking at the opposite corner.

(c) swollen wood
1 Unscrew hinges of door and take it down.
2 Smooth wood off the hinge side and/or the top until the door will fit its opening, then (after repainting) replace it.

Note Wood may be prevented from swelling in damp weather if, during dry weather, it is more thoroughly painted – particularly along all eges and bottom.

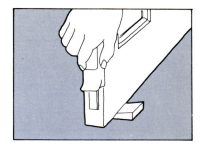

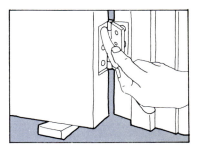

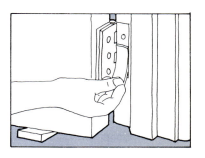

Doors

Doors

(d) loosened joint
1 Clean out the gaping joint.
2 Squeeze in adhesive (PVA or epoxy).
3 Wedge the opened door until the joint is closed up and its framework is square again. Leave till set. Alternatively, use a brace – see page 95.

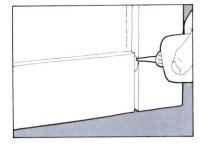

(e) distorted frame
1 To find where door is sticking, look for rubbed paint; or chalk its edge, close the door and observe where the chalk has rubbed off. (Or use carbon paper, or paper smoked over a candle-flame.)
2 Use an abrading tool to smooth the chalky part of the frame. Repaint.

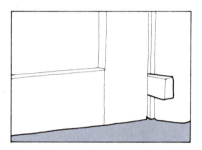

(f) multiple layers of paint
1 Use abrading tool or paint stripper to remove all paint, then sandpaper smooth.
2 Prime and paint in the usual way.

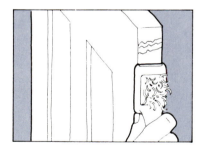

Warped or sagging

If the cause is that one side only has had a sheet of hardboard, asbestos board, etc., attached to it, fit a similar sheet on the other side. The day before using hardboard, wet the back (see page 99).

A wedge can be used to force the jamming part back into shape: you will have to leave the door closed for some days, and the door may later sag again.

A slight sag at the bottom can sometimes be corrected by putting a wedge under the opened door, unscrewing the lower hinge, slipping a piece of card into the hinge recess and re-screwing.

On very big doors (e.g., garage), screwing a castor to the bottom (by the opening edge) may solve the problem:
See also Draughts, pages 97–8.

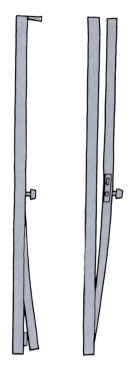

Doors

Opening impeded by floor-covering

Tools and materials
Screwdriver. Rising-butt hinges (left- or right-handed as required). Countersunk screws.
Abrading tool (or saw). Sandpaper.

Method
1 Unscrew the old hinges and replace with new ones. Rising-butt hinges come in two parts: the half with the spindle goes on the frame.
2 Before re-hanging the door, smooth (or saw) away part of the inner top corner to provide clearance – the door rises a little as it opens.
  Note These hinges need regular lubrication (just a drop, at the top). They will not solve the problem if carpet is fitted close to the door.
  If the problem is only slight, it may be simpler to remove the door and, using an abrading tool, shave a little wood off the bottom – or even merely to roll back the floorcovering and swing the door to and fro across coarse sandpaper placed underneath it.
  If the problem is severe, or if new and thick floor-covering is to be laid, or if carpet comes right up to the door, saw a strip off the bottom of the door. Use a thin strip of wood laid on the floor against the closed door to mark a line to saw.

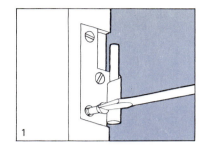

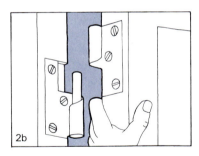

Doors

Hinge squeaking or stiff

Tools and materials needed
Lubricant or screwdriver

Method
1 Metal hinges – apply a drop of lubricant at the top.
2 Nylon hinges – slacken or tighten the screws slightly.

Draughts at sides
Use a lighted match to locate the gap if it is not obvious. If the door is not hanging properly, the large gaps occurring at some points only may be cured by re-hanging the door or by treatments suggested for sagging doors (page 96).

sagging doors (page 96).

If the door is correctly hinged yet draughts still enter, the gap can be stopped up by fitting draught excluder all round the frame. Here are the most common types (there are others): Self-adhesive foam strip, preferably with a wipe-clean surface – warm slightly, cut, and press into position without stretching it, after cleaning surface with detergent. (2) Rubber or plastic tubing to tack round (this is for wide gaps), or in metal channels to screw on. (3) Springy metal or plastic strips, V-shaped, which will last longer and will deal with gaps up to 2cm. Not all methods are suitable for sliding doors or windows; only some can be painted to match the frame.

Doors

Rain underneath

Tools and materials needed
Wood or aluminium weatherstop
Saw
Abrasive paper or abrading tool
Screws
Screwdriver

Method
1 If necessary, shorten moulding to width of door between jambs. On the opening side, cut at a slight angle to prevent jamming. Paint thoroughly the underside and back of the weatherstop if it is of wood.
2 Screw the moulding to the door and paint it thoroughly if it is wood.
Note Occasionally check that the drip-groove on the underside is not clogged.

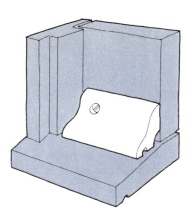

Draught excluder for inside of door

These are of several types, the easiest being made of plastic strip with a foam, felt or bristle flap hanging down (self-adhesive, or to be nailed to the bottom of the door): a bristle flap will accommodate itself to any unevenness in the threshold. A similar method can be improvised by nailing on a strip of carpet, matching the carpet in the room.
  Draught excluders to fit to the threshold need a level threshold and are not suitable for anyone infirm who might trip.
  For a more effective seal, and as the only choice for carpeted rooms, fit a spring-operated draught excluder as illustrated. (For sliding doors, choose the bristle flap type.)
  See also Worn threshold, page 99.

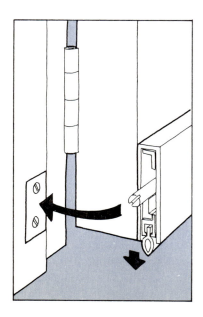

Doors

Bottom scuffed

Tacking on a thin sheet of metal is the traditional solution, but self-adhesive plastic sheeting often protects very well. If putting this on after repainting the door, use transparent sheet, which will not show.
  Another alternative is aluminium foil building tape (this can be painted).

Bottom rotted (shed, garage, etc.)

Tools and materials needed
Board to fit width of door (waterproof plywood would be a good choice)
Waterproof adhesive
Hammer or screwdriver and rustproof nails or screws
Resilient filler.

Method
1 Glue and nail or screw the board across the bottom. If the wood is too rotten to hold a screw, use bolts secured with nuts on the other side.
2 To prevent rain running down behind it, seal the gap with resilient filler. Let it overlap the top edge of the board to protect this too. (Paint would be a further precaution. Apply to back as well as front of the plywood.)
Alternative Stick bitumen-backed aluminium tape across the bottom; it can be painted. If more than one width is needed, let the upper overlap the lower one.

Doors

Panel split

Tools and materials needed
Old screwdriver
Craft knife with sawblade
Hammer
Pins
Plywood slightly smaller than the old panel, including mouldings (same thickness)
Adhesive (PVA)

Method
1 Prise out the moulding around the panel, on both sides of the door.
2 Cut the panel out, using the saw blade of the craft knife.
3 Glue and pin mouldings back on one side of the door, glue new panel to these mouldings, then glue and pin the remaining mouldings to the panel.
A simpler alternative Cover the panel with self-adhesive plastic, then paint it to match the door; or else cover all the panels in plastic of a colour that will need no painting, or with other sheet materials that can be stuck on – cork, hessian, grasscloth, etc.

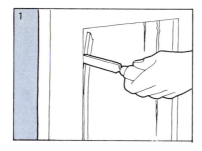

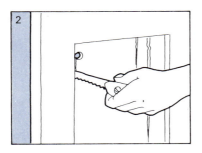

Doors

Resurfacing

Tools and materials needed
Hardboard (sizes to suit doors are available) – 2 sheets
Hardboard pins or panel pins
Adhesive
Hammer
Saw
Beading
Abrading tool
Glasspaper

Method
1 If necessary, cut hardboard to a size which will not interfere with handle, etc. Smooth edges with abrading tool and glasspaper.
2 Wet rough sides of hardboard (about 1 pint of water each). Leave them back to back on a flat floor overnight.
3 Nail hardboard to door, with pins 12cm (6in) apart and 1cm ($\frac{1}{2}$in) from edge. Start in the middle of the top, and check repeatedly that hardboard is flat.
4 Alternatively, use contact adhesive.
5 Pin on beading if required.

Threshold worn down
Car-body filler can be used to level up the surface. First cut the wood down to give a 5mm ($\frac{1}{4}$in) depth, undercutting at the edges. Drilling a few holes (1cm deep) into which to press the filler would also help to anchor it. A metal threshold strip with non-slip treads could then be screwed over the top.

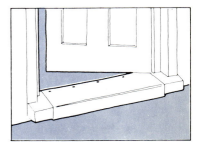

Doors

Sliding doors stiff (warped)

Method
1 Check that grit in the runners is not the cause.
2 Lift doors up and out.
3 Either replace them with their inside outside if this is possible; or stand them against a wall until they straighten; or lay flat with weights on. (But the warping may recur later.)
4 If only one side was painted, this may be the cause of warping, so paint both sides.
5 Rub candle wax on to the runners.

Glass doors
Treat as for casement windows, see page 110.

Bolt fails to engage
Re-screw either the bolt or its plate in a new position. (See also Sagging doors, page 96.)

Doors

Latch fails to engage
(a) Spring inside broken or bevelled edge of latch worn down: replace lock (see page 101). (b) Door sagging (see also page 96).

Tools needed
Screwdriver
Hammer
Chisel

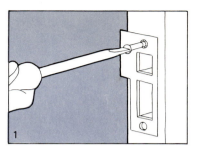

Method
1 Unscrew latch plate from door.
2 Rescrew it a little lower, altering the latch holes as required, using a wood chisel.
  Alternatively, it may suffice to shave off a little metal from the edge of the hole in the latch plate, using a metal file or a suitable abrading tool. The cause may in fact lie elsewhere. Check that the hinges are paint-free; this can prevent firm closing.
  If the lip on the plate has become bent out of its original position, gently hammer it back.

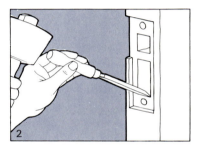

Ball-spring latch fails to engage
Whether too stiff or too loose, this kind of catch can sometimes be adjusted by tightening or loosening a screw above the ball. A roller may have a slot in it for screwing it in or out. If paint or rust has jammed the ball, use dismantling lubricant.

Handle loose

Tools and materials needed
Screwdriver
New screw of same size
Washers

Method
1 Take out the screw holding the knob to its spindle (the screw will probably be worn). Replace.
2 It may help to put washers over the spindle, between the door and the collar of the knob, if there is any gap here.

Doors

Lock stiff – mortice

Materials needed
Lubricant
Paraffin

Method
1 Hold latch in while squirting lubricant inside. Lubricate the key and keyhole too.
2 If still stiff, remove the lock from the rim of the door (see below) and undo the screw that is on the side, taking care to prevent the lock from flying apart. If nothing in the mechanism is broken, wash it clean in paraffin, grease and replace. If mechanism is broken, take to a locksmith for repair or replacement. Inserting a new spring is not difficult.

Lock stiff – cylinder (Yale type)

Materials needed
Powdered graphite in puffer

Method
Puff graphite inside (never use oil). Or rub a lead pencil on the key and turn it to and fro in the lock.

Lock replacement – mortice
Undo screws as follows: one on inside doorknob or handle (this releases outside knob too), two in edge of door (they release the face plate if one is fitted), two under this plate if fitted. The lock can now be levered out.
Note Rim locks are similar to mortice locks, but they are on the surface of the door, not housed within it.

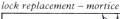
lock replacement – mortice

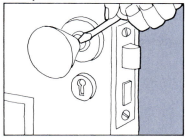

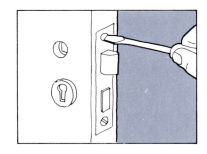

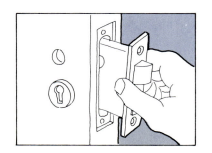

Doors

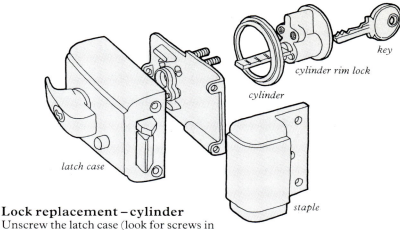

key

cylinder rim lock

cylinder

latch case

staple

Lock replacement – cylinder
Unscrew the latch case (look for screws in edge of door). Beneath is a plate with two screws holding the cylinder inside the door. Unscrew these and pull cylinder out from the other side of the door. A defective lock may be repairable: enquire before buying a replacement.

Letterbox spring broken
If the result is rattling or draughts, the former can be stopped by sticking on a strip of plastic foam or felt where the flap strikes the rim, or a blob of silicone rubber seal (prop the flap up while this sets). To stop draughts, the flap can be secured either by gluing on a pair of small magnets to flap and frame, or the two halves of a strip of Velcro (grip-tape, sold in needlework shops). Either of these will be sufficient to hold the flap closed yet will separate when letters are pushed through. Alternatively, cover the hole (inside) by tacking a square of felt to hang down over it.
  Replacing a spring involves unbolting the letterbox from the door. Tap free the rod that is on the back, to slide off the flap and spring from it, and put a new spring on. (Sometimes a slack spring can be given more tension by winding it up a couple of turns.)

Staircases

Stairtread squeaking

The cause is one piece of wood chafing on another: you may be able to see what is loose and needs fixing.

Alternative methods

If you can get at the underside of the staircase

1 Prise off any loosened block under the tread. Scrape away old adhesive and re-fix with new adhesive (such as PVA). Do not tread on the stair until the adhesive has set.
2 If a block has split, replace it by screwing on a new one or a small shelf-bracket. A brace is a possible solution to a cracked tread.
3 Sometimes the solution is to hammer a wedge (coated with adhesive) between the squeaking tread and the side of the staircase; or to refix old wedges that have loosened.

If you can only get at the top of the tread

1 Insert talcum powder between any joins (using a piece of folded paper); or use a puffer-pack of powdered graphite.
2 Use a hammer and cold chisel to part the tread slightly from the riser below it, and squeeze adhesive in.
3 Or screw the tread to the top of the riser below it, using countersunk screws.

Carpet grip loose

Re-screwing may be difficult if wood has split, but epoxy adhesive will re-fix the grip instead.

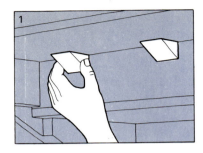
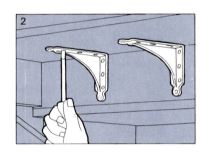
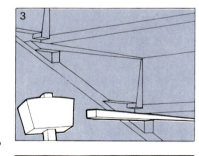
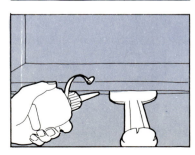

Fireplaces

Brickwork – joints crumbling

Tools and materials needed

Mortar
Trowel
Brush
Possibly, cement colourant

Method

1 Scrape loose mortar out, brush gaps clean, and soak with water.
2 Press mortar into the vertical joints first, then the adjoining horizontal ones, flush with the surface of the bricks.
3 If necessary use the trowel tip or a bit of wood to shape the new mortar to match the old – there are many variations. If the mortar is to be left flush, wait till it is fairly stiff then smooth it with a damp cloth.

Brickwork – brick loose or missing

Tools and materials needed

Hammer and cold chisel
Stiff brush
Trowel
Mortar

Method

1 Chisel remains of mortar away and brush the space clean.
2 Soak the brick and apply mortar to the space.
3 Put it in position, tap firmly down and clean off any excess mortar.
4 After a day, fill the joins with mortar, shaping or smoothing as described above.

Notes

1 To mend a broken brick, use PVA or epoxy adhesive.
2 If you need to cut a brick in half, place it on a soft pad before using hammer and chisel to tap a line along the top of it. Then one sharp blow should sever the brick. Soft ones can be sawn with a hacksaw or multi-purpose saw.

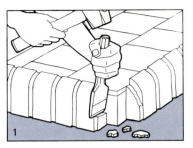

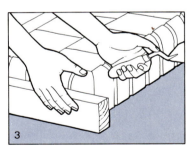
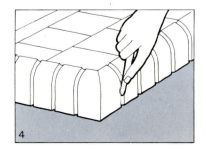

Fireplaces

Brickwork – smoke-stained

Tools and materials needed
Special cleaner or hydrochloric acid
(spirits of salts)
Soft brush

Note Never use detergent or wire brush on
bricks. Scour by rubbing with a brick of
the same colour. Special brick stains will
revive the original colour.

Method
1 Mix acid and water (1: 10) then brush on.
   Avoid soaking the mortar joins with it.
2 After half an hour, rinse off.

Warning Acid is dangerous. Keep away
from children. Do not splash your eyes.
Put acid into water, not vice versa.

Marble – chipped, stained
Use epoxy adhesive to repair marble (a
piece of polythene film left on while it is
setting will give it a shiny surface).
Stubborn stains can be removed with
hydrochloric acid (caution – see above) in
water (1: 10). Dulled marble can be
improved by rubbing with steel-wool soap
pads (wet), and repeatedly waxing (when
dry) with a colourless hard car polish.

Tiled – tile broken

Tools and materials needed
Hammer and cold chisel or old screwdriver
New tile to match
Tile adhesive (use fire cement if near fire)
Grouting
Possibly, tile cutter.

Method
1 Chip old tile out in small bits, working
   from centre outwards (take care not to
   damage adjoining tiles). Clean out the
   space.

Fireplaces

2 If the new tile has to be cut to fit, score a
   line along the top, put matchsticks
   underneath (corresponding with the scored
   line), press down evenly at each side of the
   line. If only a slight amount needs
   removing, it is easier to use an abrading
   tool; one is made specifically for tiles. If a
   small bit has to be nibbled from a tile, use
   pincers or pliers.
3 Apply adhesive thickly to both tile and
   space, but not to the sides of the adjoining
   tiles. Press in.
4 Wipe off any surplus adhesive. Fill the
   spaces around the tile with grouting. Since
   it is hardly worth buying special tile
   adhesive and grouting for just one tile,
   PVA adhesive added to any powdery filler
   or cement would do or even a mastic unless
   the tile is near the fire. Condensed milk is
   an 'old wives'' substitute that also works
   well.

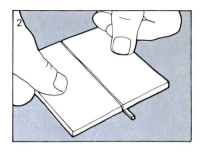

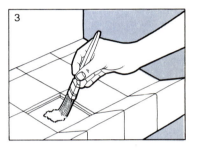

Retiling a fireplace (or other tiled surface)
Where tiles are generally crazed, but not
broken, the whole lot can be tiled over
anew without removing any. On such a
level surface, the job is very easy.

Tools and materials needed
Tiles
Tile adhesive (heat-resistant, if necessary)
Grouting

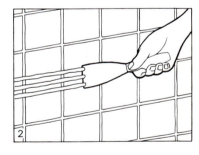

Method
1 Thoroughly clean the old tiles and dry
   them.
2 Spread adhesive over with the notched
   spatula provided with it. Do about a square
   metre at a time.
3 Place each tile on with a slightly sliding
   movement, and press down. Leave about
   1mm gap between tiles: unless the tiles
   have been made with spacing 'nibs',
   sticking small bits of card in as you go
   along will ensure uniform spaces.

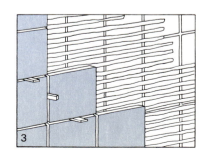

Fireplaces

4 After a few days, apply grouting to the spaces between the tiles, wiping off any surplus before it hardens.

Self-adhesive transfers in various patterns are sold for tiles, some of which would camouflage a good deal of wear-and-tear. Tiles can be painted (first, clean them with meths).

Where small pieces from tiles are missing, fill in with epoxy putty (leave plastic film over it while setting, to get a shiny surface). It can be painted to match.

Fireback cracked

Tools and materials needed
Stiff brush
Trowel or filling knife
Fire cement

Method
1 Brush the fireback clean so that all cracks are visible.
2 Scrape out cracks and undercut, using the point of the trowel.
3 Thoroughly soak cracks with water.
4 Trowel in the fireclay very firmly.
5 Smooth off with a wet finger.
Warning Smoke getting through cracks in a fireback can cause structural damage, so repair is important.

Walls and ceilings

Damp marks – low on ground-floor wall

Possible causes
(a) Earth outside heaped up above a damp-proof course or airbrick. (Damp-proof course is usually visible outside as a grey or black line above the bottom rows of bricks.)
(b) Rendering or mortar applied over the damp-proof course outside.
(c) Splashes from a gully, rain bouncing off path, etc.

heaped earth

Tools and materials needed
Spade
Stiff brush
Possibly, mortar and trowel
Hammer
Cold chisel
Waterproof building tape or a 'shoe' (see below)

Methods
Heaped earth
Shift the earth away and brush the wall clean. There should be at least 15cm clear between ground level and the damp-proof course. If any bricks have decayed at ground level, rake out joints and apply new mortar between and over the face of the affected bricks (or chip the bricks out and replace them, see page 102).

taking out decayed bricks

Rendering
Chisel off to expose the damp-proof course all the way round the house.
Gully
Either protect the wall with a patch of adhesive building tape (let upper widths overlap lower ones), paint on water-repellent liquid, or buy a shoe to push on to the bottom of the downpipe, which will direct the water away from the wall.

rendering

Note If an old house has no damp-proof course, rectifying this is a professional job: the local council may possibly provide a grant.

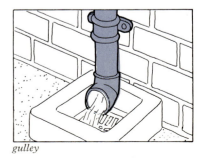
gulley

Walls and ceilings

Damp marks – on wall facing direction of prevailing rain (usually north)

Possible cause
(a) Defective brickwork
(b) Cracked rendering
(c) Internal condensation (see page 106)
(d) Porous bricks (see below)

Tools and materials needed
Waterproofing liquid, exterior grade (e.g., silicone)
Large paintbrush

Method
Liberally brush the liquid all over the porous brickwork (keep it off windows and woodwork). This should last 5–10 years.
  An alternative which may be worth the expense is to have weatherboarding, tiles or other cladding put up, which will keep the house warmer as well as drier, with less condensation likely on cold walls. Cement rendering helps, provided it is skilfully applied (if it cracks, water gets trapped behind it). Many modern masonry paints are water-repellent.
  Another alternative is a liquid plastic coating which waterproofs even walls that have fine cracks. It can also be used on roofs (tiled or flat) and other surfaces; some need a sealer first.
  If you do not want to work on ladders when tackling an outside wall, a solid wall can be treated inside, but this is a second-best solution: the masonry will remain damp and therefore cold and, unless you are prepared to take a lot of trouble, the wall behind the skirting and between floors will remain unprotected. However, at least your decorations will not be spoiled by damp marks.
  You can either paint on a waterproofing liquid (interior grade) then decorate; or line the wall with waterproof paper or with aluminium foil, using special adhesive. Wallpaper can go straight over these

Walls and ceilings

linings; but lining-paper will be needed if you want to paper over bituminous waterproofing liquid. There are epoxy emulsion paints which both waterproof and decorate, indoors or outdoors.

Damp marks – on an upstairs wall, or one with a pipe running down the outside

Possible causes
(a) Clogged gutter; or loose joint, crack or rust-hole in gutter or pipe. Look for white or green stains on wall outside, corresponding with the position of the damp marks indoors. See pages 39–40.
(b) Defective flashing (the metal strips covering joins between, for instance, garage or porch roof and wall, chimney and roof, windowsill and wall, etc.). Repairing these is usually a job for a builder.

Damp marks – above a disused fireplace
This can mean there is damp in the chimney. If the fireplace has been blocked in without any ventilation provided, open it up (the board blocking the fireplace should either be of perforated hardboard or have holes drilled in it, or have a ventilator inserted in it).
  Chimney-pots can be sealed off by a builder to keep rain out. Allow a little ventilation, however. If the chimney-stack itself is defective and letting rain in, putting it right is a job for a builder – so is curing condensation in a chimney serving a boiler.

Walls and ceilings

Damp marks – below or around windows
(see page 111)
If the marks are at a bay window, the cause may be blockage of the rain outlet on the flat roof above it.

Condensation or mildew
These tend to occur where warm, moist air strikes a cold wall. The source of this may be a kitchen or bathroom even though the trouble appears elsewhere – for instance, in an unheated bedroom beneath an uninsulated attic. Apart from obvious causes like steam from a washing-machine or bath, non-flued oil or gas appliances give off a lot of vapour. People breathe out about 1 litre (2pt) of moisture per day.

To determine whether damp on a wall is condensation or is coming from outside, sticky-tape some foil or plastic to it for a few days then take it up and observe which side of it is damp.

Walls and ceilings

Some solutions:
Prevention of steam in the house by running cold bath water before hot (preferably via a shower attachment with its head under the water), keeping lids on saucepans, installing a tube to convey steam from the tumble-dryer out of doors, a spring-hinge to close bathroom and kitchen doors automatically, plumbing-in the washing machine outlet, fully enclosing the shower.
Increased ventilation – opening windows at least once a day, opening up a blocked airbrick, fireplace, etc., putting an electric extractor fan in place of an air-brick, or into a window, putting a plastic ventilator into a window, removing some draughtstripping, changing an ordinary window to a louvred one which can be opened even in bad weather. Cooker hoods do not remove steam, unless ducted out of doors.
Warmer walls Either stick on cork tiles or sheet, or expanded polystyrene sheeting (see page 154); or put up insulation boards. Exterior cladding, especially if insulated, or waterproofing would help. Another alternative is a 60w tubular heater at the foot of the affected wall. Move a large piece of furniture if it is keeping warmth and free circulation of air from the wall. Steady warmth throughout the house, especially at night, is better than temperature changes.
Fungicides Washing walls down with household bleach in water (1: 6), or with a fungicide, may get rid of mildew but does not guarantee that it will never return. Fungicidal paints and wallpaper adhesives are a deterrent but not an absolute preventive.

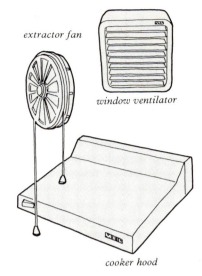

extractor fan

window ventilator

cooker hood

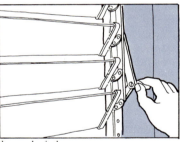

louvred window

Walls and ceilings

Skirting gaping at bottom

Sometimes a gap is designed for the insertion of carpet edge.

Tools and materials needed

Wood moulding
Saw
Panel pins
Hammer and punch (or spring-operated pin-pusher)
Resilient filler

Method

1 Saw the moulding to the length required. Where two lengths are to meet at a corner, the ends should be sawn at a 45° angle.
2 Nail to the floor at 15cm (6 in) intervals
3 Punch each nail head in below the surface of the wood and conceal with filler.
4 Fill any spaces and joins with filler. Paint when set.
Alternative Use resilient filler.

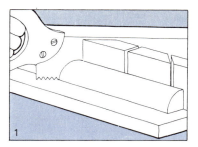

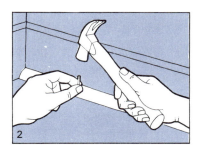

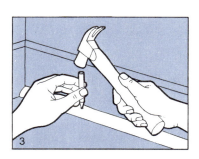

Gaps between wall and woodwork

Round door and window frames, at top of skirtings, round built-in in furniture.

   Unless the cause is merely loosened screws, fill the gaps (after cleaning out any dirt) with filler which can be painted after it has set.

Holes round pipes, etc.

These may provide an entry for cold air, damp, vermin, or escapes of natural gas (which has been known to travel along other service pipes and thus enter houses).

   They should therefore be stopped up with appropriate filler, preferably resilient. If mice are present, use a hard filler that cannot be gnawed (e.g., epoxy putty).

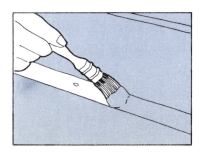

Windows

Pane broken

Tools and materials needed

New glass (same thickness as old)
Small hammer
Old knife or chisel
Pliers
Paintbrush
Putty (metal frames need special putty); or waterproof bedding tape
Putty knife (old household knife will do)
Possibly glass cutter, linseed oil
Glazing sprigs or $\frac{1}{2}$in panel pins

The new pane should be 3mm ($\frac{1}{8}$in) smaller each way than the space inside the frame. Since the space may not be dead square, measure all four sides and the diagonals too before going to buy the glass, or make a paper pattern. If glass is patterned, make sure the pattern is the right way up with the textured or the embossed side indoors. Some windows may be easier to work on if removed from their hinges.

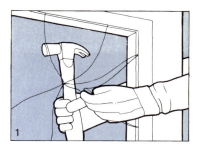

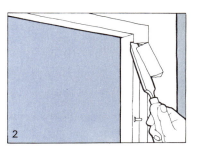

Method

1 Wearing gloves, tap out the remaining glass, working from top to bottom, with care not to let it fall where it may cause injury (pasting paper over the glass will hold the bits).
2 Hack out all old putty, taking care not to damage the window frame. Pull out and save the glazing sprigs embedded in it (or, in metal frames, the special clips and plastic pieces at the bottom).
3 Clean then paint the exposed surface (on aluminium, use metal primer or aluminium-based paint; on steel frames, use zinc-rich paint).
4 If using putty, roll it until it is pliable (if necessary, moisten it with a few drops of linseed oil), then press small bits one by one in a ribbon round the edge of the frame. Bedding tape (special self-adhesive plastic foam) is even easier: just press it on. Replace plastic pieces (if any) at bottom.

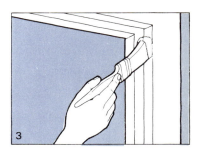

107

Windows

Or use matchsticks to support larger panels.

5 Press the pane edges into the putty, bottom first – do not press the middle of the glass.

6 Carefully tap the glazing sprigs in again (slide the hammer head along the glass) at 30cm (1ft) intervals; or replace the glazing clips in their holes.

7 Another layer of putty is then pressed in all round in a wedge shape as shown using the putty knife (wet the knife if the putty sticks to it) to make a smooth finish. The back of the wedge should be about 5mm ($\frac{1}{4}$in) narrower than the rebate. (Or use another strip of bedding-tape.)

8 On the inside, trim excess putty level with the frame, using the knife.

9 Leave putty to harden for a day before cleaning the glass with meths.

10 When the putty is firm (a week or two), paint outside to protect from rain. The paint should extend on to the glass about 5mm ($\frac{1}{4}$in) beyond the edge of the putty.

Notes

1 Some windows have a wood beading in front of the putty. This will need prising off (centre first, then ends); it can be fixed on again with panel pins and putty or bedding mastic.

2 For temporary repairs, use transparent building-tape (self-adhesive) or self-adhesive clear plastic.

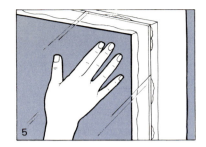

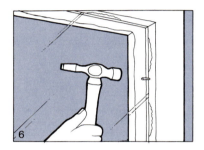

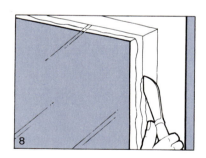

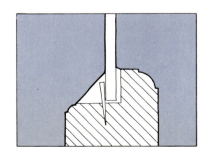

Buying glass

For glazed doors, shower screens, etc., order toughened, laminated, or wired glass which will not shatter dangerously if someone runs into it. Or use special transparent plastic, from glass merchants. (Shatterproof glass is also burglarproof.) Other glass can be protected by covering with translucent, patterned plastic film.

For greenhouses, get horticultural glass, which is cheaper because it is of lower quality.

The larger the window, and the more exposed to wind or knocks, the thicker the glass should be: 6–10mm rather than 3–4mm.

Glass for frameless sliding cupboard doors, etc. should have the edges ground by the glass merchant.

Handling glass

Glass is less likely to break if kept vertical, not flat. When carrying, have one hand under the bottom and towards the back, the other at the top of the front edge. Let the top of the panel lean towards your shoulder. Protect your wrists.

Use newspaper or adhesive cloth tape to pad edges you are holding. Also use paper to interleave two panes, and to cushion edges of panes left leaning against a wall.

Beware when turning corners or going upstairs.

If carrying glass in a car, wrap it in a blanket and don't brake suddenly. Large panes should be delivered: do not use your roof-rack.

In cold weather, glass is extra brittle.

carrying glass

Windows

Use of glass cutter
Practise first on a spare piece of glass, holding the cutter as shown. Lay the glass flat on an old blanket, etc. Lubricate the cutting wheel by running it over an oily rag.

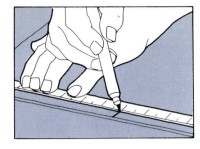

Method
1 Either mark the line to be cut on the glass with a fine felt-tip pen; or position the glass over a line drawn on a sheet of paper.
2 Use the wheel to score a single line firmly on the glass: don't go to and fro. Use a ruler or a straight piece of wood to get a straight line. Allow for the thickness of the glass cutter when positioning the ruler. Keep the cutter firmly against the ruler. Run the wheel right off the edge.
3 Tap along the back of the line.
4 Place the ruler or a thin piece of wood under the line, press down on both sides of it, and the glass should snap in two.
5 Use pliers or pincers to nibble away any small bits. (The notches on the cutter are for measuring the thickness of the glass.)

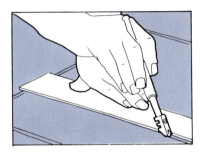

Crumbling putty
Brush the spaces clean, widen any cracks, prime, and re-putty (see page 107). Paint after 1–2 weeks.

Warning Neglecting to do this repair may let in rain and lead to a rotted or rusted frame.

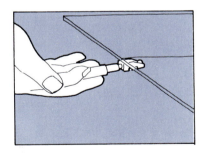

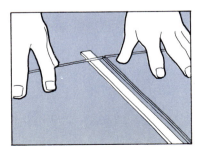

Windows

Condensation
See Walls, page 106.
   Drill some very small down-sloping holes in the bottom frame not merely to carry condensation drips out of doors but to let in a little ventilation that will reduce or even stop condensation. Pour a little wood preservative through, to prevent rot.
   The alternative is double-glazing.

Sash cord broken

Tools and materials needed
Screwdriver
New cord of same thickness as old one
Lubricant
String
Clout nails
Hammer
Panel pins
Punch (or pin-pusher)
Possibly a stepladder.

When one cord breaks, all are likely to be frail so test them by pulling each in turn. Sashes are heavy, so removing them is usually a job for two people. Waxed cord is best.

Method
1 Use the screwdriver to prise off the beading at each side of the frame. (Prise up the middle first, then the ends.)
2 Remove the lower sash, detaching from it the cords nailed into a groove at each side. (Hold them to prevent the weights from crashing down.)
3 Lower the weights to the bottom of the frame.
4 Another pair of beadings has to be prised off to reach the weights and to get at the upper sash in order to remove it. Detach its cords if they are to be renewed and lower its weights.

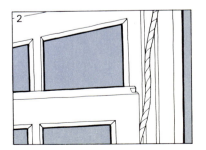

5 There are pockets at each side of the frame. Unscrew or prise off their covers in order to remove the weights. Discard the old cords attached to these. Lubricate the pulleys.

6 To insert each new cord, tie a bent nail to one end of a long string and push this over the top pulley so that it will drop down to the pocket, taking the string with it.

7 Tie new cord to the other end of the string, pull it through, and knot a weight to the bottom end.

8 With the weight pulled up, wedge the cord and pulley with a scrap of wood or a pencil while you nail the cord into the groove on the sash. The cord should be nailed well below the top corner of the sash. The distance from the top nail to the weight must be correct – otherwise the sash will not be able to be raised or lowered fully.

9 When all four cords are done and the sashes replaced (outer one first), replace the pocket covers and the beadings, punching in the heads of the panel pins.

Casement draughts

Wood-framed casements are dealt with like doors, see page 97. For metal ones use self-adhesive foam strip or snap-on aluminium draught-strips.

Casement hard to close

See Doors, pages 95–6. Do not shave off so much wood that the windows will have gaps when dry weather shrinks them again. If following the method for loosened joints, the wedging may have to be done with the window closed. In case this results in any adhesive squeezing out on to the frame, cover the latter with polythene film (plastic bag) until the joint has set.

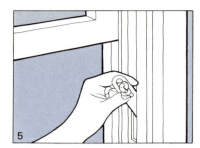
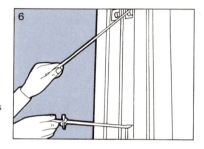

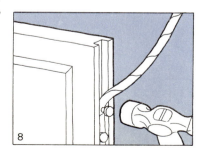

Metal fittings sticking

Use dismantling lubricant on rusted hinges and stiff fastenings. The handle of a catch that seems too firmly stuck to be moved can often be shifted by clamping on a vicegrip (see page 82) so that it is like an extension to the handle, which will give more leverage.

Windowsill (concrete) damaged

Tools and materials needed

Hammer
Cold chisel
Stiff brush
Trowel
Mortar or hard-setting exterior filler

Method

1 Chisel off all loose material, brush clean and wet the surface.

2 Trowel mortar or filler on, holding a piece of wood or hardboard against the sill to give a straight line. Coat the board with wax, grease or a sheet of polythene to keep the concrete from sticking to it. Deep cavities are best filled in two stages.

3 Slightly round the edge so that rain will run off.

4 After 2 hours, smooth with a wet trowel. (If the weather is hot, cover with a damp cloth to prevent over-fast drying.)

  If the damage goes deep, strengthen the mortar with PVA.

  If the surface is crumbly all over, use cement bandage, then paint it.

  If much mortar will have to be applied, cramp a board under the sill and if necessary use a second board as described opposite.

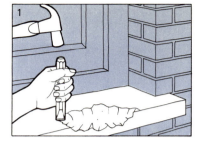
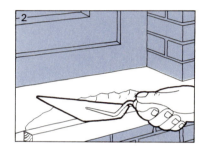

Windows

Windowsill (wood) rotted

A very extensively rotted sill can be restored as follows, after scraping away all soft wood and letting the sound wood dry: it should have preservative applied. (Check whether frame is sound or not.)

Tools and materials needed

Hammer
Clout nails
Boards
Vaseline, wax or grease
Wire nails
Two-part plastic filler
Filling knife
Sandpaper (medium grade)
Possibly, abrading tool

Method

1 Hammer clout nails partly in (to reinforce the filler).
2 Wedge or cramp a board under the sill, coated with wax, grease or Vaseline so that the filler will not stick to it (alternatively, cover it with polythene).
3 Nail another board (also coated) to the front edge of this, to determine the depth of the sill.
4 Mix together the two parts of the filler, a little at a time, and fill up the sill to its former dimensions.
5 After an hour, gently lever the boards off with the knife.
6 Smooth the surface with an abrading tool if necessary, and sandpaper before painting.

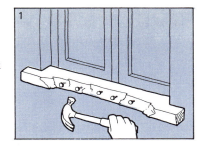

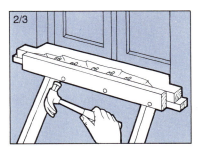

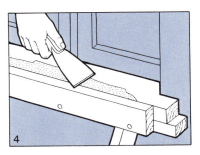

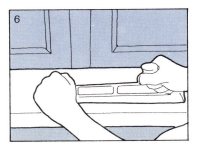

Windows

Windowsills dripping

(Look for damp marks on the wall below.)

Tools

Screwdriver (or hammer and cold chisel if sill is of concrete).

Method

Chip out any old paint or mortar that is filling the drip-groove that runs along the underside of the sill. In the case of a wood sill, re-paint to prevent rot.

Note If the sill lacks a drip groove, fix a thin strip of wood or adhesive foam strip to the underside (towards the front edge) to prevent drips running back to the wall.

If this is not possible, the wall below can be protected by pressing on to it a length of surfaced building tape which can be painted to match the sill, or the wall can be painted with waterproofing liquid.

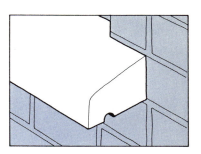

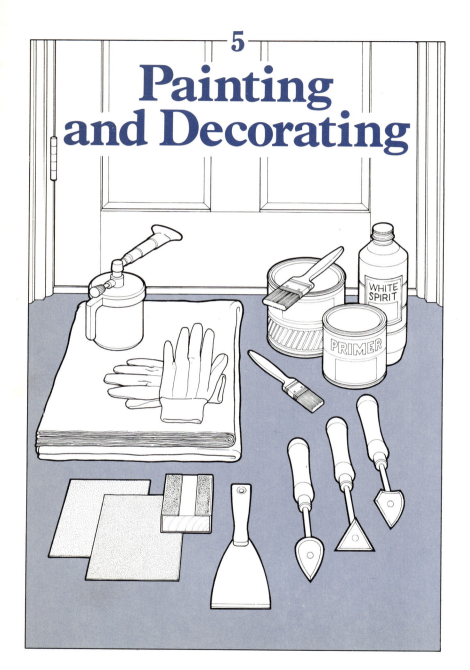

5
Painting and Decorating

Paints

Household paints are now commonly sold in metric measures, so volumes and areas are given in metric here. For approximate imperial equivalents, see page 17.

Colours

Although a manufacturer may show two dozen colours on his colourcard, the less popular ones may need to be specially ordered unless you go to a specialist paint dealer. Those who offer hundreds of colours depend upon the retailer mixing them in a special machine, and this costs more. Some skill comes into the mixing, so you may find two tins are not identical, or the colour is not exact, or not quite repeatable. You can, of course, mix colours yourself but remember that the appearance in the tin differs from what the paint will look like on the walls (emulsions deepen as they dry). Tints or stainers are sold for colouring paints (oil or emulsion).

When judging colours, bear in mind that matt finishes never seem as bright as the same colour in gloss, and that lighting alters colours and so do reflections from such things as the carpet. The colour you are painting over may affect things too. White paint seems slightly yellow if it is in shadow.

Colour names are meaningless (even white differs from one manufacturer to another and some makers' 'brilliant white' may be no whiter than another's 'white'). There are nearly a hundred British Standard colours identified by numbers not names, which should be the same.

Look at colour cards by both daylight and lamplight and from differing angles. Buy enough paint at the outset so that you can get it all from one batch (the batch number is marked on the tin) and have a little left over for touching up blemishes later. Use whatever undercoat colour the maker recommends. Mix paint from the second tin into the first when it is nearly empty in order to minimize any difference.

Paints

If you don't know what colour scheme you want, and can't afford professional help, there is abundant advice and inspiration to be had from paint makers' leaflets, home magazines, and books on home decoration.

Types
Paints are either 'oil' or 'water' (emulsion). Oil paints contain synthetic resins to give more durability (and more gloss, if wanted). Alkyd resins are the most common; the polyurethanes are even tougher (though not necessarily more weather-resistant), quicker drying and easy to use. Normally alkyd paints take many hours to dry, and overnight drying of undercoat is essential. Quick-drying brands are less likely to pick up dust but may be more difficult to brush. Apart from appearance, a glossy oil paint is often chosen for durability and the protection it gives to the surface below, though where there is a lot of condensation trickles will run down it. A few are specially formulated to be odourless.

In emulsions there are particles of synthetic resins suspended in water: they may be acrylic, vinyl (sometimes called latex) or co-polymers. Unlike oil paints, emulsions are not flammable, they have little smell, and they dry quickly; their colours are fairly fast and imperfections in the surface do not show through a lot. The glossier ones are washable. A first coat can be painted over after only two hours. They do not go over old gloss paint very well, but are excellent at obscuring a previous colour in other paint. Exterior grade emulsions may be reinforced with sand, mica, fibres, etc.

Non-drip paints in jelly form are easier to use in that runs and dribbles do not occur. They go on in a much thicker coat so often only one coat is needed. Do not stir, and brush as little as possible. (Usually these are oil-based but there are some emulsion jellies.)

Paints

Later parts of this book go into detail about which paints suit which surfaces, how to calculate quantities, and how to apply the paint.

Textures
Finishes of oil paint range through matt, eggshell (or mid-sheen) to full gloss. Those of emulsions are matt, silk (or satin) and soft gloss. Some paints have additives that give a pronounced texture, fine or coarse, which will help to camouflage irregularities and hair cracks in a surface but may collect dirt. Ready-mixed ones are easier to use, and less likely to produce uneven lumps. If you buy one with asbestos in it, get a protective mask as inhaling the powder while mixing it with water is very dangerous.

Quantities
Coverage varies among makes, the surface and the user's technique. The following is a rough guide:

Per litre
Emulsion: 15sq m
Oil paint: 15–17sq m, possibly less with polyurethane
Undercoat for oil: 10–15sq m

Non-drip jelly paints cover a smaller area but need no undercoat and often only one top coat. Porous, textured or moulded surfaces take more paint. Oil paints may need 1 or 2 coats as well as undercoat; emulsions may need more coats, particularly if glossy, but adding 10–20% water to the paint for the first coat, on a porous surfaces only, may save one of the top coats.

Costs
It is difficult to find emulsion in less than 1 litre, unless you choose a very ordinary colour like white. 5 litres may be the minimum for exterior paints. 'Bulk buys' tend to be cheaper per litre than a number of smaller cans, which might decide you to

Paints

have the same colour in more than one room. In general, supermarkets and chain stores sell at lower prices than builders' merchants or hardware shops – or even paint or do-it-yourself shops: you may find the same paint at less than half price. Sometimes there are bargain makes of emulsion paint, for example, though these may not have the covering power of better paints. The extra coats you will need may cancel out what you save by buying an obscure brand.

When considering costs bear in mind that with some paints a coat of primer may be needed first (see later sections). Also more than one coat of paint will be needed: if the surface has not been painted before; if it has only been primed (outdoors, two lots of undercoat may be needed); if you are changing from a dark to a light colour; or if you want a really vivid shade of red, yellow or green.

For the undercoat, if any, you may need to use the same paint as the top coat in the case of emulsion or matt oil; but with glossy oil paint, the maker may recommend a special undercoat, so read what is on the can. It is the undercoat that covers up the surface, and the top coat that gives most protection.

Allow extra if you have elaborate mouldings to do. Absorbent, textured or corrugated surfaces can take up to double the usual amount.

Paints

Storage
Leftovers of oil paint need to be kept airtight otherwise skin will start to form, even within an hour or so (however thin this skin is, do not stir it in but cut round and lift it off). Emulsion paints harden if exposed to air. The paint could be poured into screwtop jars if the lid of the can no longer fits tight; or float a circle of water or linseed oil on top of the paint until it is needed again; or turn the can upside down so that the paint seals any gaps round the lid (hammer the lid firmly on first). If there are any bits in the paint, fix a generous piece of nylon stocking inside the can as shown, and take paint only from within this (or strain it into a paint kettle). Store leftover paint in a cool place but ensure that emulsion paints are away from the risk of frost.

Painting equipment – brushes

For walls, use (if not a roller) a 10cm (4in) wall brush for emulsions or textured paint; wider ones are heavy to use. For oil paint, use paintbrushes from 5cm (2in) (for walls, flush doors) down to 1cm (½in) (for narrow details); a 2cm or a 1cm (1in or ½in) and a 3cm (1½in) will do for most jobs.

Cutting-in brushes for bars of windows have angled bristles; lining 'fitches' are an extra-fine version of these for painting lines. Radiator brushes have long wire handles that can be bent to get behind pipes, etc; downspout brushes have angled heads to get into awkward corners. Dustpan brushes are often used for applying textured paint, or paint on textured walls. Stippling brushes or combs are used for textured effects (an alternative is a sponge inside a plastic bag).

The bristles in good brushes feel flexible and tapered at the tip, dense and firm at the base. Only those within a metal band are likely to be really firmly fixed. Cheap brushes have fewer, shorter, untapered bristles and hold less paint; they may shed bristles. Even good brushes do this at first, so wet the bristles first, flex them on a clean surface, then dry; use them at first only for undercoat.

Pure animal bristles are best for holding a lot of oil paint and letting it flow off evenly. Cement paints damage natural bristles, however, so for these and textured walls use fibre or nylon bristles, coarse rather than fine. Nylon bristles being non-absorbent, are also better with emulsion or other water-based paint. Fine hair is used in brushes for fine lacquers, shellac varnishes, etc.

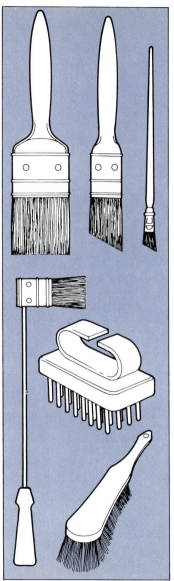

Top, left to right: standard paint brush, cutting-in brush, lining fitch. Below, left to right: radiator brush, stippler for textured paint, dustpan brush for textured paint.

Painting equipment – rollers

These cover large areas more quickly than a brush (but you will need to do the edges first with a narrow brush or pad) and need recharging less frequently. They may spatter a little, are harder to clean than brushes (especially after oil-painting) and tend to make gloss emulsion look less glossy. Narrow rollers are sold for pipes and edges but are not as good as brushes or pads for these purposes; nor are rollers so good on woodwork. Some rollers can be put on long handles for doing the upper part of walls (not ceilings, because they are tiring to hold in this position); and one attaches by tube to a 2 litre (3½pt) paint pump which saves constant recharging.

Roller heads are made of different materials. Some rollers have interchangeable heads. Choose as follows (the smoother the surface, the shorter the pile of the roller should be):

For matt oil paint	Sheepskin, wool, polyester or woven fabric.
For glossy oil paint	Sheepskin, wool, polyester or woven fabric; or mohair or foam for smooth surfaces only; short-pile synthetic fur on any surface.
For jelly paint	Mohair or woven fabric.
For emulsion	Dacron, Dynel foam or mohair for a smooth finish (the last two on smooth surfaces only); long-pile for orange-peel effect.
Textured paint, paint for textured surfaces	Long-pile synthetic fur or sheepskin (exterior grade for outdoor walls); honeycombed plastic foam.

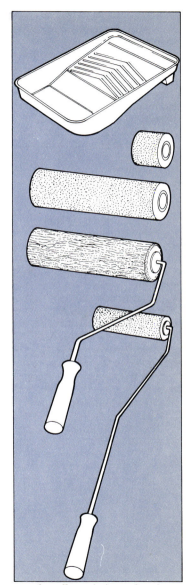

tray for roller-painting and various types of roller

Painting equipment – rollers and pads

There are also special plastic rollers to create patterned effects (diamonds, bark and so on).

Foam sleeves are so cheap they might be thrown away rather than cleaned (they do not last long anyway), particularly when full of oil paint which involves the expense of brush cleaner to remove it. Their disadvantage is that they slightly froth the paint and this can spoil the finish.

Rollers are used with sloping paint trays. Some have clips to fix them to a step-ladder, or there is a special roller bucket or paint scuttle that can be used.

Pads

The large ones provide a quick, splash-free way to put emulsion on ceilings in particular. There are small ones for gloss paint on woodwork. Most are made of mohair, much superior to synthetic pile ones that cost less. For the larger ones there are long, angled handles available, and replacement heads. Other accessories include paint trays, some with scrapers or with rollers to load the pad evenly, wheeled edges to spread paint evenly along the edges of walls and ceilings, small touching-up pads and crevice pads for window-frames, radiators, etc. Pads are not suitable for textured paints, but are very good on textured surfaces and woven materials. Paint may be better thinned.

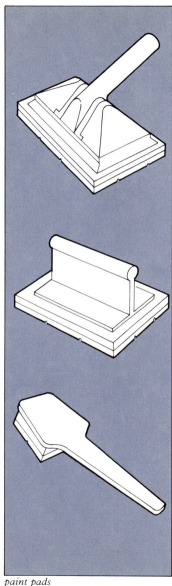

paint pads

Painting equipment – using

Loading brushes

1 Dust top of tin. Lever lid off gently (if dented it will not close well enough to prevent skin forming on oil paint). Stir deeply and for a full 5 minutes or until you can feel no solid sediment at the bottom. (Stirring attachments on power tools are quicker: immerse before switching on and switch off before taking out. Be careful with a full tin in case the paint swirls over the edge.). If you are using a can of paint that is not new, strain through an old nylon stocking. Do not stir or strain jelly paint.
2 If using a large quantity of paint, fill a lightweight, wide paint 'kettle' or bucket one-third full. A kettle is simply a paint can with a handle: an old one will do. Tie wire across to use as a brush rest.
3 Dip bristles in only one-third deep.
4 Press out surplus against inside of kettle (don't do this with jelly paint). Brush paint on to surface lightly, and lift brush away at the end of each stroke. Always start a finishing stroke at an edge, not in the middle.
5 When paint has crept further up the bristles, scrape them across the rim of the kettle to squeeze it out, or use the wire across the can.

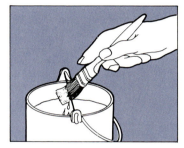

Loading rollers

1 Pour paint into tray till one-third full (having stirred and strained it as above).
2 Dip roller head halfway in.
3 Roll up and down on shallow part of tray.

Painting equipment – cleaning

Cleaning brushes, rollers, pads and hands

Emulsions, cement paints, distemper and some oil paints need only detergent and water (read the label); meths may remove dried emulsion paint.

For most oil paint, special brush cleaners are quicker and easier than white sprit because they enable the oil paint to be washed out thoroughly in water. Paint stripper will remove dried-on paint if the brush is soaked for a day, but do not use for plastic-handled pads. An alternative is brush restorer.

Certain specialized paints and varnishes (such as some polyurethanes, bitumens and celluloses) need special solvents: read what their labels say. Immediate cleaning may be vital for these. If bitumen paint does not yield to brush cleaner or white spirit, try solvent naphtha.

Cleaning brushes

Wipe surplus on to newspaper, flex bristles for a few minutes in a plastic bag with a little brush cleaner in it (if oil paint was used), rinse under tap and wash in suds. Rinse again and hang to dry before storing flat and wrapped up to keep bristles in good shape and dust-free. (Brush cleaner can be used again even when coloured by paint.)

Alternatively, wash in white spirit or (cheaper) paraffin, then work neat liquid detergent or jelly hand-cleaner well into bristles. Wash in water, then in suds, and rinse.

Brushes used for emulsion paint need only to be washed in tepid water and detergent, then rinsed. Soaking for half an hour may loosen partly hardened emulsion paint.

Painting equipment – cleaning

Cleaning rollers and pads

Press out surplus on to newspaper, and roll or press into a tray of brush cleaner or white spirit (if oil paint was used). Plastic trays can be used only if labelled as solvent-resistant. Repeat this. Remove roller head, rinse under tap (cold for emulsion), wash in suds. Rinse again and hang to dry.

To keep paint-filled brushes or rollers temporarily, either wrap in foil or polythene or else suspend in water or solvent. A polythene bag tightly wrapped round the brush will stop the brush from getting full of water or solvent. Brushes or rollers with cement paint in them should be washed at once, so should stippling brushes.

To store clean brushes, lay flat; rollers are best hung up to prevent crushing.

Cleaning hands, etc.

Rub jelly hand-cleaner well in, then rinse. Alternatively, rub barrier cream in before you start, particularly round and under nails.

Brush-cleaner and hand-cleaner are also useful to remove oil paint from clothes or floors, but first check their effect on an inconspicuous corner of the fabric. There is a cream designed specially for oily or bitumen stains. Don't wear woollen clothes when using oil paint as this paint is difficult to remove from them.

117

Masking aids

You will need either a paint-shield or masking tape if you are going to do, for instance, narrow bars on windows, mouldings on doors or walls, or woodwork adjoining a wall, floor or other surface which needs protection from the paint (unless you have a very steady hand). The shield is held over the glass or whatever needs protection while brushing the paint on: buy a metal one or use a piece of card. The tape is pressed on to the surface (taking care that its edges are firmly stuck), to be peeled off after painting is finished: the paint should still be tacky when the tape is removed; and if sun is shining on it, it must be taken off within two to three hours. Ordinary sticky-tape will not do, and even masking tape should not be used on top of wallpaper. To paint a straight line of any width, stick on two parallel lengths of masking tape and paint in between them.

Vaseline can be used to coat the edges of small handles, knobs, letter boxes, etc., but it is better to take these off before painting starts. Wallpaper edges can be masked with cellulose wallpaper paste: straying paint can be wiped off this and the paste then wiped away with a damp rag. Curved shapes could be masked by cutting out the shape in self-adhesive plastic sheet. Even better, use 'low tack' film sold in artists' shops.

If your hand is none too steady when doing fine details, remove any straying paint later, while it is tacky, with cotton-wool on a cocktail-stick or matchstick dipped in white spirit or brush cleaner. Special scrapers are sold to get paint off window panes but a razor blade will do. It is better to scrape dry paint off glass than to risk smears by wiping it off wet.

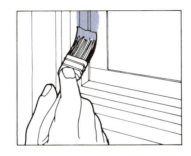

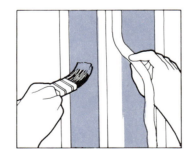

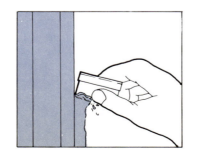

Tools

Blowlamps
Most contain a gas cartridge to be thrown away when empty, but some are refillable. Others (lighter to hold) are fed by tube from a large gas cylinder, convenient only if you can work within about 2m of the cylinder. An ignition button is preferable to having to use matches. Blow-lamps can also be used for soldering. They can be hired.

Scrapers
Stripping-knives with stiff blades, wide or narrow, should be held at a 45° angle. There is a set comprising a handle which takes two scraping blades of different size and also a putty blade for use with fillers. Scrapers used with paint stripper may also free windows stuck by old paint.

For corners, pipes and mouldings, use shave hooks (there are different shapes for curves and angles). Pull, don't push. A scrubbing brush (with natural not synthetic bristles) will help to scrape paint out of finely detailed mouldings.

There is a range of scrapers with removable blades which are extra sharp. These can even be used on their own (wear goggles to protect your eyes from flying chips of paint) though two in the range are specially shaped for use with blowlamps. One of the numerous types of abrading tool may also be useful.

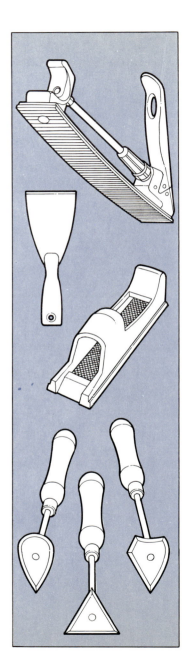

smoothing tools, stripping knife, and (bottom) shave hooks

Abrasives

Surfaces often have to be abraded a little before paint goes on, to remove loose or uneven material or to provide a grip on a shiny surface: for instance, if painting over old gloss paint or varnish. This is usually done with abrasive paper wrapped round a block of cork or wood, or fixed in a holder (which may be flexible for doing rounded surfaces); or with an abrasive block. An abrasive-coated foam block very good for doing curves or corners, and it is washable. There are other types of abrasive fabrics and meshes, made in varying degrees of coarseness, dry or wet grades.

If large flat areas are to be done, the sanding attachments for power tools can be used. Ordinary sanding discs do not last very long, are not suited to work on metal and soon clog if used for paint removal. A mesh disc is better.

Good orbital sanders, which can be hired, are better than most disc attachments (which may leave circular scratches) though they are heavy to hold on vertical surfaces. Orbitals are meant to provide a gentle scrubbing action: check that the pad is stable and does not waggle about. A third alternative is a drum sander: an abrasive belt on a foam cylinder. Wear goggles if you use an electric sander.

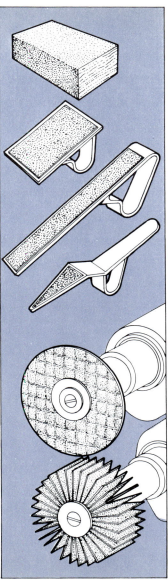

top to bottom: abrasive block, a selection of abrasive paper holders, sanding disc and orbital sander

Abrasives

Glasspaper comes in varying degrees of coarseness from 00 (the finest) to 3. Open-coat types clog less than close-coats.

Aluminium oxide paper is more durable than sandpaper. No. 36 is the coarsest and no. 180 the finest.

Garnet paper is another long-lasting alternative, cheaper than aluminium oxide: grades are 1/0–80 (coarsest) to 7/0–240 (finest).

'Wet and dry' abrasive paper (silicon carbide) is used wet to keep dust down; it is far more efficient – cleaning as well as abrading. Rub it on soap to keep it from sticking or clogging, and rinse it when it does get clogged. (One brand incorporates a soapy lubricant already.) The finest is no. 400 and the coarsest no. 60: nos. 240 and 180 are the most useful grades. It can be used during the washing-down process. Use a circular motion and sponge clean as you go. Do not use over fillers which are not waterproof.

Emery paper is for metal (steel wool can be used instead but clean up well afterwards, otherwise particles may cause rust staining); non-steel abrasive pads are preferable. Use white spirit as a lubricant.

Normally one starts with a coarser grade and finishes with a finer one. Neither should be rubbed hard. When sanding wood, run in the direction of the grain, be sure the wood is dry, and take care when doing veneered edges. If you want to halve a sheet of sand paper, do not cut it but tear it on the edge of a table sand-side up.

Ladders

When buying or hiring, bear the following points in mind.

Ladders
A two-storey-house will need a double 4.2m or 4.8m (14ft or 16ft) ladder. Very long ones, with rope-operated extensions, are less heavy if made of aluminium. Choose flattish, wide, non-slip treads. There are accessories to stop feet slipping, to provide a platform at the top, and (illustrated) to hold the ladder out from the wall (desirable when painting gutters, for instance, which will not be firm enough to keep the ladder steady). Some ladders have little wheels at the top to help raise them up the wall. Two ladders and a board connected by a special device would give you a platform to work on, and a guard rail.

To reach a dormer window it may be necessary to have a roof ladder too: a wheeled one is easier to push up the roof.

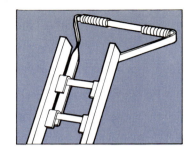

Warnings Accidents with ladders are frequent and often serious, so check that treads and ropes are sound and observe the following safety rules.

Do not use the ladder at a danger spot (sloping or slippery ground, in front of a doorway, in a windy place).

Be sure it is the right way up, the right way round, dead straight, and with extension hooks fully engaged (at least 2 rungs should overlap when extended).

Set it up at an angle of 75° (that means a 4.8m [16ft] ladder should be 1.2m [4ft] from the wall). On uneven ground, wedge one of the feet.

Tie the top and bottom to window frames or stakes, not pipes, to prevent slipping, or drive stakes into the ground in front of it.

Always have one hand holding a rung. Use a bucket and S-hook for tools, hung from a rung.

Keep your body in line with the ladder – do not lean sideways or put one foot on a windowcill. And do not stand on any of the top three rungs (so be sure your

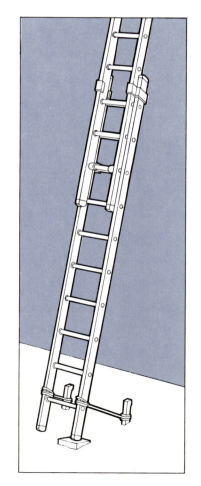

Ladders

ladder is long enough to allow for this).
Look ahead, not down or up.

Stepladders
These should have a platform and (very important) a guard rail not less than 50cm (18in) above it. When buying check that the stepladder is really square on the ground, rigid and stable. Try it out for ease of erection as some are quite awkward. Avoid any with thin, round rungs, and feet likely to come off or slip. Those that convert to ladders tend to be less reliable and much heavier, and failure to re-link properly when turning one back to a stepladder can lead to a nasty accident.

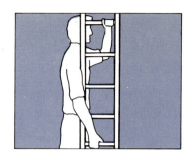

Staging and trestles
Boards can be used to make a platform between two stepladders, or a stepladder and a kitchen step-stool, but staging between two trestles is twice as wide and therefore safer. When painting a ceiling, place the staging so that your head is about 30–40cm (12–15in) from the ceiling: or higher when papering. Staging and boards are available in many lengths and are best if about 1m shorter than the length of the wall or ceiling.

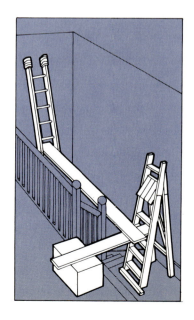

Fillers

Plaster-type fillers are usable not only on plaster but to fill cracks in walls of any kind, and can often be used in woodwork too. Some have cellulose in them. Those that are vinyl based are whiter and set harder, without shrinking. Interior grades are for indoors only, exterior ones can be used anywhere (they are fairly water-resistant). Extra-fine ones give the smoothest finish. A very durable one is so hard setting that it can even be used for metal, concrete sheds, asbestos roofs and so on, as well as walls; there is a version with flexibility for sites where there will be some movement (around windows, for instance). Epoxy putty is very easy to use for small holes in stonework, metal, etc., and sets rock hard; so do two-part fillers as used for car bodywork repairs. These are totally waterproof and so are ideal for outdoor work.

Fillers may be in powder form to mix with water to the desired thickness or made up as ready-mixed pastes in tubs or tubes (these cost more).

Mortars based on cement and sand are for outdoor walls, and special fillers are sold for wood, metal etc.

Plaster fillers or mortar can be given more strength and adhesion by adding PVA adhesive to them. For mortar, coat the surface with a 1: 4 mixture of PVA and water; and make up the mortar with a 1: 1 mixture of PVA and water instead of just water. For plaster, simply coat the surface with PVA before filling with a plaster filler. There is more about plaster fillers on page 126 (Indoor walls).

Removing old paint and paper

When to remove it
The removal of gloss paint, emulsion or varnish is rarely necessary – do it only when the paint is loose, crazed, powdery or flaking. A good test is to put sticky-tape on, then peel it off and observe whether any paint comes away with it. It may be wise to strip if there are multiple layers unlikely to stay firm.

Remove all powdering whitewash, limewash or non-washable distemper. (Anything that absorbs water rapidly when wetted should be taken off unless an appropriate primer will seal it – see pages 127–8).

Clean oiled or waxed woodwork down to the bare wood if repainting it.

Wallpaper will need stripping only if it is loose, in bad condition, or if the colours may run.

How to remove it
A sponge, stiff brush and water with detergent may suffice for distemper, some emulsions and other water-based paints (though some chemical strippers are labelled as usable for emulsions). Wallpaper stripper left on overnight will help to remove distemper, etc.

Textured paints are very difficult to remove, even with hot water or wallpaper stripper. If they have oil paint on them, chemical stripping will be needed first.

Oil paints or varnish may need either a chemical stripper (liquid or, easier, paste) or heat to soften them before being scraped off, though scraping alone may do for small areas. If an uneven surface is left, sand it, or smooth it with a filler (see page 126). Polyurethane paint is hard to strip chemically; caustic chemicals do not work on it at all.

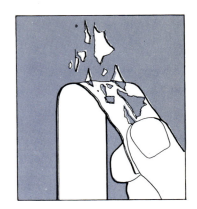

Removing old paint and paper

To get wax or oil off wood, use steel wool and white spirit, then scrub with detergent suds (not soda). Dry well. There may be wax from floor polish on the bottoms of doors and skirting boards, and oil traces by hinges, which will prevent paint from drying.

French polish can be removed with meths; cellulose lacquer or paint with acetone or cellulose thinners (these are highly flammable); other varnishes with paint stripper. (Cellulose paints are often found on kitchen units.)

To strip floorboards, hire a sander (see page 164) but even this may not be able to remove wax that has penetrated deeply (paint cannot be applied over wax). Sanding attachments for power tools are usable on other surfaces that need stripping, but see page 119.

Old paint may contain lead, which is dangerous to breathe, so wear a face-mask when scraping or abrading it.

Chemical stripping – Method 1

Tools and materials needed
Solvent stripper
(Allow 1 litre per 15sq m)
Rubber gloves
Sheet for floor
Paintbrush
Scrapers (see below)
Steel wool
Water or white spirit (depending on instructions with stripper)
Abrasive paper (see page 119)

Method
1 Wear rubber gloves (not plastic), cover floor, and do not smoke. If applying it overhead, wear goggles. Open container carefully, with a rag over the lid in case you splash your eyes.
2 Paint the stripper on liberally. Use cottonwool on a metal knitting needle tip to get into small mouldings.
3 After fifteen minutes or more, scrape off, putting shavings into a container for safe disposal. Repeat if necessary (steel wool may help).
4 Wash down with water (do not soak wood) or white spirit. Leave until dry – at least overnight.
5 Rub with medium abrasive paper, dust and then prime the bared surface.

Warning Bathe skin with cold water if you get stripper on it. Store container out of children's reach. Some strippers are flammable. Do not use on plastics.

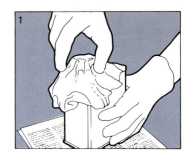
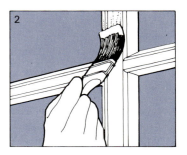
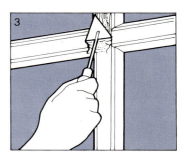
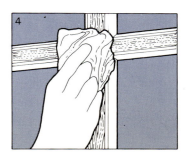

Chemical stripping – Method 2

Caustic paste stripper is usable even overhead, and is very good on mouldings, etc. It tends to slide down vertical surfaces. There is no unpleasant vapour. It is unsuitable for veneers or aluminium, or for cellulose, polyurethane, vinyl or cement paints.

Tools and materials needed
Caustic paste stripper: allow 5 l to 5sq m
Filling knife
Sponge and/or brush
Bucket of water
Sheet for floor

Method
1 Keep the room cool. Do not work in hot weather. Stir the paste, then trowel it on 3mm ($\frac{1}{8}$in) thick.
2 As soon as paste has worked through all layers of paint (test at half-hour intervals) lift it off: do not scrape the surface. If left too long it will dry and water will be needed to soften it.
3 Rinse surface thoroughly (add vinegar to the water if woodwork is involved). Leave until dry (at least overnight).

Note If many paint layers are to be removed, taking hours, the paste can be kept moist and effective by covering it with polythene sheet.

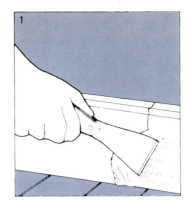

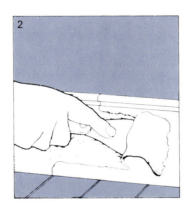

Blowlamp stripping

Quick, but needs some skill. Not suitable for plaster, plastics, thin metal, asbestos-cement, or intricate mouldings; not suitable for lead-based paints because of the fumes created, and not very good on emulsions; do not do it out of doors when it is windy; shield adjacent glass – a bit of Formica plus sticky-fixers will do.

Tools and materials needed
Liquid-gas blowlamp with flame-spreading attachment, with extra cartridges of gas for large jobs
Gloves
Sheet (not paper) for floor
Scrapers (see below)
Abrasive paper (see page 119)

Method
1 Remove any flammable things from vicinity, and keep a bucket of water handy. Cover floor and wear gloves. Open windows: this is a smelly job. Tighten connections to prevent gas leaks. Keep lamp upright for 5 minutes after lighting, or long flames may leap out. Brushing a thin paste of lime in water on to the paint will stop it building up into a sticky mass on your scraper.
2 One hand should wave the flame continually to and fro 6in away from a small area (adjust the flame to the best width) while the other follows it, when the paint bubbles, with a scraper held at a shallow angle. Do mouldings first, then flat surfaces – work from bottom to top. Keep your hand clear of paint scrapings, and do not scorch the surface or ignite the paint.
3 Rub with abrasive paper, removing all charred spots; dust; and prime.

Warning In bright light, the flame is invisible. A blowlamp can set fire to birds' nests under eaves. Never put it down with the flame pointing towards anything flammable.

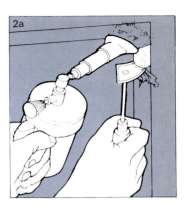

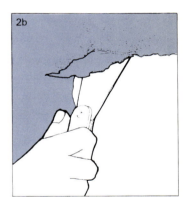

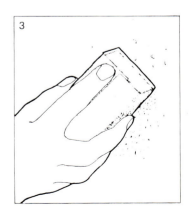

Stripping wallpaper

Many modern papers, including vinyls, simply peel off (the reverse side has a special coating) but the majority will need soaking and scraping, using a broad scraper at the angle shown so as not to harm the plaster. Wallpaper stripper or ordinary detergent is added to the water to make it penetrate better, and liberally applied – most easily with a garden syringe. Two or three lots left for half an hour will make stripping much easier: the paper may even pull off in sheets without scraping. To get water to stay put for the time needed by thick papers, add a little wallpaper paste to it, and to help it penetrate washable papers, painted papers (these may need paint stripper first), or multiple layers, scratch the surface with a wire brush, an abrader or coarse sandpaper. Really heavy, embossed papers, grasscloth or Lincrusta are best left to professionals. Stripping can be very hard work, and may take days.

Work from the top down, doing one width at a time. When the wall is bared, scrub off any remaining paste and sponge with clean water. Use a scraper lightly to remove any small 'nibs' of plaster.

It may be worth hiring a steam stripper if you have to remove a lot of oil-bound distemper, many coats of emulsion or, their principal use, thick wallpaper. Steam is produced by electricity or a butane gas cylinder and emerges through a plate that has to be held against the wall to soften the paper or paint. Hard work, and the whole room will get steamy.

Cleaning

A 'tack rag' (resin impregnated) is useful for getting off the dust that abrasives create, or use a cloth dampened with white spirit, or a damp sponge. This is essential before the final coat in particular. Merely brushing the dust off is not a good idea indoors because of the need to have dust-free air when painting: a vacuum cleaner hose is better for removing dust.

Washing down is almost always necessary on old surfaces because grease will prevent adhesion and dust will give a bitty texture. Fibrous boards or tiles should be dry brushed.

Washing down

Tools and materials needed
Bucket of water (it helps to add a
tablespoon of water softener)
Large sponge
Detergent (not soda)
Polythene sheet to protect floor
(For outside walls, a stiff broom and hose
may be useful; do not use detergent on
brickwork or stone, or unglazed tiles).

Method
1 Protect any electric fittings from water, or
turn off at main. Cover floor. Add
detergent to bucket of water.
2 Sponge on the water with detergent,
starting at the bottom and working
upwards (to prevent streaks). Don't forget
the tops of door and window frames.
Renew the water frequently.
3 Rinse well from top to bottom.
4 Leave till dry before painting.
  On metal, or if a surface is very greasy or
smoky, clean with copious white spirit first.
Steel wool can be used on metal, but
remove particles, as they may rust.
  Dark heat marks above radiators or lights
may need scrubbing. Stains which washing
does not remove may have to be coated
with aluminium sealer: these include the
marks left by burst pipes, cigarette smoke,
and past creosoting. Marks from mildew
can be removed with household bleach.

Indoor walls – preparation

If a fireplace has been in use, chimney-
sweeping should be done before
decorating, of course; and if the ceiling or
picture-rails are to be painted, do these
before the walls (window frames, skirtings
and doors are done afterwards through
their preparation should be done in
advance).
  Remove or cover wall-lights (turn off at
mains, before unscrewing them, and cover
any bare wires with insulating tape).
Unscrew any other wall-hung fitments
such as shelves or clocks. Move furniture
and curtains out of the way, protect floor
coverings, and turn off radiators.
  Unless the present surface – whether new,
painted, or papered – needs stripping,
washing down or priming (see pages 124,
left and 127–8), brush it down. If paper has
any loose edges, stick them down; if you
strip it off, wash remaining adhesive off the
wall. Water keeps the dust down when
sanding and so forth, but after any wet
preparation method, allow a day or so for
drying, especially if oil paint is going to be
used. After any dusty work, allow a day for
the air to clear. Deal with defects as
described on pages 126–7.
  If some walls are to be treated differently
from others, do light painted ones before
dark, and painted walls before papered
ones.

Indoor walls – filling

A packet filler is the most common filler for plaster, but where there is a lot to be done, plaster is much cheaper. Mix with only enough water to make a stiff paste. Adding a little PVA adhesive gives extra strength and makes priming unnecessary. In addition to other gaps, fill any around electric sockets or along skirtings. Some textured paints can act as filler.

Tools and materials needed
Filler
Putty knife, filling knife or trowel
Abrasive papers (see page 119)
Possibly, hammer and cold chisel
Primer (see pages 127–8)

Method
1 Scrape any loose or soft material away from the gap or crack and widen it if it is too narrow for you to be able to work filler into it. In the case of plaster or cement surfaces, dampen the space unless instructions on the pack do not advise this. Some big holes or gaps by woodwork may be part-filled with, for instance, crumpled paper lightly packed, before putting any filler in. (For very big holes see page 127.)
2 Press in the filler (after mixing it as instructed on the pack) with the knife or trowel. Plaster fillers tend to shrink, so slightly overfill with these unless instructions do not advise this.
3 If the gap is wide, you may need a cold chisel and hammer to undercut the edges as shown. Then brush water in (unless instructions advise against this), and press the filler in behind. If the gap is deep, it is better to use two thin layers, scratching the first one to give the second one a grip and leaving to dry (unless instructions advise against this) before the second layer goes in.

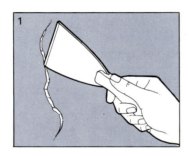

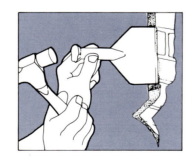

Indoor walls – filling

4 Smooth the surface with a wet trowel or brush, damp sponge or a wet rubber-gloved finger. Leave till hard (this may be hours or days) before rubbing down with medium abrasive paper (followed by fine in the case of plaster) then priming and painting.

Filling a damaged corner
1 Nail a thin strip of wood down side A as shown (or sticky-tape cardboard on) and apply filler on side B, up to the strip.
2 When filler is hard, remove strip and hold (don't nail) it on side B, while filling side A up to it. Slightly round off the corner before leaving to harden.

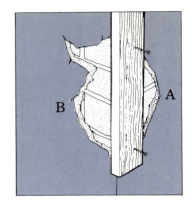

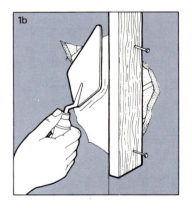

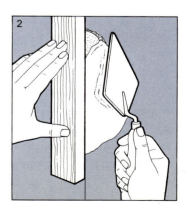

Indoor walls – other problems

Widespread hair cracks (in plaster or paint) Cover with thick lining paper (see page 148), to be primed if oil paint is to go over it.

Widespread irregularities Hang embossed or woodchip ('ingrain') paper (see page 148); or camouflage with textured paint (but remember that many of these will be permanent, or very difficult to remove).

Bulging plaster Likely to crumble if it sounds hollow when tapped. Cut away and treat as for large hole, see below.

Plasterboards gaping at joints This means boards need re-nailing (conceal heads with filler). Use damp paper tape and special ready-mixed adhesive filler to seal the joints.

Large hole, laths missing behind Tuck in crumpled chicken wire, stiff paper dampened and crumpled, or a square of metal mesh to provide a hold for plaster. Start with small dabs of plaster, gradually building up as they harden.

Adding sand to the first layer of plaster mix will strengthen it. When the hole is almost filled, make crisscross marks on the plaster, leave for a day, dampen, then add a final coat well smoothed with a damp trowel or brush. Some holes can be plugged by covering wet newspaper in filler and pushing this in as the base layer.

Large hole in plasterboard Dampen all round the hole, dab thin plaster on, press moistened bandage over, plaster this with several thin coats. Smooth with a damp trowel.

Mildew Use bleach as described on page 139 (moulds) or, better still, a fungicide. (Strip any wallpaper first.)

Panelling, mouldings, etc – missing bits May be replaceable with matching patterns.

Vinyl paper Cannot be painted: strip off.

Heavily embossed paper Do not paint it in very dry weather because unless paint dries slowly it may shrink the paper and pull it away.

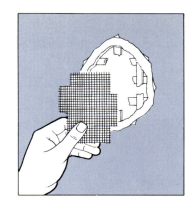

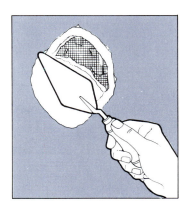

Indoor walls – other problems

Tiles Glazed ceramic, see page 145. Imitations – plastic, see page 145; enamelled, treat like gloss-painted surfaces.

Cellar walls (damp) Epoxy emulsion paint will keep damp out.

Exposed brickwork See page 138 (Outside walls). Consider a clear seal, possibly tinted, as an alternative to paint to keep it clean.

Indoor walls – primers

The need for these is much the same as on outdoor walls (see page 140). In addition, the following surfaces will need priming if oil paint is going to be used:

Lining paper, Anaglypta, insulating board
Thinned emulsion

Non-washable wallpaper
Multi-purpose primer or plaster primer

Non-washable wallpaper if colours or gold 'bleed'
Aluminium primer (may be difficult to obscure with other paint)

Washable or previously painted paper if absorbent
Multi-purpose primer (gently wash, rinse and dry first)

Plasterboard, paper-faced board
Multi-purpose primer, wallboard primer or wallpaper adhesive

Hardboard
Multi-purpose or plaster primer (rub down first if very shiny, using fine dry abrasive paper)

Asbestos insulating board (use no abrasives)
Alkali-resistant primer – necessary even with emulsion paint

Tobacco or smoke stains
Aluminium primer (after cleaning with meths)

Indoor walls – primers

Polystyrene sheeting or tiles
Acrylic primer or emulsion paint (two coats)
Joints between plasterboard panels
Multi-purpose primer

Indoor walls – paint types

Emulsion paint is the most usual choice though oil paint can be used (except over polystyrene sheeting or tiles, on very fibrous wallboards or tiles or on new walls); matt or eggshell oil paint stands more wear and washing than emulsion, but is harder to put on. The glossier the paint, the easier it is to sponge clean but its highly reflective surface may be unpleasing on large areas of walls. Windows will have to be open for some time while oil paint dries.
  Other alternatives are:
Textured Porous though thick. Some come in powder form and others are ready-mixed. Some are in white only but can be painted over. One brand is a particularly pure white, very fire-resistant. Various effects obtainable by stippling, swirling sponge over, etc. Outdoor paints containing sand, powdered stone, etc., could be used indoors. Textures catch the dirt and not all are washable. Many are hard to remove, and you will never be able to paper over them.
Anti-condensation Also textured (with cork granules). Whitish colour; can be overpainted with any porous paint. Sold by boat shops.
Fire-retardant Effective only if made to Class 1 of British Standard 476. A good choice for kitchens; over polystyrene sheeting or tiles; on plasterboard.
Fungicidal To inhibit mildew, moulds, etc., for a year or more – but cause of damp must be cured first.

Indoor walls – painting

To calculate the area of the walls in a room, measure the lengths of the walls and add together; multiply by the height from the top of the skirting. Deduct 2sq m for each doorway, and also the area occupied by windows and fireplace.

Tools and materials needed
Stepladder (or two with boards)
Paint
Brushes and/or rollers
'Kettle' (see page 116), bucket or paint-tray

Method
1 Start near the main window and work away from it. Try not to work in artificial light but, if you must, remove shades and put in 150W bulbs. Keep the room dust-free (if it is possible, dampen the floor). Follow the same system as for outdoor walls (pages 141–2).
2 When painting walls from a platform of boards, paint right across the wall, then lower the boards and do another band below this one, and so on. Leave the edges of the bands irregular.
3 Oil paint: brush top coat on in two directions but end in same direction as undercoat, upwards for gloss, downwards for matt. Brush any runs outwards before they set.
4 Emulsion paint over paper: if large blisters arise, slit with a razor-blade and insert adhesive.
5 Wall-plugged holes: keep free of paint if they are to be used again (otherwise, fill).

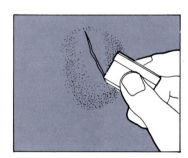

Ceilings – preparation

Preparation, priming (rarely needed) and choice of paint are very similar to those for indoor walls.

Remove any light fittings that may get splashed (turn off at mains first, and tape bared wires) or enclose them in large plastic bags. Furniture may be conveniently gathered in the centre of the room where staging or boards stretched between trestles or stepladders can go over it. Cover it and the floor with plastic sheeting (mop split water off this wherever it might cause a fall).

To decide whether the present surface needs stripping, washing down or repairing, see pages 121, 124, 138–9. Distemper in particular will call for scrubbing off. Stick down any loose corners of ceiling paper; or, if you strip it all off, wash away its adhesive too. If washing leaves bubbles in ceiling paper, slit each with a razor-blade and stick back when it has dried.

Ceilings – repairs

Cracks and holes Fine all-over cracks may involve papering the ceiling (see pages 152–3) though some textured paints act as filler. Big holes or cracks will need treating as on page 127.

Ceiling irregularities and joins in plasterboard ceilings become conspicuous when lights are turned on, so papering is often done even when there are no cracks.

Cracks where walls and ceilings join can be hidden by sticking coving round.

Ceilings – repairs

Ceiling tiles Polystyrene ceiling tiles or sheeting are sometimes used to cover up a ceiling in poor condition: this also helps to conserve warmth, curb condensation and subdue noise. It is important that the special adhesive should be spread all over the tiles: mere blobs will leave air-gaps which could speed any fire that broke out (polystyrene – unless specially treated – is a fire hazard, unlike mineral-fibre ceiling tiles). Polystyrene can be painted, but use only emulsion, preferably fire-resistant, for oil paint dissolves polystyrene and increases fire risk even if a primer is applied. Tiles can be painted before being put up, which is easier; or left unpainted. The last ones to go up will need trimming with a razor-sharp knife; arrange matters so that these occur in the least conspicuous part of the room. Do not press tiles into place with your fingertips as this will mark them, but use a piece of polystyrene.

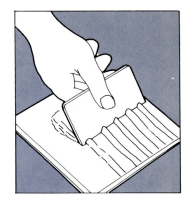

If a tile comes loose, put some adhesive in a plastic bag, push its open end under the tile and squeeze the adhesive out.

Clogged mouldings Use a fine spray to wet 50cm (18in) at a time, wait for half an hour then scrape out with a screwdriver and brush clean. (Hard work: 3m (3yd) could easily take a day.) It may help to have wallpaper stripper in the water if the old paint was distemper, etc. (If it was oil paint, chemical stripping will be needed: wear goggles.)

Missing bits of mouldings Many patterns are still made and can be bought by the metre to stick on or, if heavy, screw on. If only a small detail is missing, take a Plasticine impression of a nearby piece, grease and then fill this with plaster and when hard stick the new piece into the gap with thin plaster as an adhesive.

Heated ceilings Use Fibreglass tape for bridging any gaps.

Fibrous (acoustic) ceiling tiles Emulsion paint applied by spray is best.

Stains from water leaks Apply aluminium primer, see page 140.

Ceilings – paint types

Beams See Woodwork, page 133.
Non-washable distemper (Identifiable by the chalky traces it leaves on your fingers when you touch it.) Unless stabilizing primer will suffice (see page 140), remove it with a sponge or brush, frequently changed water containing water softener or wallpaper stripper, a wide striping knife and a bucket or dustpan held up to collect the stuff.
Polystyrene-covered ceiling Pull tiles away and get off as much adhesive as possible with a brush and hot water. To remove the remainder, cover with wallpaper stripper and after a few minutes both paint and paste can be easily scraped off together. Texture-painting the ceilings will cover any lingering traces.
Painting a ceiling when walls are not going to be decorated after it Use non-drip (jelly) paint, or ceiling tiles painted before being put up. Alternatively, sheets of newspaper held with masking tape can protect the walls.
Unsatisfactory ceilings (too high, dilapidated and so on) Consult a builder about having a lightweight false ceiling suspended below the present one, over part or all of the room; or about resurfacing with plasterboard or insulating board. Alternatives are a new ceiling of plywood or tongued-and-grooved boards screwed through to joists; or a false ceiling of translucent plastic with lighting above. Acoustic tiles or cork will muffle sound in the room (not sounds from outside).

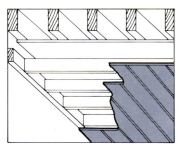

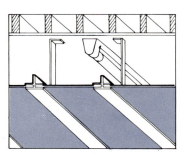

Ceilings – painting

Tools and materials needed
Pair of trestles or stepladders
Boards or staging
Paint
Rollers and/or brushes
'Kettle' (see page 116), bucket or paint-tray

Method
1 Turn off heating (fast, uneven drying leads to trouble). Place boards or staging near to and parallel with the main window, moving them back bit by bit. If you must work in artificial light, put in 150W bulbs. Keep the room dust-free.
2 Use a brush to paint a line where the ceiling meets the wall.
3 Paint bands 50cm (18in) wide parallel with the window. For a smooth surface, finish each off by brushing back from the wet edge into the dry area (do not re-load brush for this) to obliterate brush marks; do not do this with textured paints, however.
4 If using a roller, make crisscross strokes over a square then finish off the square with straight strokes running towards the windows. Use a brush for mouldings.
5 If painting ornate mouldings in two colours, first cover the whole thing in the colour of the raised parts. When this paint is dry, use an artist's brush to touch in the background colour. Make a padded stick as shown to support your wrist while doing tricky bits.

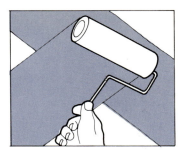

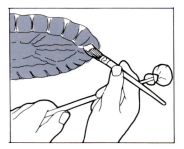

Woodwork – preparation

Before deciding to paint over it, consider the natural beauty of wood: pages 135–7 deals with varnishes, seals, etc., that will reveal instead of covering it. Some methods are more economical than paint and easier to apply. However, transparent finishes are not durable or protective as paint out of doors.

Before starting, make sure windows and doors are in a good state, if necessary attending to hinges, locks, sashcords, cracked panes, loose or crumbled window putty, sticking doors and so forth before redecorating begins. Rot or woodworm must of course be eradicated.

The painting of exterior woodwork should be done in fine but not hot weather; all wood must be dry before paint goes on. New softwoods (those from coniferous evergreen trees, such as 'deal') or elm outdoors need a coat of paintable wood preservative two days before painting, especially on end grain. Wood exposed by paint-stripping should be coated. Take special care with the bottoms of windows and sills.

Woodwork – preparation

Old paint may need only cleaning and rubbing down (see page 121), unless there are many old layers or any of it is in such poor shape that this part must be stripped (see pages 122–3) and then immediately coated with preservative or primed to keep damp out. Strip mildewed paint. Strip multiple layers from door or window edges if the build-up might cause sticking.

Primers

Priming is vital outdoors, and even indoors most new and all stripped wood will need a primer. Out of doors, use low-lead primer made to British Standard 5358; indoors, use lead-free primer for any surface which a toddler might bite or suck, now or in the future. Acrylic primer is usable outdoors or in. Alternatives (not so good) are varnish, linseed oil or multi-purpose primer: they may be adequate indoors.

Brush the primer firmly in the direction of the grain (after gentle sanding if it is softwood). Do corners and joints thoroughly. End grain needs two coats because damp entering here will get under the paint film elsewhere (PVA adhesive thinned with 20% water is an alternative seal). Plywood should have two coats. When the primer is dry, carefully rub off any small 'nibs' you can feel, but do not rub away the primer. For open-grained woods like oak, thin the primer with white spirit. Aluminium wood primer is used for resinous or oily woods like cedar or teak, or where condensation or other damp troubles exist, or over some preservatives. (First wipe oily wood with white spirit.) Paint as soon as the primer is dry (up to two days).

Woodwork

Grain fillers and stopping

The grain of coarse wood will need filling with a special filler if a good finish is wanted. This is a whitish or wood-coloured paste that hardens, applied with a circular motion. It is then rubbed with medium abrasive paper. Minor holes and blemishes are filled with patent stopping in paste form, ruffed level when hard. Use exterior-grade oil stopping wherever conditions are damp. You can make your own stopping with sawdust and adhesive, and add stain to it if you wish. Filling and sanding will give end-grain a paintable surface. Chipboard needs oil-based filler because it is so porous.

Repairs

Cracks, gaping joints and holes in any wood See page 121. Deal with these before any washing down or after priming. Ordinary plaster-type filler (fine grade) will do indoors except where conditions are going to be damp: for method see page 126. Outdoor work needs exterior grade stopping. Ordinary putty (which is linseed oil plus whiting) can be used but prime the wood first and let it dry before putting the putty in; otherwise the wood will absorb the oil from the putty and it will crumble. Leave for two or three days before painting. So-called plastic wood tends to shrink. Do not fill gaps between the uprights and cross pieces of panelled doors: these joints should be properly repaired because the movement of the door puts a strain on them. Take special care to fill gaps out of doors (even, for instance, behind mouldings on doors) in order to stop rain penetrating; and in any room that suffers from condensation, take special care over bottom joints of window frames and doors.

Woodwork – preparation

Chips in old paint. Fill in with undercoat (using an artist's brush). After a few days, rub down with abrasive paper. Alternatively, use fine filler. (If the chips have bared the wood below, this will need priming first.)

Soft patches (wet rot). If large, replace with new timber, treating this and the adjoining area with preservative. Small patches can be cut out and replaced with wood stopping or epoxy filler.

Clogged drip-grooves (on the undersides of outdoor window sills). Scrape out and prime.

Worn woodwork (eg., stair treads). Use exterior-grade wood filler to level it before painting. The wood will need priming. This filler will stand up pretty well to the heavy wear of footsteps.

Problem surfaces

Oak window sills The coarse grain tends to open in sunlight and this pushes paint off. An alternative is simply to use a wood preservative or exterior-grade varnish (see page 137). Do not use steel wool on oak because it causes stains.

Knotty wood Shellac knotting is a quick-drying varnish that stops resin seeping out of knots, particularly important on wood that is in sunlight. Knotting containing aluminium pigment is very effective. Apply on and slightly around the knots with a small brush or bit of cloth, before priming. Two thin coats are needed. Very large or resinous knots should be removed and the hole filled. Shellac knotting coloured white will be easier to conceal under light paints. (Preliminary heating with a blow lamp helps, because this draws the resin out – wipe it away with white spirit.)

Woodwork – preparation

Nail and screw heads To prevent rusting and staining, apply primer, knotting, or oily filler after screwing or punching them in just below the surface of the wood.

Waxed wood Remove wax polish by rubbing hard with white spirit and steel wool or other scouring pad in the direction of the grain. Clean with kitchen paper and repeat several times (use fresh paper each time). Test a small area with paint. If it fails to dry, repeat the process or else coat all over with knotting before painting.

Wood previously treated with preservative, or smoke-stained Use aluminium primer (one or two coats) or shellac knotting. A very thick and soft coating of creosote may be impossible to seal off, even with special anti-tar coatings. There is a paint that will go over creosote, etc.

Unfamiliar timbers (possibly oily or resinous) Having prepared the wood, test-paint a small part, leave for two days and draw the edge of a coin over. If this easily removes the paint, the timber is not suitable for painting. Aluminium primer may solve the problem – do a similar test.

Woodwork accessible to toddlers Check that the paint contains no lead because this can cause brain damage if chewed or sucked. (Very little is sold now.)

Wood in humid conditions (eg., greenhouse). Buy special paint from boat shops; or greenhouse paint; or simply use wood preservative.

Surface moulds and blue-stain fungi Use mould-resistant paint, after treating the wood with fungicidal preservative.

Woodwork – paint types

Oil paint is the usual choice, with whatever undercoat is advised on the tin (if you want speedy drying indoors, use emulsion instead of undercoat, or acrylic primer, but the finish will not be so perfect or durable); or soft-gloss emulsion (most of these are for indoor use only; they are more inclined to look dirty; and remember that they take weeks to become really hard). High-gloss paint gives maximum protection, especially out of doors and at windows subject to condensation. Other paints suitable for particular purposes include the following.

Polyurethane paints (gloss or semi-gloss) contain some oil but stand up to a good deal of heat, stains, alcohol and hard wear (but not weather) and so are particularly useful in the kitchen or for shelves and table-tops. Use no undercoat but thin the first coat with a little white spirit. Two-part plastic paints are even tougher but more troublesome and expensive: a hardener has to be mixed in to make them set and particular care is needed when preparing the surface.

Enamel and lacquer are descriptions for oil paints formulated to give a particularly smooth, hard and high gloss. They are useful for smaller jobs like doorknobs, toys, smaller whitewood furniture, etc. They are quick-drying, and available in extra-small tins for decorative touches.

Flame-retardant paint might be a good choice where there is a lot of wood panelling or flammable boards.

Blackboard paint is usable also for exposed beams, but special matt black paint has a better finish.

Floor paints are extra tough; or boards can be painted with polyurethane.

Non-drip paint (jelly type) is handy for overhead work or the sloping surfaces of, for example, louvre doors and shutters.

Whenever painting outdoors, check that your chosen paint is recommended for exterior work.

Woodwork – quantities

Multiply width by length of each surface and add together. In the case of window frames, multiplying width by height of the whole window will give the right answer for frames with deep mouldings; halve this for very simple, narrow frames (such as metal ones).

Woodwork – painting

Tools and materials needed
Stepladder or alternative
Paint
Brushes
'Kettle' (see page 116)
Possibly, paint shield or masking tape and window wedges to hold sash windows up
Tack rag (see page 118)

Method
The room should be dust-free (dampen the floor if this is possible). Wipe the surface clean just before painting.

1 Paint mainly in the direction of the wood grain. On vertical parts, paint the last strokes upwards to avoid runs. Be sure edges are coated and also all undersides and tops of outdoor fitments or others liable to damp. When painting windowcills out of doors, open windows (otherwise part of the cill will be missed). Draw any excess off bottom corners, using an unloaded brush.

2 Use the tip of the bristles to 'lay off': that is, after painting a brush-width in one direction, brush back (without re-loading), if possible at right angles to the first strokes. Final very light strokes can be made, but always finish in the direction of the grain or of the length of the area being painted. Runs and sags are caused, not by a thick film, but by an uneven film, so always

Woodwork – painting

aim to apply paint evenly over the area of the work.

3 If doing narrow mouldings, window bars or skirting tops, use a cutting-in brush lightly loaded and lightly held. Use a poking action at inner corners, with a very lightly loaded brush, then draw away any excess. A padded stick (see page 130) may help you to keep a steady hand.

4 A day later, or whenever the paint has hardened to the point where your fingernail will not scratch it, rub undercoat lightly with abrasive paper and then clean with a tack rag before applying top coat in the same direction. If more than a day or two elapses before the top coat is applied, the undercoat must be left till hard and then rubbed down firmly.

5 Mouldings, knobs, etc. to go on to built-ins or other furniture in a contrast colour can be painted before being fixed on.

Note An extra coat of paint may extend the life of the paint on woodwork by at least one third.

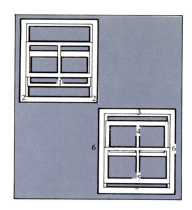

Some tips to remember

Windows
Do not get paint on sash cords. If you want to close casements soon, do first the parts that will touch when closed. (When dry, dust with talc before closing.) When painting window bars, do first the edges adjoining the glass and then the fronts: do not overload with paint. Let the top coat of paint on window bars extend 1–2mm on to window glass so as to seal the putty well; and let the paint from picture rails and skirtings extend a little on to the wall if the wall is going to be papered later.

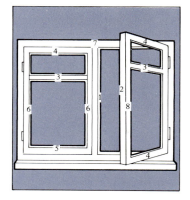

Doors and windows
Keep the paint film fairly thin on edges that close against one another and on mouldings. Normally, do the handle side last. Do surrounding frames, cills and edges after doing the fronts (see illustrations). Keep paint off hinges, bolts, etc.

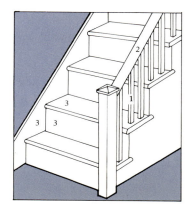

Woodwork – painting

Panelled doors, etc.
Do any mouldings lightly and before the wide panels they are on, and try not to get their paint on the panels. The drawing shows the order in which to paint the other parts. To paint mouldings or panels in a contrasting colour, use masking tape on the surrounding area (when its paint has dried hard).

Frames adjoining masonry
The masonry line is unlikely to be dead straight. Do not attempt to paint right up to it, but finish with a straight line of your own making.

Out of doors
A solid coat is more important than a smooth finish, so paint all areas that were stripped, primed, etc., then paint the entire surface.

Indoors
Extra undercoats, with rubbing down, will give a first-class finish on, for instance, windowsills.

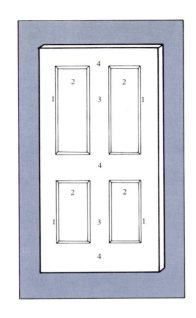

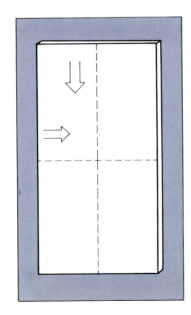

Woodwork – alternatives to paint

Wood can be protected and given a transparent finish (matt, semi-gloss or gloss) by a variety of materials, such as oil, wax, varnish or polyurethane seal.

To reveal the natural surface of furniture or other woodwork, old paint, wax or varnish can be stripped off (see pages 122–3). Naturally, defects like knots will then become visible too. It is not easy to strip finishes off veneered wood, so avoid this if you can. To discover what the wood may look like when stripped, find an unpainted edge and scrub it clean.

One or two applications of wood-colour restorer or special wood bleach may then be needed to deal with discoloration, followed by washing off later – or use oxalic acid (1 part in 7 parts water), taking the precautions mentioned on pages 122–3.

Stains
Indoor wood can then be stained if desired (in wood colours, or in bright colours), still revealing the grain, and this can be waxed or varnished. Do not, however, use any oil-based filler for repairs below a stain that will not soak into this; try to stain the filler before you use it. Stains are of three main types, the first two in the form of crystals or powder to be dissolved, others already liquid:

Water-based – like fabric dyes (cheap)	If the wood swells after applying these, rub down when dry. Water stains can be lightened after applying, by rubbing with a dampened cloth.
Spirit-based	Quick-drying. Can be lightened with meths-dampened cloth. (All teak-coloured stains are spirit-based.)
Oil-based	Ready to use, fairly quick to dry. Some dry glossy.

Woodwork – alternatives to paint

Stains should be wiped or brushed on in the direction of the grain (one coat only) after sanding the wood and, in the case of water-based stains, wetting it. Most can be wiped over a day later. Test first on an inconspicuous part, for the colour will be affected by the wood itself. Spirit stains are very flammable. They should be kept off plastics and clothes.

Stains for exterior timber are different: they need to be weatherproof and fungicidal. Do not use them indoors as some are poisonous. Teak and oak do not take stain well unless weather has bleached them white.

Gloss stains are a combination of stain and varnish; or you can colour varnish yourself with tubes of stainers. Coloured varnishes, however, tend to obliterate the grain, unlike stains which sink into it.

Oils

Teak oils, containing resins, are for use on any natural hardwood indoors – possibly stained but not waxed or varnished. (Linseed oil has been superseded for this purpose because it attracts dirt and goes dark; so does heavy waxing.) New wood will need several coats rubbed in with a cloth. (Burn oily rags out of doors: they are a fire hazard even in a dustbin.) For later upkeep, only a damp cloth is needed, or light waxing if preferred. Some teak oils contain silicones to give extra resistance to water and stains. Any filler used should be oil-based.

Seals

For an oiled look but a more heat- and stain-resistant finish, use well-thinned polyurethane seal wiped on and off with a cloth (2–3 coats), smoothing each coat with steel wool. This, too, can be waxed, if desired.

Woodwork – alternatives to paint

Varnishes

These can give an even deeper gloss (but are also obtainable in a flat and eggshell finish) and more protection. Most dry overnight. They may 'bloom' (produce a whitish film) if the air is damp or cools off rapidly. They are used on hardwoods or stained softwoods. Out of doors their life is only a year or two even when three coats are used; marine varnishes are among the best but may go yellow or brown. Therefore varnishes are best used only where there is some protection, such as on a door under a canopy or porch. Varnishes peel on weathering and then need stripping (use paint remover, or scrape dry); also the wood may develop black spots of mould and white patches which have to be sanded off and possibly treated with fungicide. Polyurethane varnishes are not recommended out of doors.

Clear spirit varnish is used only where a cheap, quick-drying, indoor finish is wanted; oil varnish is rather better. Those containing shellac are superior; and some have the advantage of being almost colourless. The most practical finish is polyurethane, clear or tinted, glossy or matt, brushed on (or sprayed from an aerosol) with no filler or sealer between it and the wood. Several coats are usually needed, the first one thinned. Dry and lightly rub down each coat. Glossy types may need a third coat but will then be more durable than matt ones. There is a non-drip jelly version, and extra-durable grades for floors. Two-part polyurethane or other plastic coatings are even tougher but give off fumes as they harden.

For a mirror-like finish to varnish or polyurethane, rub down when hard with fine abrasive paper and apply burnishing cream. A more liquid version of this, called polish reviver, is for restoring high gloss to french polish or cellulose. For a satin or matt finish, rub with fine steel wool and wax.

Woodwork – alternatives to paint

Stains for outdoors
Creosote is a cheap, tarry preservative for fences and sheds (keep it away from plants and clothing); the darker the colour the more durable the result.
Other wood preservatives are available in natural or bright colours or green, quick-drying and long-lasting. Some are formulated specially for cedar shingles.

These are applied to new or stripped wood, and show the grain (also any defects). They won't last longer than paint – if as long – but are easy to apply and renew. They should not need stripping, but may have to be sanded after two or three treatments. They are very useful on cladding and fences and gates, but less satisfactory on existing softwood windows, which may distort more easily, and they don't protect the putty.

Outdoor walls – preparation

Once painted, most walls cannot be restored to their natural state again. So be sure you really are prepared to repaint the walls regularly. An alternative may be a good clean, with or without a clear seal (tinted if desired). Or use a surface tinter.

Painting in hot weather is as inadvisable as doing it in wet, windy, misty or frosty weather, so it makes sense to leave outdoor painting until early autumn, when summer should have dried out all surfaces. Beware of dew and night frosts.

Meantime, attend to cracked or clogged gutters and down-pipes, and dripping windowsills: look for dripmarks on the walls. Do the repairs to walls that are listed below, and fill gaps between walls and door or window frames with mastic. If gutters and the boards behind them are to be painted, do these before the walls. Downpipes and window frames should be prepared for painting now though the actual painting is done after the walls. If possible, detach or prune creepers, and protect nearby plants with polythene sheeting. If woodwork is not going to be painted, use masking tape to protect its edges.

With luck, brushing down may be all that is needed to ensure a surface that is clean, smooth and dry. Use a stiff bristle brush, not a wire one. But if any paint removal (page 121), washing down (page 125) or repairs involving wet materials (below) has to be done, do it well in advance so that the wall can dry before being painted, especially if oil paint is going to be used. If primer (page 140) is to be applied, however, do not leave more than a day or two before painting over this.

Outdoor walls – surface repairs

Here is a guide to the most usual defects in walls that may have to be remedied. Where cracks and gaps are concerned, the filling method is described on page 126, while really large ones are dealt with later (special problems). Some gaps or flaking surfaces may be dealt with by applying a cement-and-resin impregnated 'bandage' which will go over any shape and is waterproof when set.

Brick	White stains (efflorescence) particularly in spring	Brush off repeatedly. See also Special problems, opposite.
	Green stains (may appear only in winter), due to algae or moss	Cure the cause (damp). See also Special problems, opposite. (Green marks made by copper are hard to remove.)
	Cement marks	Apply cement solvent or acid (even vinegar).
	Crumbling mortar	Bricklaying mortar used fairly dry (scrape out loose mortar first).
	Cracks and holes	Bricklaying mortar.
	Broken bricks, stones	Stick together with PVA or epoxy adhesive.
	Cracks in stone	Epoxy putty or mortar.
Concrete	Stains, cracks and holes	As for brick.
	Gaping joints	Specially formulated mastic, or epoxy adhesive mixed with sand.
Asbestos cement	Broken sheets	Epoxy adhesive plus glass fibre bandage. See also Special problems, opposite

Outdoor walls – surface repairs

Half-timbering	Patchy colour	Apply black preservative wood stain.
	Gaps at joins	Fill with non-setting mastic.
	(See also Woodwork, page 132.	
Tile cladding	Cracked tiles	Cement bandage or self-adhesive building tape will suffice for first-aid repairs.
	Broken tiles	Stick together with PVA or epoxy adhesive. Put replacements on the clips that held the old ones.
Weatherboarding or cedar shingles	Discoloured natural wood	Sand and apply a clear or coloured restorative: water-repellent, fungicidal and with a sheen. Do not varnish because this will prevent penetration of future restoratives.
	Cracks	Use oil-based moisture-resistant wood-filler, rub down and paint (or seal, using preservative stain first if desired).
	(For painting information see Woodwork page 134.)	
Plaster (including stucco)	Cracks and holes	Exterior grade filler, or mortar with PVA adhesive added.
Cement rendering	Cracks and gaps	Cement mortar with PVA adhesive added.
Pebbledash, roughcast, etc	Small gaps	As for cement rendering but while the mortar is still soft throw matching gravel on and press in. See Special problems, opposite.
Painted surfaces		As it is difficult to be sure what paint has been used previously (some types are now obsolete), and cement types in particular can give rise to problems, scrape a little off to post to the technical department of your chosen paint firm and ask what surface preparation and paint type they recommend. If paint needs stripping, see pages 122–3. (Multiple layers: see Special problems.)

Outdoor walls – special problems

Moss, lichen, moulds (what looks like dirt may be mould). In dry weather get off all you can with a wire brush, then apply household bleach in water (1 part to 4 of water). Leave for a few hours then rinse. When the remaining moss looks dead and dry, brush or scrape off then repeat with bleach. This may have to be done annually before rainy weather sets in but applying a water-repellent solution (see page 105, Damp walls) may discourage recurrence. Longer-lasting fungicides are available. Some paints contain fungicides, and emulsions harbour growths much less than cement ones. An acid-based brick cleaner may help.

Chronic efflorescence Usually, rain helps the white marks on new brick walls to disappear or they can be brushed off, but occasionally a leaky pipe or faulty damp course may lead to continual efflorescence (the soaking out of salts that are in bricks) or the lime from adjacent concrete, limestone or mortar may leach on to bricks. Hydrochloric acid (spirits of salts) can be used to clean up, but test its effect on a small part first. The acid is dangerous (wear rubber gloves and goggles, and keep bicarbonate of soda handy to put on skin if splashed). Unless bought already diluted, mix one part acid to 5 of water in a glass jar, wet the brickwork and gently brush the acid well in using a long-handled plastic broom. When the stain has gone, rinse the wall. Keep the acid well out of children's reach. Alternatively, use proprietary brick-cleaner.

Salty atmosphere Paint containing epoxy resin withstands seaside conditions well but is expensive.

Rust stains can be removed with oxalic acid crystals in warm water – 30g to $\frac{1}{2}$ litre (1oz to 1pt) – applied repeatedly, then sealed when dry with an oil-based primer before painting. (The acid is poisonous; wear rubber gloves, and also goggles if working overhead.) The cause may be serious: consult a builder.

Outdoor walls – special problems

Tricky surfaces Even when intact, the following surfaces may spoil the new paint later.

Very shiny surfaces (such as glazed bricks or tiles, granite, marble and some other stones). They need to be cleaned with meths, rubbed down with coarse 'wet and dry' abrasive paper, left till joints are completely dry, and primed quickly before getting contaminated. Thin the primer with 10% white spirit if necessary: alkali-resistant primer adheres well. Tile paint or polyurethane paint will adhere best, often without primer.

Multiple layers of old paints (water-based, not oil) can be bound together in one, provided they are not flaking or hollow, by using a special proprietary paint over its special sealer for this purpose.

Asbestos cement presents problems because it is particularly absorbent and alkaline; avoid using abrasives (or wear a mask) because asbestos dust is dangerous to lungs.

New walls need time to dry out: three months before using even porous paint (see page 140).

Note There is a firm that specializes in wall and floor paints for difficult situations, waterproofing, fillers, cement colourants, masonry cleaners, etc.

Outdoor walls – primers

Coating a surface with special priming or sealing fluid, usually oil-based, is not invariably needed but is desirable if the surface is bare or is very porous, powdery, alkaline or stained – though not even then if a paint is chosen that can survive the hazard in question.

Primers have to be brushed or rolled well in (you may need to wear goggles for this work) and left for a day before being painted, though some are quick-drying. They are often flammable. Multipurpose primers may be convenient but are something of a compromise. Coverage varies greatly, from 6 to 18 sq m per litre. Specific primers used for outdoor walls are:

For porous masonry, cement or plaster – if no other problem is present
Also where limewash or non-washable distemper has been imperfectly removed
Stabilizing solution or penetrating primer; possibly thinned with white spirit. Diluted PVA adhesive makes a suitable primer on indoor plaster.
Powdery surfaces
Masonry sealer or penetrating primer.
New rendering, concrete, new cement-based filler (if to be oil-painted; unless using polyurethane paint)
Alkali-resistant primer.
Surface previously tarred, bitumen painted or with other staining in it (including water stains)
Aluminium primer (effective only if the stain is neither fresh nor thick). Or PVA adhesive diluted with an equal amount of water. Or acrylic emulsion. Or special sealer.
Glazed bricks, tiles, plastic or other very smooth surface
Alkali-resistant or plaster primer.

Outdoor walls – paint types

Paints for wood or aluminium cladding are dealt with under Woodwork and Metalwork.

Most paints for outdoor walls are water-based emulsions (or cement paints) although oil paints and some oil-free 'masonry paints' can be used. Three factors are important where walls are concerned. If new, their bricks, concrete or plaster may still be damp. They (or the mortar used in their construction) may contain a lot of alkali. And, of course, outdoor ones are exposed to rain which often contains atmospheric dirt or the spores of moulds.

On new, damp walls only matt, porous paint should be used (and only after 3 months), otherwise the damp will not be able to evaporate. On alkaline walls (unless primed) only alkali-resistant paint should be used.

Paint type	Porous	Alkali-resistant	Weatherproof
Cement	Yes	Yes	Moderately
Emulsion			
PVA copolymer	Yes	Some	Very if exterior grade
Acrylic	Yes	Yes	
Vinyl	Yes	Yes	Not always
Oil paints			
Matt	Some	No	No
Glossy	No	Some	Yes
Imitation stone	No	No	Yes
Masonry paints			
Pliolite	Yes	Yes	Yes
Chlorinated rubber	No	Yes	Yes
Bituminous	Some	Yes	Yes

Outdoor walls – paint types

Bituminous paint, usually black, is for waterproofing (thick compounds are used particularly for roofs). An alternative for walls, not quite so waterproof, is a clear silicone-based **water-repellent** but it is difficult to paint over this for a year or two.
Ordinary emulsion or **gloss oil paint** can be used on outdoor walls if labelled as suitable for exterior use, but special paints are better. Painting outside walls is such a performance that extra durability is desirable. One-coat paints halve the work, of course, but are less durable out of doors.
Pliolite paints can, unlike emulsions, be used even in cold or damp weather.
Cement-based paints are fairly durable but tend to look dirty soon. They come as powders which need mixing, and they cannot go over old paint other than cement paint. One can be applied with a spattering machine (this can be hired) to give a sandy, 'Tyrolean' finish; doors and windows will need masking.
Reinforced emulsions are resin-based paints containing powdered mica, ground stone, sand, nylon fibres, etc., to give a texture (coarse or fine), greater rain-resistance and very long life. They fill in minor cracks, and many contain fungicides. A good choice for flat roofs covered in asphalt, etc. Some come as a paste that has to be diluted.
'Elastic' paint forms a thin coating of rubber-like consistency, bridging fine cracks and providing a smooth, self-cleaning finish. It can go on wood, metalwork and roofing felt too.

Outdoor walls – painting

Quantities
To calculate the area of each outside wall, multiply width by height. Unless they are particularly large, make no deduction for doors and windows as these will compensate for any bays, porches, etc. To estimate the height of a wall, look at the rainwater pipes: each section is 2m (yd) long as a rule. The walls of an average two-storey house will be 6m (yd). For gable ends, square the width of the wall then divide by two.

Painting

Tools and materials needed
Ladder or platform tower (for two-storey building)
Paint
Brush or roller
'Kettle' (see page 116) or bucket (and S-hook if using a ladder)

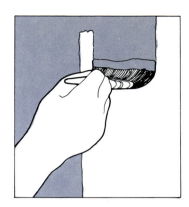

Method
1 Begin with whichever wall the sunlight has just left and move round the house in the same direction as the sunlight. Start at the top right corner (unless you are left-handed) and, tackling the wall in squares about 50cm (18in) wide (or 1m [1yd], if using a roller), work from top to ground level, then move the ladder along. Do not leave the squares with dead-straight edges, nor take a lengthy break in mid-wall, or the joins will show.
2 For a smooth finish, paint each square downwards; then across, except when using jelly paint or emulsion (do not re-load the brush for these cross strokes). Jelly paint should be brushed as little as possible; emulsion paint can be brushed on in any direction. Finish the bottom edge with a few light strokes upwards. If using a roller, make diagonal crisscross strokes until the square is covered, then finish off with straight lines. On a textured surface, the paint is jabbed or stippled on with a short-bristled brush.

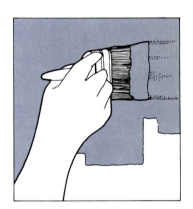

Outdoor walls – painting

3 Tackle the next square before the edge of the previous one has dried, otherwise the join will show. Brush into the previously applied paint.
4 Wipe off any splashes before they harden (if any do harden, use a razor blade on window panes, and water or paint stripper on other surfaces). If a downpipe needs protection during wall painting, make a tube of paper or card and sticky-tape which you can slide down as you go. Other adjoining surfaces can be protected by masking tape.

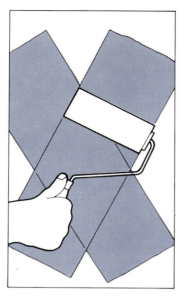

Metalwork – preparation

Paint is often essential to protect metal (particulary iron and steel) from corrosion or tarnish as well as to decorate it. Alternatively, clear varnishes (as for woodwork) can be used on copper pipes, brass doorknobs or other things indoors.

Do not do this work in damp or misty weather.

Cleaning and rubbing down (or stripping old paint, if required) are done as described on pages 121–2, and rust removal as on page 143. A stiff wire brush is useful for iron or steel, a softer one for other metals. White spirit is needed to remove even the slightest trace of grease or fingermarks, before the metal receives its first coat. Rub the white spirit on with emery paper and clean it off thoroughly. It is important not to have metal dust flying about.

Small iron or steel objects can be stripped of paint by immersing overnight or longer in a solution of caustic soda; add 1kg (2lb) slowly to a plastic bucket three-quarters full of water. Take great care and wear rubber gloves and goggles. Wash off in another bucket of clean water, rinse well under a tap and dry quickly to avoid re-rusting. Dispose of caustic by flooding with water down the drain, but don't let the paint skins block the drain. Don't try this with other metals.

For steel window frames, old putty may need replacing with special metal casement putty after cleaning and applying a rust inhibitor to the steel.

Repair leaking or clogged gutters and pipes as indicated on pages 39–41.

Other metals, too, may have cracks, pitting or dents requiring attention. Special metal fillers and adhesives are available, epoxy adhesives and putty are excellent (motor accessory shops sell these for car bodywork repairs): soldering may be called for, but clean up well after this otherwise paint will not stick. Do not attempt repairs to metal windows.

Before painting radiators, turn them off to cool. With some paints it is necessary for

Metalwork – preparation

them to stay off for a week after painting, but others require heat to 'cure' the finish. Unscrew hot-air grilles or other metal fittings that are detachable as it is easier to paint these on a table.

Metalwork – primers

The main purpose of metal primers is to inhibit corrosion, so priming is particularly necessary out of doors. Primers also aid adhesion, for which reason it is often best to apply them before putting any repairing filler on – read the makers' instructions. New radiators and windows come ready-primed.

A primer is used on new, or newly stripped, metal or on patches where old paint has chipped off. Prime edges and the tops of corrugations first, otherwise the full coat of primer may not stay on them, and make sure all nooks and crannies are coated. Wrought iron in particular should have two coats. Paint soon after priming and avoid making any fingermarks, otherwise corrosion may start up. Suitable primers include the following (there are others, but many contain lead, which is best avoided):

Steel, iron
Zinc phosphate (two coats if conditions are severe) or zinc-rich

Zinc, galvanized iron or steel
Etch primer followed by zinc chromate or zinc phosphate or zinc-rich.

Aluminium
Etch primer (if metal is new) followed by zinc chromate.

Copper, brass, bronze
If indoors or if clear-lacquered, no primer; otherwise etch primer followed by aluminium primer.

Lead, chromium
Etch primer only.

Tin
Etch primer followed by zinc chromate.

Metalwork – rust removal

Use a scraper, abrading tool and wire brush to get loose bits off (wear goggles if working overhead), followed by emery paper; or use wire-brush attachments with a power tool – disc shape for flat areas, conical for small spaces. If there is any chance that rust may be hidden under seemingly sound paint, strip it. Next apply a chemical rust remover – either a caustic jelly or an acid liquid which has to be wiped off; or a paint with phosphoric acid, lead and resin in it which is left on and forms a permanent coating that reduces further corrosion. Take safety precautions with these. A pipe cleaner will help to get these chemicals into small angles. If a simple remover is used, a primer will be needed immediately to inhibit future rust. Another alternative is an oil-and-mica paint which isolates rust particles from the metal, and provides a damp-proof coating to iron before it is painted.

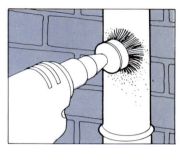

Metalwork – paint types

Although emulsion paint can go on to metal (except hot pipes and radiators), oil paint is usually chosen: polyurethane is very good. The water in emulsion paint may rust iron or steel unless they are very thoroughly primed first. Gloss or other exterior grade oil paint is desirable (even indoors) if metalwork is exposed to damp or steamy air. Some other paints worth bearing in mind are as follows.

Bitumen or bitumen rubber Used mainly to waterproof the insides of gutters and tanks or to protect railings, corrugated iron, etc. In the case of tanks containing drinking water, check whether the paint is of a grade suitable for this use. Only black or dark colours; has a tendency to soften in hot weather unless coated with aluminium paint; will not go over other old paint. This paint is also useful to protect metals that might be corroded by drips coming from some other metals, masonry or timber. Berlin black is a matt version for wrought iron, stoves, etc.

Bituminous paints, in black and a few colours, give cheap but not very attractive protection to outdoor metalwork.

Metallic paints, have powdered aluminium or other metals in them to give the effect of silver, gold or bronze. As well as being decorative, they protect against moisture and deflect heat. Cheap ones, however, will darken in colour. Some are in aerosols; and artists' shops sell them in paste form, in tubes. Usable on other surfaces, not only metal.

Radiator paints are formulated to resist any colour change due to heat, though many ordinary gloss paints are adequate except perhaps in white.

Fireproof aluminium paint will withstand even hotter temperatures and is used on boilers, flues, etc. Usually, no primer is needed. Metallic paints decrease the heat output of radiators.

Bath enamels are designed to withstand hot water. The best are two-part epoxy paints needing careful application. Bath

Metalwork – paint types

enamels are suitable also for sinks, cooker fronts, etc. There is a touching-up enamel, sold in small jars, for repairing chips.

Varnish can be used on metals instead of paint (avoid cellulose lacquers, which discolour), not only to prevent tarnish or dulling but to inhibit corrosion too, except on outdoor iron and steel. There is a polyurethane lacquer, sold by motor accessory shops, usable for such purposes not only on chrome but also on aluminium, brass, etc. An anti-rust lacquer for larger areas of iron or steel can be used on its own or painted over.

Metalwork – painting

This is similar to painting woodwork. Some points worth remembering:
1 Do not paint heavily any pipe joints or nuts which you may later want to unscrew; nor hinges, latches, bolts or other parts that need to move freely.
2 If possible, detach window fasteners or other fittings in order to paint them. Otherwise, use masking-tape round them
3 Be sure to paint undersides (even of feet) of things like garden furniture. The thin edges of metal objects also tend to be under-painted.
4 Use a piece of card to shield walls when painting pipes. It is important to paint all round them.
5 If there are places where rainwater or condensation may collect on the new paint, try to arrange for it to drain away, perhaps by drilling a hole or by using a waterproof sealing compound to divert it.
6 Thin tin is slightly flexible and so may crack paint on it. Polyurethane may be best. Do not press hard when rubbing down any undercoat.
7 Oil paint cannot be applied direct over old bitumen paint. Seal it with aluminium primer.

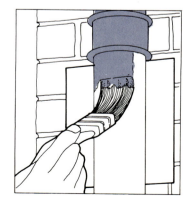

Metalwork – painting

Heating-oil tanks If black paint rubs off in white spirit it is bitumen based and you may have to use the same again. Otherwise gloss paint is better and is not affected by the oil if it spills over. Clean rusty patches well and double-prime.

Iron railings Cast iron (moulded shapes) does not corrode easily, but clean and prime in usual way. Mild steel (bars, tubes, rods) corrodes quickly if not galvanized, especially near the sea. Remove all rust and put on two coats primer, undercoat, and two coats gloss.

Gutters Badly rusted metal gutters are best replaced with PVC. Clean and paint brackets thoroughly with gutter removed.

Other surfaces

Building boards

Hardboards The smooth surface should be rubbed with sandpaper. If using oil paint, apply acrylic primer first, or hardboard sealer, usable also on cardboard. Emulsion paint needs no primer. Tempered hardboards (for floors and outdoor use) always need priming, and are often sold ready-primed. Transparent seals can be used instead of paint.

Softboards (insulation boards) are very porous and should be sealed with thinned emulsion paint or acrylic primer before painting with emulsion or oil paint. Primer and paint should be fire-retardant if the board is used as a lining for walls.

Asbestos boards need alkali-resistant primer or a well-thinned coat of emulsion followed by oil paint or emulsion. Do not abrade asbestos if you can help it, but if this is essential take the work outdoors if you can, wear a face mask, and use wet abrasive (dry the board completely before proceeding with primer and oil paint). The same applies to asbestos flue pipes.

Other surfaces

Floors, steps and hearths
Painting principles are similar to those for exterior walls (in the case of concrete or tiled floors) or woodwork (in the case of board floors).

Specially formulated floor paints can be used not only on wood or concrete, but on some plastics (test a corner first), lino, composition, stone or brick. An alternative to paint is a clear seal. Rubber, vinyl and some other floors may be softened by some paints, so read warnings on labels carefully. Old thermoplastic floors may contain bitumen which can 'bleed' into paint or floor seal.

Plastics
Unless otherwise stated, the best choice will probably be polyurethane paint (preceded by cleaning with meths, abrading with fine paper and applying zinc chromate primer). But first test the paint on an inconspicuous corner for some hours, because some plastics can be dissolved by some paints.

Type of plastic	Some like uses	Notes
Acrylic (eg, Perspex)	Baths, ornaments, roofing	Do not abrade
Polystyrene (shiny, brittle)	Wall tiles	Do not abrade. Paint may cause crazing
Rigid PVC	Gutters, drainpipes, cladding	No primer or undercoat needed. Do not paint while new: wait a year
Nylon (slightly resilient)	Curtain tracks, taps	Paint may not adhere well
Polystyrene foam	Ceiling tiles	Emulsion paint only, preferably flame-retardant

Wallpapering – materials

Types of paper
Ordinary wallpaper comes in a range of qualities according to the grade of paper, the standard of printing (the best are hand-blocked), the number of colours, and so on. While the beginner would not be wise to start with an expensive paper, the cheapest may not be the easiest to hang either, as they are easily torn when wet with paste. On the other hand, washable papers, which include vinyls, are easy to hang.

Lining paper
Lining paper is used under paint or wallpaper to help disguise crazed, irregular, or much-repaired surfaces. It also creates a better surface on which to hang a decorative paper, and it is advisable on walls which have gloss or emulsion paint on them and are to be wallpapered. It comes in different weights; a heavier one is likely to be more effective and less easy to tear than the cheapest. Lining paper is sometimes available tinted to go with the final decoration.

Foam-polystyrene 'wall veneer' is intended to reduce condensation on cold walls and to make them feel warmer. It can be painted with emulsion but not oil paint.

Relief papers
Woodchip ('ingrain') papers provide a random surface texture. This helps to disguise poor plasterwork, having both extra thickness and a camouflaging surface. Some come with a decorative finish, most are for painting over.

Other relief materials include very heavy papers with a pattern formed by embossing. High- and low-relief and plastic-surfaced materials are available.

Estimating
Most wallpaper comes in rolls 10m (11yd) by 53cm (21in) approximately. But dimensions differ according to type, so check the sort you intend to use before estimating your requirements.

Wallpapering – materials

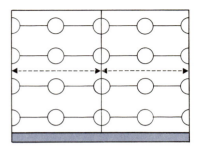

To estimate, divide the height of the room from skirting to ceiling or picture rail into the length of the paper to find out how many complete strips a roll will yield. Then divide the total distance round the room by the width of the paper to find the number of strips required. A ready reckoner may be available at the wallpaper retailer. Unless doors, windows, etc., are many or large, they can be ignored, as some spare paper will be needed for unavoidable wastage. But if the spare ends of the rolls are extra long, you can take this into account. On the other hand, a pattern with a large repeat may involve extra wastage when aligning the pattern (the length of the repeat should be given in the pattern book). Some patterns are printed with a 'drop' and allowance may have to be made for this.

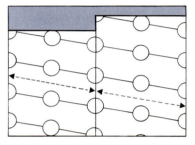

Estimate correctly so that you buy all the paper at the same time: paper from different batches may vary in colour, so check the batch numbers when purchasing.

Adhesives
Many manufacturers offer a range of pastes, to be chosen according to the type of wallpaper. Most are mixed into cold water, though a few wallcoverings require a ready-mixed or hot-water adhesive.

Standard paste is used for ordinary papers and, with less water, for heavier ones. For heavier papers still, and for washable papers and vinyls, heavier pastes are required. Many contain fungicide to prevent mould growth under an impermeable surface; these should be kept away from food, children, animals, and your eyes.

Check the suitability and coverage of the paste when buying the wallpaper.

Paste is mixed by stirring the powder into a measured quantity of water, then leaving it for a quarter of an hour to thicken, stirring occasionally. Mixed paste will keep for several days, but it will start to deteriorate eventually. A paste available in small packages may save you from buying more than you need.

Wallpapering – equipment

A special folding paperhanging table can be bought or hired. A kitchen table will do instead, but it is unlikely to be large enough for convenience, especially when papering a tall room. Better is to use a piece of board about 2m by 60cm (6ft by 2ft); or temporarily take down a flush door and remove the handles, etc.; and support either on a table or pair of trestles.

A hop-up can be hired or simply made. Or use a strong footstool or wooden box, or a stepladder. For a large room, use a pair of stepladders with a stiff plank between.

A paintbrush 10cm (4in) or more in width is used to apply paste. For smoothing the paper, a paperhanger's brush is needed: a good quality one, with long dense bristles, makes it less easy to tear the paper. A poor substitute is a new soft broom-head.

Scissors at least 25cm (10in) long and a seam-roller are the only other items of special equipment apart from a large synthetic sponge (better than a cloth for wiping away wet paste, though damp and dry cloths will also be needed). An apron with a large pocket at the front for tools will be a great convenience.

If you do not have a spirit level of the kind which can be used vertically, a plumbline can be bought or else improvised from fine string and any kind of small round weight.

Buckets for paste and for water for cleaning up, a measure and a pencil, and a length of wood for a straightedge complete the equipment, though a steel straightedge and a razor blade or sharp craft knife may be needed for certain wallcoverings. Stretch wire or string across the paste bucket to rest and wipe the brush on.

All equipment should be kept as free as possible of paste during use, and immediately afterwards should be washed with plain tepid water and dried. Metal tools, unless rustproof, should be oiled before storage.

Wallpapering – equipment

147

Wallpapering – preparation

The walls should have been cleaned or stripped and then repaired as described on pages 121–7 before decorating the woodwork. New plaster, which should be left for six months before papering, should be lightly sanded. If you are to hang decorative wallpaper, apply the final coat of paint to the woodwork and leave it to harden completely (at least a week) before paperhanging. The paper will then overlap any paint on the plaster and give a neat edge; also, paste can be wiped off oil paint, but paint cannot so easily be removed from paper. But if you are hanging lining paper which is to be painted, hang it and paint it before putting the finishing coat on the woodwork.

If lining paper is to be painted over, it can be hung just like decorative paper (see pages 149–52). Though professionals hang it horizontally if it is to be papered over, it is easier to hang it vertically. But plan the positions of the joins in such a way that they do not occur where the joins in the top paper will come (see below). And if you are not certain that you can hang it without overlaps, leave the very slightest gap between the strips.

Leave lining paper to dry at least overnight before painting or papering over it.

Before lining or papering, painted walls should be rubbed with an abrasive block or wet-or-dry paper to provide a key for the paste.

Bare plaster may be highly absorbent (try it with a wet finger), in which case it should be sized – that is, treated with a coat of either proprietary size or diluted paste according to the paste manufacturer's recommendations – and allowed to dry thoroughly. Sometimes, painted walls too have to be sized: check the instructions for the wallcovering you have chosen.

Wallpapering – planning the work

Where to start
On a conspicuous area, such as a chimney-breast or the longest wall, ensure that the paper is hung symmetrically, with either a joint or the centreline of a strip in the middle – especially if using a paper with a large pattern. Avoid having to hang very narrow strips at the ends of an area: for example, if a chimneybreast is just under three strips wide, hang one strip centrally so that the wall is covered with one whole strip and two with some trimmed off each, rather than with two whole strips and two awkwardly narrow pieces.

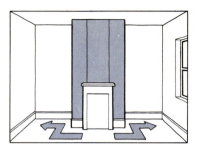

With a plain or random-patterned paper, start work at the window or other source of light and work away from it so that any slight overlaps do not cast long shadows. But with a large-scale design, start in the centre of the most prominent area, so that the pattern gives a symmetrical effect. And when cutting lengths, try to ensure that a complete motif comes at the top of the wall.

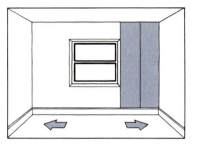

Aim to finish in the least noticeable place you can, as the pattern may not match at the end.

Plumbing lines
Corners in a room are unlikely to be perfectly vertical or straight, nor are the sides of window frames, etc. So when starting a room (or a fresh area of one), always begin by marking a vertical line on the wall as follows.

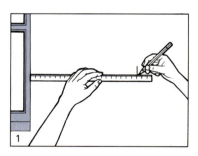

1 Make a pencil mark the width of the paper away from the corner (or the side of the door, etc.) less 1cm ($\frac{1}{2}$in).
2 If you are using a spirit level, rule with it a continuous line the full height of the wall.
3 If using a plumbline, drop the line through the mark and either make pencil marks on the wall or carefully hold a straight piece of wood against the line to use as a ruler. Start from this line, trimming the paper to ensure a neat junction with the woodwork, etc. (see page 150).

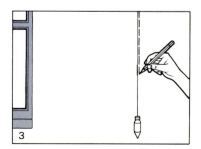

Wallpapering – hanging

Cutting

As paste needs to stand for a time before use, mix it before cutting up the paper.

Cut several lengths of paper the height of the area to be papered plus about 10cm (4in); do enough for one wall. Lay them face down on the table with one end overhanging, overlapping each alternately so that the top of the table is covered. This way, you will avoid getting paste on the table itself, which could damage subsequent lengths of paper. If the paper curls excessively, draw it gently over the edge of the table to flatten it.

With a very small or random pattern, the lengths can be cut one after the other. But if there is a large repeat or drop (see page 146), make each piece long enough to give room for manoeuvre when matching the pattern at the edges. You may avoid waste by cutting lengths from two rolls alternately.

If the ceiling finish cannot easily be wiped clean of paste, add 5cm (2in) to each length (see page 150).

Pasting

1 Start pasting at one end of the first strip of paper. Apply the paste along the middle of the strip, then brush it outwards to the far side.
2 Pull the strip towards you so that it just overhangs the edge of the table, and brush more paste outwards to the near side. Brushing inwards or down the edges will get paste on to the front of the paper.

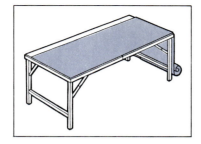

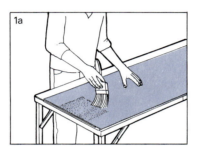

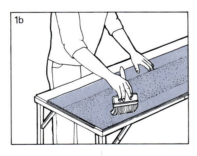

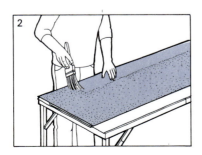

Wallpapering – hanging

3 Fold the pasted paper back on itself with the edges aligned, move the length along, and do the other end.
4 Fold the second end back on itself almost to meet the first end. Long lengths can be concertinaed. Do not crease any folds.
5 If extra length has been allowed, fold over the first 5cm (2in) of the top of the length before doubling the length back on itself.

Heavier papers need to soak for a while after pasting, so do several lengths and hang them in the same order. Light papers can be hung straight away and may tear if soaked too long.

Throughout, avoid getting paste on the table-top.

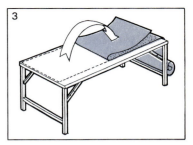

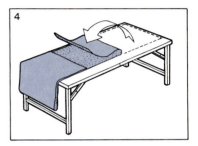

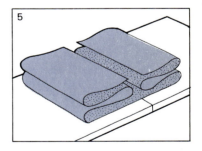

Wallpapering – hanging

Hanging a length

1 Carry the paper to the wall over your arm. Standing on the hop-up, etc., and with the paper against the wall, hold the top corners of the length (having made sure that it is the right way up), and let the fold drop open under its own weight.
2 Slide one edge of the paper to the pencil line you have made, keeping the other side of the strip away from the wall.
3 Brush downwards with the paperhanging brush, then from the middle outwards to each side.
4 Pull the bottom fold open and brush downwards and then to each side, pushing air-bubbles outwards as you smooth the paper on to the wall. Avoid making sharp creases.

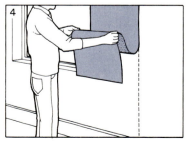

Wallpapering – hanging

5 With the brush, push the top edge of the paper well into the angle between wall and ceiling, then mark the angle across the paper with the back of the scissors.
6 Pull the top of the paper away from the wall and cut along the marked line.
7 If the top 5cm (2in) have been folded over to protect the ceiling from paste, pull away the loose strip.
8 Brush the trimmed end of the length back into place after wiping paste away from the ceiling if necessary, using a damp sponge. Trim the bottom of the length similarly.
9 Slide each of the following lengths up to the previous one, checking that there are neither gaps nor overlaps before trimming. If the paper does not slide easily, it is probably because the paste has been applied inadequately, or it has started to dry, or the wall should have been sized.

While at work, do not drop pasted trimmings on the floor: fold them sticky-side inwards and keep them in a cardboard carton, etc. Unpasted offcuts and scraps may be useful for completing small areas and, later, for repairs.

Doors and windows

At the sides of frames of doors, windows, etc., work similarly: brush the paper into the vertical angle, score it with the scissors, pull it back, trim it, and brush it back finally, not forgetting to wipe away paste as you go.

At the corners of such frames, snipping diagonally inwards will make it easier to fit the paper accurately before trimming.

Areas over doors and windows can be left until last and papered with leftover ends of rolls if they are long enough. At least with random or small-scale patterns, minor inaccuracies may not matter in some such places.

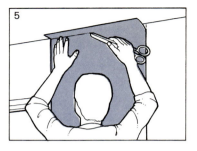

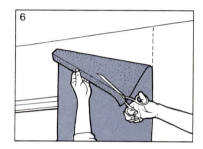

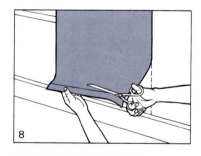

Wallpapering – hanging

Corners

Do not try to make a piece of wallpaper turn a corner of a room, which is unlikely to be straight or 'true'.

1 Measure from the edge of the last complete piece of paper to the corner, checking that the measurement is the same all the way down.
2 Add about 1cm ($\frac{1}{2}$in) to this figure (to the greatest if there is a difference) and cut a length of paper to this width.
3 Paste and hang it next to the last length you hung and brush the cut edge well into the corner.
4 Then hang the offcut on the other side of the corner, matching the pattern vertically. Check with the plumbline or spirit level that the uncut edge is vertical and adjust as necessary (any overlapping will not be noticeable in the corner).

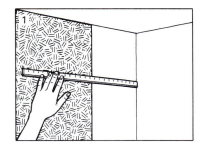

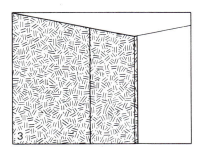

External angles

1 At a chimney breast, etc., deal with the internal angle as described.
2 Cut the piece of paper for the side of the chimney breast about 3mm ($\frac{1}{8}$in) less than the widest measurement of the side.
3 The outermost length of paper on the face of the chimney breast should be cut 2cm (1in) oversize and folded round the corner to overlap the paper on the side.

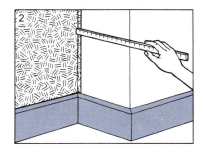

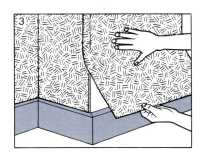

Wallpapering – hanging

Reveals

The simplest way to paper a window reveal, alcove, etc., is as follows.

1 Paper the sides, with 1cm ($\frac{1}{2}$in) overlaps on to the main wall and on to the top of the reveal.
2 Hang the last complete length on the main wall to the side of the reveal and cut away surplus paper neatly.
3 Mark where the edge of this strip comes over the top of the reveal.
4 Peel back this paper from over the top of the reveal, and paper the top of the reveal, running the paper from front to back, ensuring that its edge corresponds to the mark, and overlapping the wall over the reveal by 1cm ($\frac{1}{2}$in).
5 Brush the overlaps down firmly and replace the peeled-back paper. Any discontinuity of pattern should not be noticeable, especially if the pattern is not large in scale and the area is in shadow.

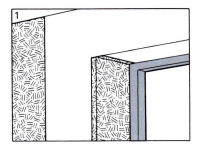

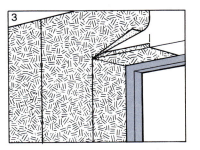

Obstructions

1 To fit wallpaper round a light switch or similar obstruction, cut a star or cross after having hung the top half of the strip.
2 Mark the outline of the switch with the back of the scissors and trim neatly, and brush the paper into position.
3 Flush switches can be temporarily unscrewed from the wall – after the mains have been turned off – and the paper brushed underneath with the points cut off to prevent contact with live parts.
   For obstructions which come at the edge of a length of paper, such as a protruding cill, make diagonal cuts to allow the paper to lie flat against the wall, mark, trim, and brush into position.

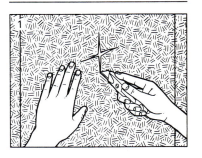

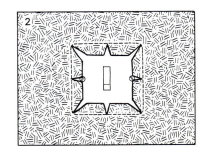

Wallpapering – hanging

Rolling seams

Gaping seams and peeling edges are prevented by the use of the seam roller. Use it after hanging a few lengths, when the paste has become more tacky – usually about 20 minutes, but experiment to find the right timing. Run the roller up and down firmly but not so hard as to mark the paper: be extra cautious with paper with any kind of relief surface. Wipe off any excess paste that may be squeezed out. Avoid making sharp creases or wrinkles with the roller, as these will be permanent.

Overlaps and repairs

1 Wallpaper tends to pull itself on to the wall as it dries, so bubbles and uncreased wrinkles should disappear. But if any remain – probably because the paper was not properly pasted or soaked for long enough – the remedy is to make a cross-shaped cut across the bulge, using a very sharp blade; turn back the corners; and carefully paste the wall. Replace the peeled-back paper and roll well with the seam roller after a few minutes.

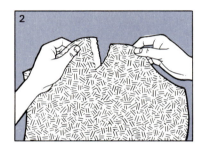

2 Occasionally, patching or overlapping is necessary, either during hanging or to repair damage in use. Tear rather than cut the paper (both over and under an overlap) so that there are no conspicuous straight lines or sharp steps. Tear the edge which will lie on top in such a way that the backing paper will be hidden and the printed surface will merge with the paper on the wall. Remember to align a prominent pattern.

3 To patch wallcoverings, such as vinyl, to which paste will not stick, a special overlap adhesive may be available. Otherwise, cut an oversize patch and sticky-tape it over the damage, matching the pattern. Cut through both layers of wallcovering with a sharp blade; pull away the patch and tape; remove the damaged piece and replace it with the patch, using adhesive.

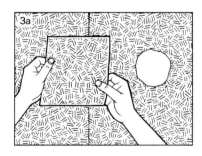

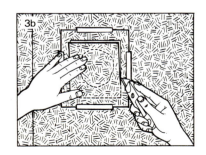

Wallpapering – ceilings

Papering a ceiling is not easy. Unless you are doing it for the sake of a pattern, consider the following alternatives to lining paper.

Extra-careful filling of cracks, etc., may suffice, as faults are less likely to be noticeable on a ceiling than on walls. They will be more inconspicuous if you use a coloured or, better, textured paint on the ceiling (see page 128).

A ceiling should be papered (and painted) before any other decoration in the room is completed.

Hang the lengths of paper parallel to the window-wall unless doing so will leave a lot of pieces to go to waste.

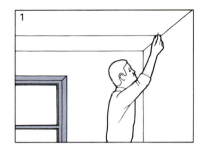

Tools and materials needed

Paperhanging equipment and materials
Two stepladders or trestles and long stiff plank
String
Drawing pins

Method

1 At a distance of 1cm ($\frac{1}{2}$in) less than the width of the paper, stretch a string across the room parallel to the wall, fixing it at the ceiling with a drawing pin at each end.

2 With a pencil and straightedge, mark a starting line across the ceiling, using the string as a guide.

3 Cut the paper into lengths, allowing extra for trimming. Paste it, folding it concertina-fashion with 30–45cm (12–18in) folds.

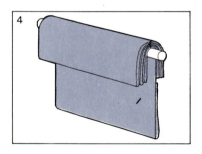

4 Support the folded paper with a part-used roll of paper, a cardboard tube, or the head of a broom (clean) held by someone else.

5 Starting at one end, apply the paper to the ceiling between the line and the wall, unfolding the concertina as you go and making sure the edge is against the line.

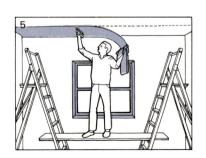

Wallpapering – ceilings

6 When the paper is in position, trim the ends and edge in the usual way, but leave 1cm ($\frac{1}{2}$in) overlapping the walls if they are to be lined or otherwise papered.
7 Butt the following lengths against each other, using the technique described on page 151 when you come to the light fitting.

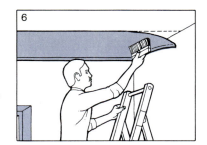

Wallpapering – staircases

The main problem when a staircase has to be papered is to get at the highest wall area. An arrangement like that in the picture is usually needed, but make sure that whatever you do is secure and safe.

Start paperhanging at the highest corner, using the normal technique for corners (see page 151). As the extra-long strips needed will be heavy, they may tear or stretch, so it is advisable to have someone to support the paper from underneath while you are working on the top of the length.

Wallpapering – special papers

Ready-pasted papers
These are cut to length in the usual way, soaked for the recommended period in a special water trough, and slowly unrolled from the trough while being applied to the wall like ordinary paper. Special paste is used where overlapping is necessary.

Ready-pasted papers do not call for a table, paste bucket, or paste brush.

Paste-the-wall materials
For these the paste is applied to the wall (using a foam paint roller if you wish) and the paper is applied from the roll without being cut into lengths first. It is smoothed down with a damp sponge, so neither a paperhanging brush nor a table is required.

Paste-the-wall and ready-pasted papers can, like vinyls, be stripped by simply pulling the surface from the wall without soaking or scraping. The paper backing which is left can be used as a lining for decoration or else easily stripped like ordinary wallpaper (see page 124).

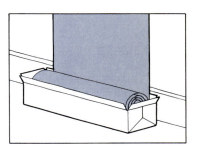

Woven materials, etc.
There is a variety of wall coverings consisting of a paper base with a surface created from such materials as hessian, raffia, wood, textile fibres (woven and unwoven), cork, and foil. Most are expensive and not for the beginner except, perhaps, on small areas. Follow closely the manufacturer's instructions about adhesives, lining, trimming, etc.

Wallpapering – foam polystyrene

Though foam polystyrene 'wall veneer' can be hung like wallpaper, closer joins will result from the following method, which is also necessary for a few fabric wallcoverings.

Tools and materials needed
Foam polystyrene 'wall veneer'
Adhesive
Wallpapering equipment
Sharp craft knife and steel straightedge

Method
1 Paste the wall, not the material, doing enough for one width at a time.
2 Hang a length of material, brushing down and trimming as for wallpaper.
3 Hang the next length of material overlapping the first by 1cm (½in).
4 Cut through both layers of overlapping material, using straightedge and knife or razorblade. To avoid tearing, the blade must be very sharp, and dipping it in hot water will help.
5 Pull away the offcuts and smooth the material down, putting more adhesive under the edges if necessary.

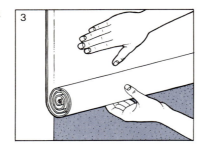

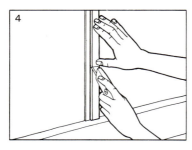

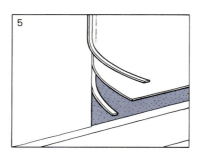

Wallpapering – alternatives to paper

Cork tiles

Tools and materials needed
Tiles
Adhesive
Craft knife
Metal straightedge
Seam roller
Perhaps hardwood moulding, stain
Perhaps fine glasspaper, fine saw
Perhaps lining paper, etc.

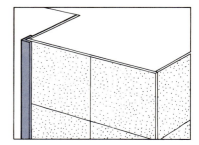

Method
1 Unwrap the tiles and spread them out in the room where they are to be hung for at least 24 hours.
2 If walls are painted, line them with heavy lining paper, preferably brown. If they are porous, size them with one part of PVA adhesive in five parts of water. Allow to dry.
3 If using a contact adhesive, apply it to the back of the tile and to the wall with the spreader provided. Other types of adhesive, suitable for some tiles, are applied to the wall only.
4 Apply the tile to a plumbed line on the wall. Rub it well down, then use a wallpaper seam roller, especially at the edges.
5 Where necessary, cut tiles with craft knife and straightedge. (For method of fitting, see page 155.) Where a tile meets an internal angle, cut it 1mm oversize to ensure a tight fit.
6 At external angles, where the tiles are unlikely to be touched, the front tiles should overlap those on the other face, and the edges can be rubbed down and slightly rounded with glasspaper. Where damage is possible, protect the angle with hardwood moulding stained to match the cork.

Flooring materials

Some flooring materials, such as sheet vinyl, can be used on walls and other vertical surfaces (the sides of a panelled bath, for example). Apply them as to a floor, using drawing pins for temporary fixing if necessary.

Ceramic tiles

Ceramic tiles in the readily available size of 11 cm sq ($4\frac{1}{2}$ in sq) are thin and light enough to be easy to cut and fix, and most have built-in lugs to ensure correct spacing. They can be put on any firm sound surface with special adhesive (a flexible type on wood). Tiles with one or two rounded edges are made for external angles.

Tools and materials needed

Tiles
Adhesive
Grouting
Tile cutter
Straightedge
Two long battens
Spirit level
Adhesive spreader (often provided with adhesive)
Pincers
Plumbline

Method

1 Nail a perfectly horizontal batten with its top one tile's width above the bottom of the wall (the lowest point if it is not level).
2 Nail another batten vertically with one edge on the centreline of the wall (but see page 168 to avoid having to cut awkward sizes).
3 Spread about 1sq m (1sq yd) in the angle of the battens with adhesive.
4 Starting in the angle, press the tiles into place, sliding them slightly. Continue until half the wall is covered, checking from time to time with a batten and spirit level that the tiles are horizontal. Then remove the vertical batten and complete the other half.

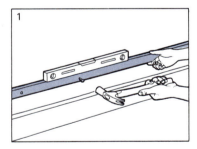

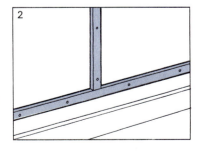

5 To cut tiles to fit round the sides, score a line with the cutter against a firmly-held straightedge, then snap the tile by pressing it on a tabletop with matches underneath the score. Small pieces and curved shapes can be nibbled away with pincers after scoring, smoothing with an oilstone or file if necessary.
6 Later, rub grouting into the crevices with a pencil-end, etc, and polish the tiles.

Alternatives to ceramic tiles are plastic tiles or tile-effect enamelled hardboard. Though less durable, these may be easier to put up in certain situations, and they may reduce condensation.

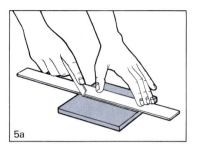

5a

5b

6
Floors and Flooring

Floor structure

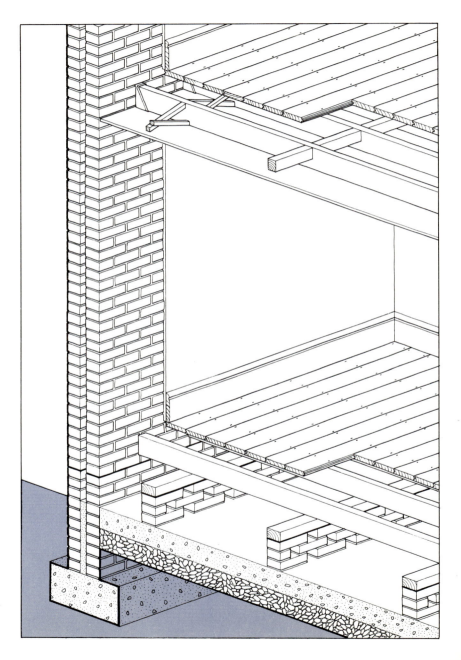

Floor types

The great majority of floors are of either wood or concrete. Other materials used in the past, such as stone flags laid directly on the earth, present special problems if they need attention, and expert advice should usually be sought.

Wooden floors

Wooden floors consist of boards (or, sometimes in modern buildings, sheets of chipboard) nailed to joists. The ends of the joints are supported by various means: dwarf walls built just inside the house walls, steel hangers set into the brickwork, etc., or they are let into the walls themselves. On the ground floor, they have intermediate brick supports; on upper floors, they are deeper and have cross-shaped struts to increase their stiffness.

The edges of the boards are usually tongued-and-grooved both to hold them flat and to stop draughts. Better quality floors are made of narrower boards and superior timber. If meant to be seen, they may be 'secret nailed' so that no nailheads show.

A wooden floor in good condition is warm and comfortable to walk on, and it is easy to lay pipes and wires underneath and to fix most floorcoverings to. It can be sanded and sealed instead of being covered.

But wood can deteriorate, especially in damp conditions. For this reason, it is wise to check the condition of a wooden floor before doing any elaborate and expensive floorcovering job. Examine the boards and skirting against the exterior walls for any signs of rot or damp: if you find any, the woodwork below is likely to be affected. Stand at various points on the floor and bounce with flexed knees: if the floor seems excessively springy, the ends of the joists may have started to rot.

If your suspicions are aroused, take up a board or two so that you can examine the underfloor more closely. One near an outside wall will enable you to check the condition of the ends of the joists, where

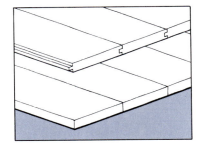

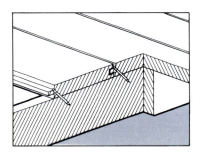

trouble is most likely. Feel for damp, and press a pointed knife into the wood near the wall: if it goes in too easily, rot has started, and a surveyor or other expert should be called in. A powerful torch or inspection lamp and a small mirror held at an angle of 45° to act like a periscope will enable you to see a long way between joists.

Even with a floor that seems to be in good condition, such an inspection may be worth making if you intend to lay a floorcovering which will not be moved for a long time, especially if it is the ground floor – and see the caution on page 163.

Concrete floors

Though hard and usually cold, concrete floors are durable, and the most serious problem such a floor is likely to present is dampness. This may be present if the concrete was cast over hardcore (compacted rubble) laid directly on the ground, allowing moisture from the soil to soak upwards. This will not occur if there is a damp-proof membrane between the concrete and the screed (the layer of finer material which forms the surface). Such a membrane, of polythene or a bituminous material, is now compulsory in new buildings, but if your home is more than about 25 years old, you cannot count on one being present.

A damp floor may not seem so if it has been covered with a material which has allowed moisture to evaporate as it rose (this includes quarry tiles and parquet), but once an impervious floorcovering has been laid, problems are likely. And a floor can be dry at some seasons but damp at others.

It is not possible to check for dampness without a special instrument, but a rough-and-ready test can be made. Take a piece of waterproof material, such as polythene or foil, and sticky-tape it to the floor round the edges. Leave it for a few days. If there are then signs of wet on the underside, the floor is definitely damp; unfortunately, absence of wetness does not prove that the

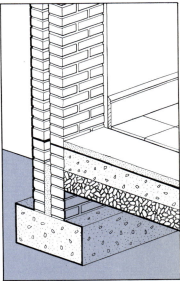

damp-proof course between screed and concrete

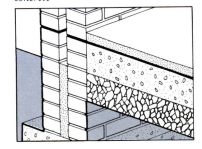

Floor types

floor is definitely dry. (Moisture on the top of the polythene or foil suggests condensation from within the building.) The only floorcoverings that can be laid on damp concrete with any safety are quarry tiles, a few vinyl tiles, and matting of a kind which allows the concrete to 'breathe'.

The proper solution to the problem is to apply a damp-proof membrane to the concrete in either sheet or liquid form or to lay asphalt. This has to be taken up to meet the damp-proof course in the walls and usually has to be covered with a cement screed. Because of the added thickness, this major job involves trimming doors, re-siting joinery, and so on, and it is one for a builder or specialist firm. But there are proprietary liquids which can be used on top of the existing concrete. They are not the most thorough solution, but if you think they may be an answer to your problem, consult the manufacturers of both the material and the floorcovering you are considering. As a stopgap measure, you can cover the floor with thick polythene stuck down with double-sided adhesive tape.

Upper floors of concrete, and ground floors not in contact with the soil, should not be affected by damp. But fresh concrete contains moisture, and no impervious flooring should be laid on a newly constructed floor until it has dried out: an allowance of at least one month for each 3cm (1in) of thickness is usual.

Tools

Some tools used for repairing floors and laying floorcoverings are too specialised and expensive to be worth buying for very occasional use. It should be possible to hire them. Among them are the following.

Knee kicker A device for stretching carpet when laying it. Spikes at one end bite into the carpet, and the pad at the other is 'kicked' with the knee while kneeling. It is not needed for laying foambacked carpet.
Flooring saw The curve of the edge makes it possible to cut down into the surface of a wooden floor.
Flooring cramp Used only when laying or re-laying a large area of floorboards, this grips a joist while a screw is turned to tighten a number of boards at once.

Other tools are cheap and versatile enough to be worth buying.
Tack lifter Used for shifting tacks from fitted carpet by levering them from underneath the carpet. Useful for many other levering jobs.
Jemmy or **wrecking bar** With a chisel-like tip at one end and a crook at the other, this greatly eases the removal of floorboards. The crooked end is shaped like the claw of a hammer for pulling out large nails. One about 60cm (2ft) long is convenient.
Nail punches Indispensable for dealing with nailheads. Buy sizes to match the nails to be dealt with.
Straightedge Purpose-made straightedges are available, but a 60cm (2ft steel rule has more uses, and any straight strip of stiff metal will serve.
Scraper A patent scraper with renewable blades will be needed for stripping and smoothing angles and corners of a board floor which an electric sander will not reach.

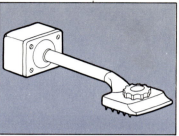

knee kicker

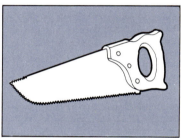

flooring saw

flooring cramp

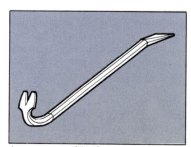

jemmy or wrecking bar

Wooden floors – repairs

Raising floorboards
If you have to raise a floorboard that is in good condition, it is worth going to some trouble to avoid damaging it, so that it can be replaced with minimum trouble and expense. This is particularly true if the floor is to be sanded and sealed, as a damaged board will be unsightly.

Start by looking to see if any boards have been raised and replaced in the past, in case they are in a position which will suit your purpose, as such boards may be easier to get up, especially if they have been re-fixed with screws instead of nails. Likely places are over a central lighting fitting in the room below, and near electric sockets, radiators, etc., which have been installed since the house was built.

Where possible, raise a short board rather than a long one. Long boards which extend under the skirting may be difficult to shift without damaging it and they may have to be cut off short.

Because of the danger of accidentally damaging electric cables under the boards, turn off the electricity at the mains before starting work. This will prevent shocks and short circuits, but proceed with caution nevertheless, especially when using a drill or saw which extends beneath the under-surface of the boards.

Wooden floors – repairs

Tongued-and-grooved boards
Most wooden floors are made with tongued-and-grooved (t&g) boards. Check yours by trying to push a thin knifeblade between two boards: if it goes through easily, the boards are square-edged.

To raise a t&g floorboard, it is necessary first to remove the tongues at the sides. (A board can be simply forced up, but it will be badly damaged in the process.) With a short board, cut away the tongues all along both sides. With a long board, it should be necessary to cut them away for only 50 cm (2 ft), as the rest of the tongues should split off when you start to lever up the board.

Choose one of the following methods according to the tools available.

Alternative methods
1. Obtain a floorboard saw and, using the curved side of the blade, cut straight down into the gap between the boards. Clean grit out of the crevice first to avoid blunting the saw.

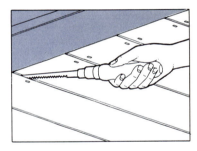

2. Use a narrow-bladed saw, such as the sawblade of a craft knife, between the boards. There may be a gap at one end where you can make a start. Otherwise, drill a row of small holes next to each other until you have made a slit long enough to insert the blade. When the sawcut is long enough, you can change to a longer saw. Do not cut into joists (use the saw as horizontally as possible above them), and watch out for electric cables and pipes – feel for them with the back of the sawblade.
3. Drive a bolster between the boards to cut through the tongues, working your way along the length of the board until enough has split off.

Wooden floors – repairs

Levering boards up

Always lever floorboards from the sides – not the end, which will split. Drive a bolster or other stout tool into the gap with a hammer, starting near the end. Lever the board upwards until it has shifted slightly, then do the same at the other side. Work at each side alternately until you have raised the board enough to get a second tool underneath it. You can then use another lever or the head of a claw hammer to lever the board upwards more vigorously.

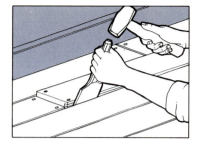

With the nails at the end free, put a piece of wood, etc., under the raised end of the board from side to side, and lever the board as close as you can to the next joist. As the board 'gives', move the wood along, levering as you go, pulling the nails out of each joist in turn. It may help to bear down on the raised end, but not so heavily as to risk snapping the board.

Continue until the whole board is free, or cut it across at right angles at the centre of a joist.

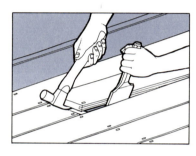

If it proves difficult to make a start when levering up a board, check that the tongues have been completely severed at the end. If they have, try one of the following ways of shifting the end.

1 About 2½cm (1in) from the end and from the side, drive a thick screw into the board (not through the joist), leaving the head standing above the surface, and use the claw of a hammer or a jemmy to lever up the end until you can carry on in the usual way.

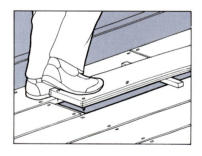

2 Drive the nails right through the board, using a thick punch. (This method can be used for any stubborn nails along the length of the board.)

3 If all else fails, bore a large hole through the board, avoiding the joist, and force the board up with a lever in the hole. This method will involve replacing the end of the board (see page 161).

Wooden floors – repairs

Removing a short length

It is sometimes necessary to raise a short piece in the middle of a board which cannot be removed as a whole – perhaps because the ends are obstructed by fitments.

At each end of the piece, cut it through 2½cm (1in) away from the centreline of the joint, which is where the nails will be seen. Use a narrow-bladed saw as in Method 2 on page 159, but incline the saw slightly away from the joist so as to make an angled cut. Saw away the tongues of the boards similarly (cutting through one may be enough). Lift out the cut piece.

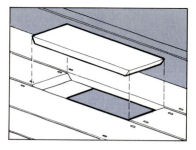

To replace such a piece, use two strips of wood at least 5cm by 2½cm (2in by 1in) and longer than the width of the board. Nail or, screw these flush with the top of each joist, and nail the piece of board to them.

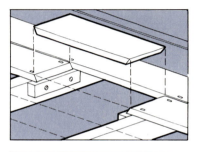

Replacing boards

The best nails to use for floorboards are floor brads. These taper, so that they pull out easily once they have been shifted. But oval wire nails are good enough for small jobs. Use the same length as that of the original nails.

Before replacing a board, pull out any nails left in the joists. Any that will not move can be bent to and fro with pliers until they break, and the stump can be hammered in. Remove nails from the board and brush or scrape all dust from the edges of the boards and the tops of the joists.

Place the new nails alongside the holes left by the old ones. Drive them in vertically to make later removal of the board easier, but where the nails are close to the edge of the joist (as where a board has been cut across), drive them inwards at an angle to avoid splitting the wood.

Where a board has started to split, use screws (making starting holes and countersinking them) to avoid making it worse. And use screws where there is any likelihood that you will want to take the board up again – perhaps to get at wiring or plumbing.

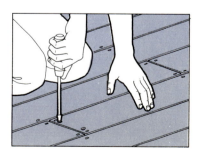

Wooden floors – repairs

Replacing a board

A badly split, splintered, warped, or otherwise damaged floorboard should be replaced if the floor is to be sanded and sealed or if it is too uneven to lay a floorcovering on. If possible, use wood of the same thickness for the replacement. This may be difficult to buy new if the floor is old enough to have been made before metric timber sizes became standard: in this case, try to obtain a secondhand floorboard, perhaps from a demolition site. Otherwise use a piece of board which is as close as possible to the right thickness. For the sake of stiffness, it is better for it to be too thick, but a too-thin board will do for a short length and is easier to adapt.

Tools and materials needed

Saw
Shaping tool or plane
Hammer
Nails
Punch
Perhaps scrap plywood or hardboard

Method

Cut the board to the right width, allowing a slight excess so that the sawn edge can be smoothed with shaping tool or blane. Cut it to length. When it fits snugly in place, check the thickness.

Board too thin Pack each joist with pieces of plywood, hardboard, card, etc., until the board is slightly higher than the existing floorboards. (This is to allow for the packing to compress slightly when the board is nailed down.) Tack the packing in position with a small nail in the middle and nail down the board. If it lies slightly above the floor surface, level it with shaping tool or plane after punching in the nails.

Board too thick Mark the position of each joist on the back of the board with a pencil. Make sawcuts about 1cm (½in) beyond these marks and as deep as the board is thick: do this carefully, as cutting

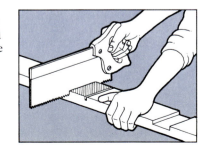

too deeply will weaken the board. Remove the excess wood with chisel and shaping tool making frequent checks with the board in its place. Then nail the board in position, finally levelling it if necessary with shaping tool or plane.

Loose board

Tools and materials needed

Hammer, punch, and nails
Or screwdriver, drill, and screws

Method

Drive home all existing nails and punch them below the surface. If this does not work, drive an extra nail into each joist. Or use screws, especially if the board is beginning to split; countersink them.

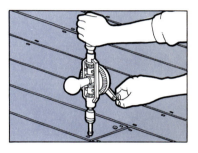

Squeaking board

Squeaking is caused by a board rubbing against the next one or on a joist or by a loose nail. So tackle it by securing the board as described above. If the board still squeaks, try one of the following.

1 Drive a short, thick countersunk screw between the boards to jam them together.
2 Insert talcum powder between the boards, using a folded piece of paper, to act as a lubricant; or use a puffer pack of powdered graphite.

Gaps between boards

Gaps between floorboards occur when the wood has dried out and shrunk since the floor was laid. They can be a nuisance for any of three reasons: draughts, more likely with square-edged than with t&g boards; appearance, important only if the floor is to be sanded and sealed; and unevenness, which makes it difficult to lay many floorcoverings and causes uneven wear thereafter. In the last case, the answer may be to cover the whole floor with hardboard

(see page 163), but if gaps are not widespread and the floor is generally in good condition, they can be filled. A more drastic solution is to take up all the boards and re-lay them.

Re-laying floorboards

Raise one board (see page 159), then lever up the rest, damaging them as little as possible and stacking them in such a way that they can be replaced in the same order. Scrape dust from edges of boards and tops of joists and remove nails.

Replace the boards a few at a time, cramping them together tightly with a pair of flooring cramps before nailing. Lever the last board tightly into position and fill the remaining gap with a length of suitable wood cut and planed to fit closely.

Filling gaps

Start by picking the dirt out of the gaps (though tight-packed dirt can be an effective filler).

For a large gap, use a length of wood shaped to a slight taper. Coat it with adhesive and hammer it into the gap. When the adhesive is hard, level the wood with a plane or shaping tool.

For narrower gaps, use either newspaper boiled to a pulp and with water-based adhesive added, or wood filler in a colour to match the boards if they are to be seen. Work the filler well down into the cracks, leaving it slightly too high, and sand it smooth when it is hard.

filling a gap – wide

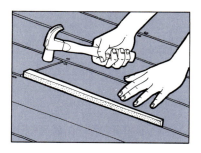

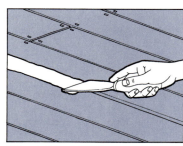

filling a gap – narrow

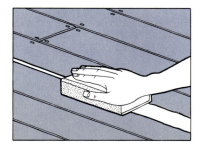

Irregularities

Any surface irregularities in a wooden floor should be put right: if the boards are visible, they are unsightly, while even if hidden, they may damage any floor-covering laid on top or make it wear prematurely.

Knots Being both harder and less prone to shrink than the rest of the wood, these may stand above the surface of the floor, especially an old and well-worn one. Do not try to level them with abrasive paper, which will have more effect on the surrounding wood and so make matters worse. Instead, use a plane or shaping tool or sharp chisel.

Nailheads If these are standing up because of wear or because the boards have shrunk since they were laid, they should be hammered level or, preferably, punched just beneath the surface. If the boards are to be exposed, fill the holes left after punching with a coloured wood-filler. Make sure there are no old tintacks round the sides of the room: use a tack-lifter and pincers on them.

Warped boards Warping is more likely to have occurred with square-edged than with t&g boards, making the sides of the boards stand up. Level them with plane or shaping tool, working across the grain for speed if appearance is unimportant. It is sometimes effective to take up a warped board and replace it upside down, using extra nails to help to flatten it.

Splintering If an old board has developed a splintery surface, try glueing the loose pieces back: use a wood adhesive, cover the area with sheet polythene, and weight it down until the adhesive has set. Or take the board up and replace it upside down.

Surfacing with hardboard

Hardboard can be used to give a smooth, level, and draughtproof floor surface. It is advisable to use it on wooden floors before most of those floorcoverings which are stuck down, both to make adhesion more successful and to prevent uneven wear. For this purpose it is generally laid rough side up, but check the directions for a particular material.

'Exterior' or 'tempered' hardboard should be used in damp places such as kitchens. This type can itself serve (smooth side up) as a floorcovering: finish it with a suitable coloured or clear floor seal.

Use 3mm ($\frac{1}{8}$in) hardboard in 1220mm (4ft) square sheets.

Two days before using the hardboard (three days for exterior board), condition it by wetting the rough side of each square sheet with $\frac{1}{4}-\frac{1}{2}$ litre ($\frac{1}{2}-1$pt) of water, and stacking the sheets with the rough sides against each other. This ensures that the board will shrink and flatten itself rather than swell and buckle.

Tools and materials needed
Hammer
Punch
Tenon saw
Narrow-bladed saw
Hardboard
25mm (1in) ring-shank nails

Method
1 Sweep floor thoroughly. Hammer or punch in any protruding nailheads. Level any high places (see page 162).
2 Place first sheet in centre of room (see page 168 for advice on positioning). The edges should not coincide with joins between floorboards. Nail round the sides, placing the nails 1cm ($\frac{1}{2}$in) from the edge and 10cm (4in) apart. Drive more nails in all over the sheet, 10cm (6in) apart each way, starting in the middle.

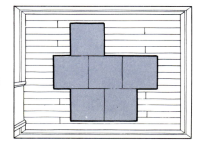

Surfacing with hardboard

3 Fix subsequent sheets similarly, working outwards from the central sheet. Stagger the joints in one direction, and pair the nails at the edges of adjacent boards.
4 Trim the sheets for the sides of the room, using a narrow-bladed saw for tailoring. See page 169 for methods of fitting. While being sawn, hardboard should be supported, preferably by a helper, to prevent it from tearing.

If the hardboard is being laid to serve as a floorcovering, the nails along the edges should be 15cm (6in) apart and those elsewhere 20cm by 40cm (8in by 16in) apart. They should be punched below the surface and the holes filled with a matching wood-filler.

Warning Covering a wooden floor with hardboard (or with any other air-proof material such as building paper or vinyl floorcovering) stops it from 'breathing', and any dampness in the floor or in the space below may be trapped. This can rapidly cause rot in the floor and its supporting timbers. So before doing such work on a ground floor, it is more than usually important to make sure that there are no sources of damp on the outside of the house and that the airbricks are in order (see page 104). If the space beneath the floor is unventilated, airbricks should be fitted by a builder or – at the least – a floorcovering used which allows some ventilation (see page 158).

Note, too, that any such fixed covering will make it very difficult to get at cables, pipes, etc., below the floor. If necessary, make access panels in the hardboard and screw, rather than nail, them down.

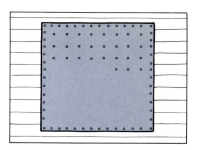

163

Wooden floors – sanding and sealing

Wooden floors that are in good condition can be sanded and sealed as a cheap and attractive alternative to covering them, though the floor will not be warm, soft, or quiet, and the seal may not stand up to very hard traffic indefinitely. Sanding is also a way of smoothing a floor which is to be covered.

Sanding

Sanding needs to be done thoroughly, as any stains, etc., in the boards will be made permanent and conspicuous when the seal is applied.

Very small areas, such as the surround to a carpet square, could be done with an orbital sander or discs used with an electric drill. But most floors will call for a special machine rather like a lawnmower, which is hired. The hire firm will supply abrasive sheets to fit it and charge for them according to the number used.

Before sanding, carry out any repairs needed to the floor (see pages 159–62), though some filling, etc., may turn out to be necessary afterwards. Go over all the boards, punching nailheads just below the surface. If this is not done, not only may the nailheads tear the abrasive sheets, they will also – being harder than the surrounding wood – leave bumps on the surface. For the same reason, use a plane, chisel, or shaping tool on upstanding knots: these may also have to be planed down during the course of sanding as the surrounding wood is abraded away.

Bare boards should present no other problems, but boards which have already been stained may be difficult to sand down to raw wood, so be prepared to use a stain or coloured seal on them so that dark patches do not show up. If wax polish has been used, this should be removed by scrubbing or with white spirit and steel wool, otherwise it will clog the abrasive.

Do as much as you can of the preparatory work before you take delivery of the sanding machine – otherwise you will be

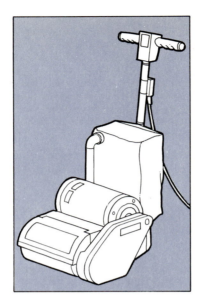

Wooden floors – sanding and sealing

paying for its hire while it stands idle.

Most of the dust from sanding is collected in the bag on the machine, but a lot of fine dust escapes, so the room should be completely emptied and all doors in the house kept shut while the machine is in use. For the same reason, the job should be done in advance of any redecoration. You may want to wear a dust mask, and as the noise can be objectionable, it is advisable to give near neighbours warning.

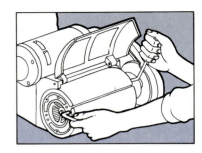

The hire firm will show you how to fit the abrasive sheets to the drum of the machine: the ends are fitted into slot in the drum and are gripped by turning simultaneously two keys in opposite directions. If the sheets are very stiff, roll them between your hands.

The coarsest abrasive may be needed only to remove paint or to level very uneven areas. If will be particularly effective if the machine is used at an angle to the boards, when it will remove a lot of wood quickly. But try a medium abrasive first, and avoid sanding to excess: heavy scoring, particularly across the grain, can be difficult to smooth and may show up when the seal is applied, and accidentally grinding away too much wood will make the floor uneven.

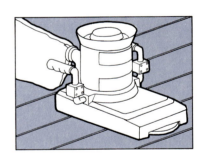

In general, overlap the area just sanded, and finish with the finest abrasive used along the grain. Do not run over the cable – you can drape it over your shoulder.

The machine will not sand right up to the edges of the floor: one side is designed to work up close to the wall (be careful not to damage the skirting), but some areas in corners, etc., cannot be reached. For these you can hire an edge-sander – a heavy-duty disc sander. Or use an electric drill and abrasive discs: hold the drill at such an angle that one side of the disc is in contact with the floor, and keep the disc moving to avoid making circular marks on the floor. Finally, use a patent scraper with renewable blades, followed by hand-sanding with abrasive on a block.

Wooden floors – sanding and sealing

Sealing

There is a choice of seals suitable for wooden floors: clear or coloured, matt or eggshell or glossy. For the most natural appearance, stain followed by clear seal may be preferable to a coloured seal, though the time and work involved are greater. Either method is the answer if the floorboards turn out after sanding to vary in colour. Just a pale-shaded stain close to the natural colour of the wood will ensure a more even effect, while a darker material will disguise obstinate discolourations.

At least two coats are usually required. A quick-drying material is obviously preferable. Second and subsequent coats may have to be applied within a certain time, otherwise the previous coat will have to be sanded. Check the directions for a particular brand: the first coat may have to be diluted, and you may need to apply gloss before a last coat of matt or eggshell.

Use a wide paintbrush (at least 5cm [2in]), preferably a new one, as old paint loosened from an imperfectly cleaned one may cause streaks. Or use a lambswool roller.

Vacuum-clean the room thoroughly before starting – avoid making footmarks on the floor. Apply the seal in the direction of the grain, and try to keep a 'wet edge' to avoid overlaps – where you can't, stop at the edge of a board. And work towards the door!

If using a two-pack seal, mix no more than you can use in one session.

Unsealed cork tiles are treated similarly. They need several coats because they are absorbent. Chipboard can be sanded and sealed, as can existing parquet.

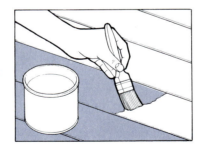

Concrete floors – repairs

Cracks and holes

Small cracks and holes in concrete floors are repaired with a cement-based filler, larger ones with sand and cement, which can be bought pre-mixed. If mixing your own, use three parts of sand and one of cement and combine them thoroughly while dry. Make the heap into a volcano-shape and fill the crater with water. Tip material from the sides into the water gradually until all is absorbed, then mix thoroughly.

If the right amount of water has been used, the mixture will hold the marks of a shovel, etc., without collapsing. If it is too wet, sift in sand and cement mixed together and work them in. If it is too dry, add water, preferably with a watering-can fitted with a rose. It is better to use too little than too much water in the first place.

Especially if it is a wide gap with sloping sides that you are filling, add PVA adhesive to the mixing water and paint the sides of the hole with diluted PVA. This will ensure a firm bond and neat junctions (and give a smooth and dust-free surface). Otherwise, wet the sides of the hole.

Use a trowel or steel float to put the cement in place. On a large area, spread it about with a wooden float or broad block of wood, levelling it with a strip of wood from side to side of the hole. A steel float is used to give an extra-smooth surface, but stop before water starts to come to the surface, as this will create a weak and dusty finish.

On a hot day, cover a large repair with polythene to stop it from drying too quickly.

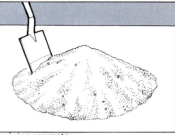

mixing concrete

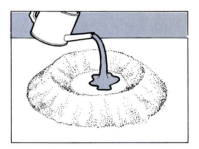

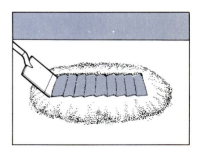

Concrete floors – repairs

Levelling
Most floorcoverings demand smooth and level concrete, free of cracks, pitting, and traces of old repairs. This can be achieved by 'screeding' the whole area with sand and cement, but it is easier to use a special levelling compound.

Such compounds smooth themselves, so no trowel-marks are left, harden quickly, and can be tapered to a 'feather edge' where necessary. They can be used on materials other than concrete, but not on sloping floors. The maximum thickness is 6mm ($\frac{1}{4}$in), so large faults have to be filled as above before levelling compound is used.

Tools and materials needed
Steel trowel
Bucket
Stick for mixing
Levelling compound

Method
1 Mix powder with water (or liquid supplied, according to brand).
2 Tip some of mixed compound on to floor.
3 Spread over floor with trowel to maximum thickness of 6mm ($\frac{1}{4}$in).
4 Allow to harden before laying flooring (it can be walked on within a hour or two).

Surface treatments
Where a concrete floor is not to be covered, as in a garage or workshop, its surface can be improved in a number of ways.
Dustiness, probably the result of badly-made concrete, can be stopped by brushing on a special liquid (the most lasting way), or waterglass (obtainable from chemists), or diluted PVA adhesive.
Seals, of the kind used for wooden floors, will give a more presentable appearance.
Floor paint comes in a range of colours and can be used on other surfaces.
Levelling compound can be left exposed.
Emulsion paint will wear through very quickly but it is cheap and easy enough to renew frequently.

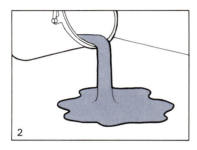

Floorcoverings – selection

The existing floor
Most floorcoverings can be laid on most types of floor, but there are some limitations. When in doubt, consult the manufacturers of the floorcovering.

Damp concrete and stone Unless you can cure the dampness thoroughly or temporarily (see page 158), the only permanent materials to use are some vinyl tiles (which are slightly porous) or quarry or some ceramic tiles. Otherwise use matting such as rush or maize (page 181).
Quarry tiles These may have been laid on a damp basis, so test before using an impervious floorcovering over them (see pages 157–8). Also, they may be uneven and so may have to be levelled with compound (left).
Parquet As this too can 'breathe', it may have disguised the fact that the floor beneath is damp. If parquet has been impregnated with polish over the years, materials which have to be stuck down may not adhere to it. Covering with hardboard or an impervious floorcovering may make the blocks bulge and buckle if they are on damp concrete or an unventilated wooden floor. But parquet can be renovated by sanding and sealing (pages 164–5).
Heated floors These are not suitable for cushioned vinyl, some rubber-backed carpet and carpet tiles, cork, or parquet tiles. Underfloor hot-water pipes laid too near the surface may also cause trouble.
Board floors If smooth, these will take almost any material. The main exceptions are quarry and ceramic tiles unless the floor is strong enough to bear their added weight. If boards have been treated against rot or woodworm, vinyl should not be used on them. And if in doubt about the condition of the floor or the ventilation underneath, see page 157.

Floorcoverings – selection

Old floorcoverings Loose-laid materials (carpet, lino) should always be removed. Fixed ones (vinyl tiles, etc.) may have to be scoured of polish or levelled with compound (page 166) or both.
Porous materials Bare hardboard, plywood, or chipboard may need priming with adhesive before laying self-adhesive tiles: check the manufacturer's instructions.

Sheet or tiles?

In many floorcoverings, there is a choice between sheet or tiles in comparable materials. Other things being equal, tiles have the advantage of being easier to lay, particularly in a room with a complicated shape, whereas sheet material can be laid with fewer joins or none – an advantage in wet conditions as well as for the sake of appearance.

Check that a sheet material comes in a width which will not involve excessive waste. With tiles, check the size against the dimensions of the room for the same reason. And, as many tiles are sold in packs of a certain number, check also that you will be able to cover the floor without having to buy a whole pack for the sake of a single tile. Sizes and packaging differ, so it might be worth choosing another brand or even material, though a few spare tiles may well be useful for future replacements.

Floor coverings – preparation

The thinner and less resilient a floorcovering is, the more important it is to lay it on a level and smooth floor.
Wooden floors Carry out any necessary repair and levelling work (pages 159–62). Clean the floor thoroughly, and scrub off any polish with detergent or white spirit, especially if an adhesive is to be used. Paint or varnish may have to be stripped (page 122).
Concrete floors These too should be cleaned and repaired (pages 165–6). Any 'nibs' on a new floor should be chipped off. Very greasy concrete can be cleaned with a product made for garage floors and obtainable from some motor-accessory dealers. If the surface is loose or dusty, adhesives may not stick (page 166).

Before you start

If cleaning and repairs have made the floor damp, allow time for it to dry out. And check the floorcovering manufacturer's instructions about 'conditioning': most materials have to be left in the room for a day or two to acclimatise before they are laid.

If the new floorcovering will raise the height of the floor, take down any inward-opening doors, and trim their bottoms before replacing them (see page 97).

Tiles – setting out

With the floor prepared as necessary, start by finding the centre. Tiling should generally be started from this point, not from one of the walls.

1 Measure two opposite walls and mark the centre of each, ignoring any bays, projections, etc.
2 Stretch string between drawing-pins at these points, and mark a line on the floor with chalk, using a piece of wood against the string as a straightedge.
3 Do the same with the other walls.
4 Check that the two lines are at right angles to each other. An easy way of doing this is to mark points 90cm (3ft) from the centre in one direction and 1.2m (4ft) in the other, and measure the distance between them: if this is 1.5m (5ft), the lines are at right angles (other units of measurement can be used). Redraw one of the lines to get a right angle if necessary.
5 Starting in one of the angles at the centre, lay out a row of tiles (without fixing them down) as far as you can towards one wall. If the gap which remains is less than about a quarter of a tile-width, you will have to start tiling with the centreline of the middle tile on the centreline of the room.

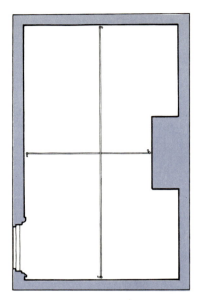

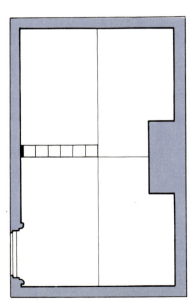

Tiles – setting out

6 Make a similar check in the other direction. There are thus four ways of using the centre of the room as the starting point for tiling while avoiding excessively narrow pieces at the sides (see diagram).
7 If the shape of the room is complicated, lay more tiles 'dry' to make sure that no awkward fitting will be involved.

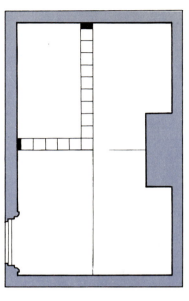

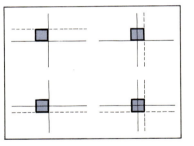

Tiles – laying

With most types of tiles, it is best to lay the first three in an L-shape, beginning at the starting point you have determined as just described. Either continue outwards towards the walls until you can no longer lay a complete tile, and then fill in that quarter of the floor from the centre towards the corner; or work outwards from the centre, making a growing triangle of tiles and then working into the corner.

It is important to lay the first tiles very accurately, as any error here will get worse as you proceed. So take great care at this stage, pushing the tiles up against a straightedge to ensure that they are square and in line.

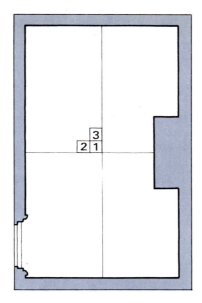

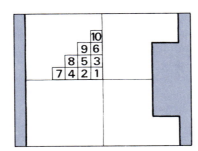

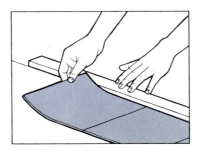

Tiles – laying

Make sure that each tile is the right way round if you are using a material with which this matters: carpet tiles with a nap have to be laid alternately, and other materials with a directional pattern, such as marbled vinyl, look best if the tiles are alternated. You may find arrows on the backs. With patterned tiles, the design may match better on one side than another.

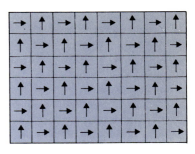

Trimming
Some vinyl tiles can be cut with scissors, but for most materials a trimming knife with removable blades is best.

As a rule, cut from the top surface downwards. An exception is carpet tiles, where the backing is cut first. Some of those have a bituminous backing which is slightly tacky: use methylated spirit to clean the knife blade.

Cork tiles need a sharp blade if tearing is to be avoided.

Fitting round the sides
Lay all the tiles you can without cutting. Then tackle those round the sides of the room. For those tiles which are cut from the top, use the following method.

Put a tile (A) exactly on top of the nearest whole tile already laid (B). Place a spare tile (C) so that it overlaps tile A and has one edge firmly against the wall. Either cut or mark tile A, using tile C as a straightedge. One piece of tile A will fill the gap perfectly, the cut edge going against the wall.

For those materials which have to be cut from the back, turn tile C upside down, overlap it with tile A, and cut or mark it with the edge of tile A. Or use measurements.

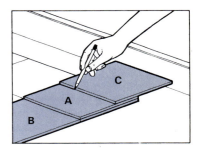

Tiles – laying

Fitting round obstructions

To trim tiles to fit such obstructions as pipes and pedestals, it is best to make a template of stiff paper or thin card, having laid as many straightforward tiles as possible. Mark the top of the template if there is any likelihood of confusion, and bear in mind the direction of the tile where necessary.

Application

Smears and spills of adhesive (if used) should be removed immediately, so keep on hand a damp rag or tin of solvent as appropriate.

Vinyl tiles The most popular are now self-adhesive. For other kinds, use an adhesive made or recommended by the manufacturer of the tiles. Using the toothed plastic spreader which is often supplied, cover an area no bigger than can be dealt with while the adhesive remains workable.

Cork tiles Ready-sealed and vinyl-surfaced tiles are generally fixed with a special contact adhesive, bare ones with an emulsion. Avoid marring the surface of the last sort before it has been sealed.

Carpet tiles Though some are described as 'loose lay', these have to be pushed very firmly together to prevent movement. Kneel on the laid area while doing so to prevent buckling. If you are laying an area of more than about 9sq m (10sq yd), every third row in each direction should be stuck down – or more frequently if the floor surface is slippery. Either use suitable double-sided adhesive tape down the middle of the tiles in those rows, or put spots of latex adhesive on the corners of each tile in the row. At a doorway, stick the tiles down and fit an edging strip (page 180). Also stick down tiles round the edge of the room, under heavy furniture and furniture with castors, and where traffic is heavy.

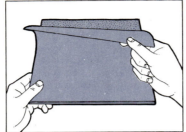

self-adhesive tile

spreading adhesive

carpet tiles

Tiles – repairs

Vinyl and cork tiles It is difficult to repair damage to these. Replacement is the best course, so keep a few spares in hand. Though the new tile will be conspicuous at first, it should fade or discolour to match the rest in time.

Prise up the damaged tile, being careful not to harm the adjoining ones. Scrape away adhesive remaining on the floor, using a stripping knife, and fit the replacement with an appropriate adhesive.

Old cork tiles were often fixed with pins and had tongued-and-grooved edges. Cut through the tongues with a sharp trimming knife and steel straightedge before levering up the tile and pulling out the pins with pincers.

If levelling compound was used under tiles and has pulled away, make up the depth with a filler or squares of card.

Carpet tiles A damaged or worn carpet tile can be exchanged with one from a less conspicuous place in the room.

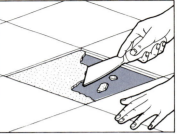

vinyl tile

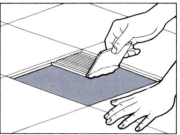

cork tile

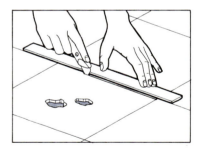

Sheet vinyl – laying

Sheet vinyl is obtainable in widths of 2, 3, and 4m, so it should be possible to cover most rooms without the need for seams. Some types can be laid loose, others have to be stuck down with either double-sided adhesive tape or fluid adhesive. Adhesive can be applied in a band round the sides, or all over, which is preferable where there is heavy traffic.

Vinyl should be left in the roll where it is to be laid for at least 24 hours so that it reaches room temperature. After it has been unrolled, cut it roughly to fit, leaving about 8cm (3in) surplus all round. Then leave it for a further hour before starting the final trimming.

If vinyl cannot be marked with a pencil, use a felt-tip pen where needed. It is cut with a trimming knife or strong scissors.

Where seaming is required, allow enough extra length for pattern-matching at the join if necessary. And check the manufacturer's literature for information on shrinkage: if the particular material is liable, the seam will have to be overlapped and left for a time before final trimming (done by cutting through both layers of the overlap at once). Re-check for pattern match. Material which is stuck down all over will not shrink.

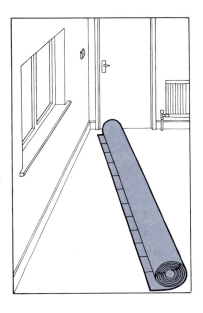

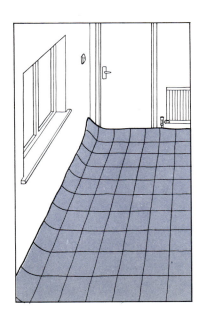

Sheet vinyl – laying

Tools and materials needed
Trimming knife
Scissors
Straightedge
Block of wood about 10cm by 5cm (4in by 2in)
Pencil or felt-tip pen
Screwdriver
Bradawl, etc.
Vinyl
Edging strip

Method
1 Where there is a long unobstructed wall which can be used as a starting point, lay the vinyl up to it.
2 Brush the vinyl all over with a soft broom to make sure it is lying flat on the floor.
3 Use the block of wood to push the vinyl into the angle between the floor and the first wall to be trimmed.
4 Trim away the surplus by (a) using the knife freehand, or (b) with a straightedge, or (c) marking the vinyl and cutting along the mark.

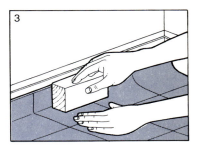

Sheet vinyl – laying

5 In an internal angle where surplus material runs up both walls, cut off the corner of the vinyl until it will lie flat on the floor. Then trim as above.

6 At an external angle, cut the surplus vertically as far as the corner (at a slight angle if the corner is not square). Cut away all but 2cm (1in) of the surplus before final trimming.

7 At doorframes, etc., make vertical cuts at each angle, press the vinyl into the angle between wall and floor, and trim. Or else make a template of stiff paper, or use a patent shape-tracer.

8 Where you cannot easily get at the angle between wall and floor, as in the toe-space below a kitchen cabinet, make vertical cuts about 30cm (1ft) apart as far as the angle. Draw the material back, lay a straightedge along the ends of the cuts, and trim.

9 At doorways, trim the vinyl so that the edge is half way under the door. Fit an edging strip (page 180).

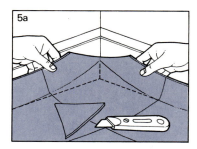

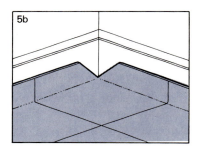

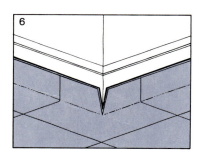

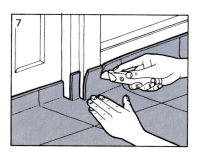

Sheet vinyl – adhesives

Use a suitable adhesive, as an unsuitable one may damage the material.

Double-sided adhesive tape of a kind made for flooring is an alternative to liquid adhesive. It is unrolled in position, the backing is peeled off, and the vinyl is applied and rubbed down.

To stick down the edges of sheet vinyl, all trimming having been completed, roll back about 30cm (1ft) from the wall and apply a 10cm (4in) band of adhesive to the floor. A notched spreader can usually be obtained with the adhesive. Seams are dealt with similarly, but with a 20cm (8in) band of adhesive.

If the whole area is to be stuck down, roll back the floorcovering to the middle of the room and spread adhesive on the floor. Replace the floorcovering, then treat the other half of the sheet similarly. Use a soft broom to flatten the vinyl and remove air bubbles. It may be necessary to avoid walking on the floor for a period.

Edging strips

At a doorway, etc., an edging strip is necessary, both for appearance and to prevent damage. Buy one to suit the thickness of the floorcovering and fix it with the screws provided.

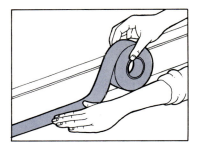

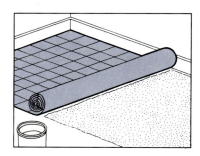

Sheet vinyl – making a template

In a room, such as a lavatory, which is small and contains many obstructions, it is better to make a template of the whole floor than to wrestle with a sheet of vinyl in situ. Spread the piece of vinyl out in another room where it can lie flat.

Tools and materials needed

Trimming knife
Scissors
Rule
Pencil
Compasses
Stiff paper
Perhaps felt pen

Method

1 Take a sheet of stiff paper large enough to cover the whole floor and lay it down.
2 Trim it round the sides and round obstructions, leaving a gap of about 1cm ($\frac{1}{2}$in) all round. Fix it with weights or drawing pins.
3 Set the legs of the compasses about 3cm (1½in) apart. Make a circle on the paper so that you can re-set them to the same gap.
4 Run the point of the compasses along the wall (holding them carefully at right angles to the wall) so that the pencil makes a line on the paper parallel to the wall.
5 Trace round obstructions similarly.
6 Round circular obstructions, such as pipes, mark a square with the ruler held against the pipe.

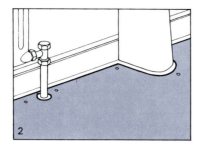

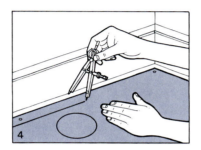

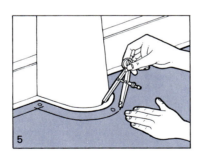

Sheet vinyl – making a template

7 Lay out the template on top of the vinyl, fixing it with adhesive tape, drawing pins, or weights.
8 Run the point of the compasses along the pencil line on the template so that the pencil (or felt pen) marks the outline of the room on the floorcovering. Use the ruler as a straightedge where you can.
9 Where a square has been marked for a pipe, use the same ruler to mark a smaller square on the floor covering, find the centre, and draw a circle with the compasses, having set them to the diameter of the pipe.
10 Cut the floorcovering to shape. Where it has to be slit from the edge to a hole, try to cut along a line in the pattern.

Warning Be careful when replacing furniture, etc., on a newly-laid vinyl floor. If you have used adhesive, wait for the recommended time. To avoid damage to the vinyl when sliding heavy things across it, put underneath them an upside-down piece of surplus vinyl or (better) carpet.

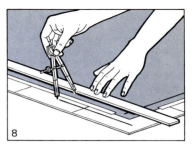

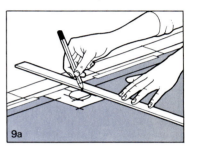

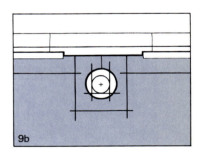

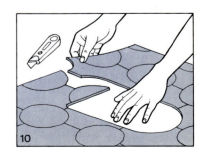

Sheet vinyl – repairs

Vinyl can be repaired only by patching, so it is a good idea to save your offcuts – especially as patterns and even materials can go out of production.

Materials and tools needed
Trimming knife
Stripping knife
Drawing pins or adhesive tape
Spare vinyl
Adhesive, or double-sided adhesive tape

Method
1 Cut a piece of spare material larger than the damaged area.
2 Put it in place on the floor (matching the pattern if necessary) and tape or pin it down.
3 Cut round the damaged area through both layers of vinyl. Keep the knifeblade vertical and follow a line in the pattern if there is one.
4 Remove the patch and offcut and pull up the damaged vinyl from the floor.
5 Scrape away any adhesive from the floor.
6 Spread adhesive on the bare floor and for 5cm (2in) under the existing vinyl. Or use double-sided adhesive tape.
7 Put the patch in place and rub it well down.

Ceramic tiles – laying

Kits now make it much easier to lay ceramic tiles than it used to be. Consisting of primer, adhesive and grouting, they can be used on almost any permanent floor-surface. A concrete floor must contain a damp-proof membrane (page 158) and if new must have had at least a month to dry out. A wooden floor must be strong enough to take the extra weight without flexing. If necessary, it can be strengthened by covering it with 12mm plywood fixed with countersunk screws (not nails) 30cm (12in) apart all over (see also page 163). The floor must be clean, dry, and free of grease or polish before you start to lay the tiles.

Tools and materials needed
String, pencil, rule, etc. (see page 171)
Wide paintbrush
Stick for stirring
Steel trowel
Tile cutter (can be hired)
Pincers
Tiles
Ceramic floor tile fixing kit
Perhaps scrap 3mm ($\frac{1}{8}$in) hardboard

Method: laying
1 Set out the tiles dry to determine the starting point (see page 168). As colours may vary, mix the tiles in all the packs together to give a random effect.
2 Brush the whole area liberally with primer.
3 While the primer is becoming touch dry, immediately clean the paintbrush with water and mix the adhesive with water.
4 After the mixed adhesive has stood for 20 minutes, stir it again, and tip on to the floor enough to cover about 1sq m (10sq ft), spreading it with a trowel. (Mixed adhesive will stay usable for about four hours, after which it must be discarded.)
5 With the spreader which comes with the kit, go over the adhesive to create an evenly ridged surface.

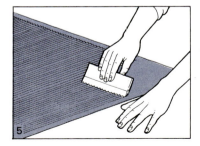

Ceramic tiles – laying

6 Place the tiles in position with a slight twisting action, ensuring that the whole of the back of each is in contact with the adhesive.
7 As you go, check that all tiles are level and square. On completing each area, which must be before the surface of the adhesive has started to dry, remove surplus from the adjoining floor, from the face of the tiles, and from between the tiles.
8 Cut tiles to fit the sides. Very narrow or irregular shapes can be formed by nibbling with pincers. Cut edges should be rubbed with abrasive.

Method: grouting

The tiles should not be walked on for at least 48 hours. If this is not possible, either do half the floor at a time, or lay out flat boards to spread your weight. Grouting should not be done less than 12 hours after the tiles have been laid.

1 Mix the grout with water to a thick paste.
2 Spread the paste over the tiles and work it into the joints with the flat side of the spreader from the kit, leaving it level with the tops of the tiles. Complete grouting within about 45 minutes.
3 Remove the surplus, allow the grouting to harden for an hour, and wipe over the tiles with a damp rag.

Many tiles are made with spacer lugs to ensure that they are laid with the correct gap between them. With others, place a slip of hardboard between each – cut a supply in advance.

If there is a raised pattern on the backs of the tiles, it may be necessary to cover them as well as the floor with adhesive.

At doorways, if the tiles form a step, protect it with a strip of hardwood.

Do not flood the floor with water for a week or two.

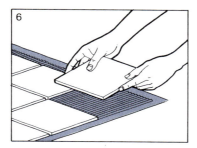

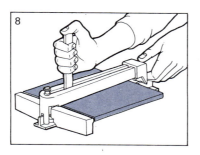

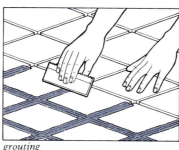

grouting

Ceramic tiles – repairs

Ceramic tiles and quarries are replaced similarly, using either tile adhesive or sand and cement as previously used. Before starting, check that you can get a matching replacement.

Tools and materials needed
Hammer
Cold chisel
Trowel or stripping knife
Scrap wood
Tile
Tile adhesive, or sand and cement and PVA adhesive

Method
1 Carefully break up the cracked tile, remove the pieces, and chip away adhering grouting, cement, etc., from the hole.
2 Check that the replacement tile will not stand above the surrounding ones.
3 Spread the bottom of the hole with tile adhesive or sand and cement mixed with diluted PVA.
4 Tap the tile into position, ensuring that it is flush by means of a strip of wood.
5 Work extra cement, etc., into the gap round the sides. Wipe the surface with a damp cloth.

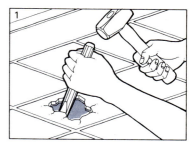

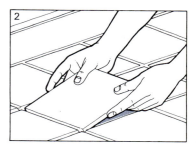

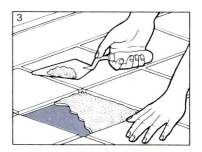

Parquet – types

There are three ways of providing a parquet (or similar) floor.

Wood strips can be solid or laminated and up to several feet long. They have tongued-and-grooved edges and ends and are glued or secret-nailed (see page 157) to wooden floors or glued edge-to-edge on concrete floors. Some can be used on top of joists as a replacement for floorboards. One other material is backed with cork and covered with vinyl.

Wood blocks are similar but shorter and generally thicker, and always solid. They are mostly used on solid floors. They can be laid in the patterns illustrated.

Wood mosaic consists of small strips of thin wood laid out in a basket pattern and made up into panels about 50cm (18in) square, backed with a felt-like material. This is stuck to the floor (though special double-sided adhesive tape can be used with one make). Boards may first have to be covered with hardboard or plywood (page 163).

Blocks are available planed only, but other types may be sanded, or sanded and finished. The more you have to do to the laid floor, the more the trouble and expense, and sanding (done as for floorboards, see page 164) could be risky on some of the thinner materials.

As with all floorings, you must start with a sound, well-prepared floor, though some types which involve a bituminous adhesive may tolerate a slightly damp concrete floor – check with the manufacturer.

from top to bottom: herringbone pattern: brick pattern; basket pattern

Parquet – laying

Though a fully professional result is not easy to get with wood flooring, the mosaic type is among the easier to lay. One ready-sanded make is laid as follows.

Tools and materials needed
Trimming knife
Fine saws
Wood mosaic panels
Manufacturer's adhesive
Cork expansion strip (concrete floor only)
Quadrant moulding
Stirring stick
Scrap wood for spreading adhesive

Method
1. Prepare floor by levelling, smoothing, and cleaning. Loose-lay some panels to check for fit (see page 168). Starting point is corner furthest from door.
2. Stir adhesive thoroughly and spread on first area of floor.
3. When adhesive is tacky, lay panels. On wooden floor, leave 1cm ($\frac{3}{8}$in) expansion gap at sides of room; on concrete, lay cork strip against skirting.
4. To trim panels, cut through backing between strips, using trimming knife. Tailor intricate shapes with saw, using templates or shape-tracer.
5. Fit quadrant moulding round sides to hide expansion gap.
6. Sand down any slight high spots and finish with floor seal (see page 165).

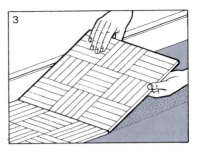

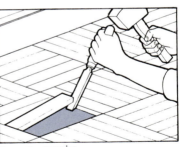

parquet – repairs

Parquet – repairs

If replacement strips are available for a parquet or similar floor, lever up the damaged one and replace it, using similar adhesive. Check that it is level with surroundings, sand carefully, and seal.

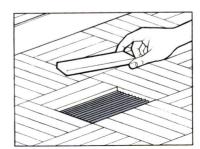

Carpets – types

Woven

If you intend to have a large new wall-to-wall Axminster or Wilton (the main types of woven carpet), you would be unwise to economise on such an investment by trying to lay it yourself. But if, for example, you have moved house and want to fit an existing carpet in a smaller room, this is more feasible.

You can lay woven carpet either by the old 'turn and tack' method, which is cheap but leaves a rippled edge, or with tackless grippers. These are strips of plywood or metal set with rows of angled pins. The grippers are set around the sides of the room with nails (hardened ones for concrete) or adhesive; some have the nails started in position. The carpet is stretched and hooked on to the angled pins, which penetrate the backing, and the edge of the carpet is tucked down into a gap left between the back of the gripper and the wall.

Woven carpet has to be stretched – to keep it flat, to stop movement, and to make the pile stand up.

Woven carpet also requires an underlay. This evens out slight irregularities in the floor and so prevents patchy wear, and it makes the carpet softer to walk on. And if there are gaps between the boards, underlay will prevent draughts from carrying dirt up into the carpet and marking it. Underlay also acts as an insulator, keeping the room warmer; but if you have underfloor heating, check that the underlay you are buying is suitable.

Tufted

Most tufted carpet is now foam-backed, so it does not need an underlay. It is easier to lay than woven carpet, as it is not stretched and does not need either tacks or grippers. It does require a liner to stop the backing from sticking to the floor and tearing when the carpet is lifted. Special paper or other materials are cheap, or you could use strong brown paper.

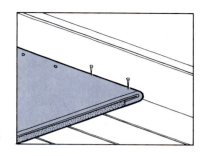

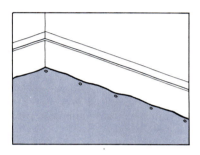

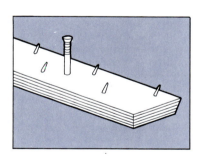

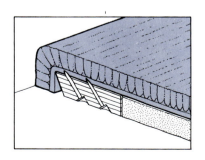

Carpets – types

Other types

Less conventional types of carpet include both pile and felt-like materials. Many of these are made up into tiles (see pages 167–70). Otherwise, check the manufacturer's instructions about laying.

Planning

When you have decided on a carpet of suitable quality for the room, you will need to allow about 10cm (4in) surplus all round – more if there is a pattern to match at any seams. Except for the simplest room, it is a good idea to take to the dealer a plan with all measurements, including diagonals. The illustration shows how many would be taken by a professional carpet planner for a room with a complicated outline.

Where seams are unavoidable, they should as a rule run the length of the room, be along rather than across traffic paths, and be at right angles to the window. If a small strip has to be used to make up the width of the room, it should be on the side opposite the door. Pile should face away from the main course of light and towards the door and must always be in the same direction in adjoining lengths.

Before starting work, check that you have done all that is necessary to give a sound, level, and clean floor (page 167).

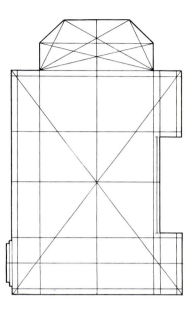

Carpets – laying foam-backed carpet

Tools and materials needed
Trimming knife
Scissors
Measure
Carpet
Paper or other underlay
Single- and double-sided adhesive tape
Latex adhesive

Method
1 Cover the floor with paper underlay to within 5cm (2in) of the walls. Join it if necessary with adhesive tape, and fix it at the edges with double-sided tape.
2 Apply double-sided tape all round the outside of the room, leaving the backing in place.
3 Spread out the carpet, lining it up against the longest uninterrupted wall and letting the surplus run up the other walls.
4 If the manufacturer recommends leaving the carpet loose for a period, cut it only roughly to fit.
5 To fit, cut through foam and cloth backing with trimming knife, using scissors to cut pile if necessary.
6 Make vertical cuts in the surplus to tailor the carpet in angles, round obstructions, etc. Use paper templates where helpful.
7 Apply latex adhesive to cut edges of cloth backing to prevent fraying.
8 Roll edge of carpet back, peel backing from adhesive tape, and smooth carpet on to tape with hands.
9 Complete laying, smoothing carpet on to floor without stretching.
10 Fit edging strip at door (see page 180).

In a large room, or where there is heavy traffic or much movement of furniture, lay extra adhesive tape 75cm (30in) apart along the length of the room, cutting through the underlay to do so.

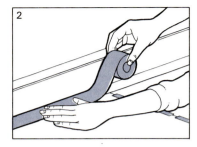

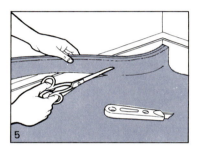

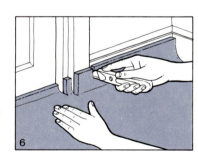

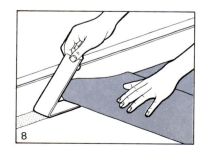

Carpets – laying woven carpet

1 Using grippers

Tools and materials needed
Hammer
Nail punch
Saw
Measure
Knee kicker
Trimming knife
Tacks, or adhesive carpet tape and perhaps latex adhesive
Carpet
Underlay
Gripper strip
Perhaps recommended adhesive and brush

Method
1 Nail or glue grippers around room except across doorway, leaving gap between grippers and wall of just less than thickness of carpet. Finish driving nails home with punch.
2 Round curves and other shapes, cut strip into short lengths (minimum of two nails in each).
3 Lay underlay right up to inside edge of grippers. Tack or stick it round sides to prevent movement. Seams should be joined with adhesive carpet tape (if foam) plus latex adhesive (if felt).

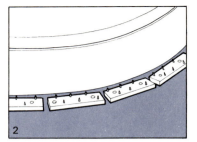

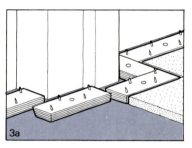

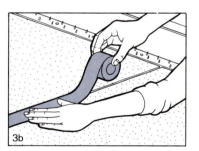

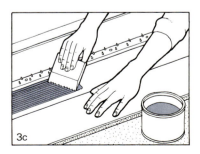

Carpets – laying woven carpet

4 Unroll carpet. In one corner, hook it on to pins for about 30cm (1ft) along each wall, pressing it down on to pins with side of hammer and leaving 2cm (¾in) of the surplus riding up the walls.
5 Stretch carpet towards opposite corner, using the knee kicker (see illustration 9). Hook carpet on to pins at this corner for about 30cm (1ft) along each wall. Then hook the carpet on to the pins along the wall between the two corners.
6 Return to starting corner and repeat process from there to other adjoining corner.

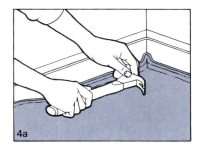

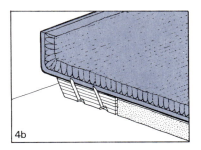

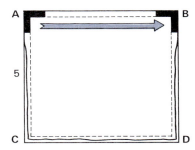

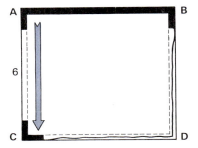

Carpets – laying woven carpet

7 Repeat from there to fourth corner, stretching carpet across width of room as you go.
8 Stretch carpet across room towards last wall, hooking it in place.
9 Now that all sides are fixed, look over carpet for any irregularities and re-hook as necessary.
10 Trim off surplus, leaving enough (about 1cm [½in]) to tuck down behind back of grippers. At the doorway, leave surplus for trimming when you fit edging strip.

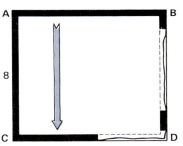

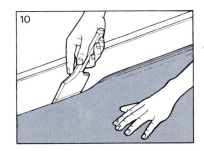

Carpets – laying woven carpet

2 Turn-and-tack fixing

Tools and materials needed
Hammer
Tack lifter
Pincers
Trimming knife
Knee kicker
Tacks (1cm [½in] plus some 1.5cm [¾in] for folds)
Carpet
Underlay

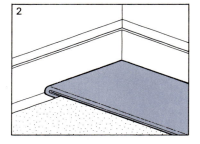

Method
1 Lay and fix underlay as above, leaving 5cm (2in) gap all round.
2 Turn under one edge of carpet so that it touches edge of underlay.
3 Starting at longest wall, tack carpet in place, with tacks 10–12cm (4–5in) apart and about 2½cm (1in) from wall. Stretch it as you go.
4 Stretch the carpet towards opposite wall (shuffle it with rubber-soled shoes if no knee kicker is available). Starting at the centre of this wall, fix it temporarily with tacks about 50cm (18in) from the wall every few feet. Turn the edge to meet the underlay.
5 Working from the middle outwards, tack carpet finally as along first wall.
6 Fix carpet along other walls similarly, using the longer tacks through corners.

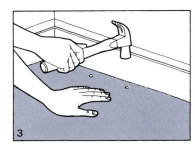

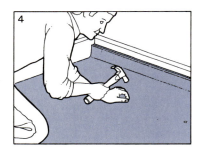

Doorways

At doorways, an edging strip (or 'binder bar') gives a neat appearance and protects the edge of the floorcovering. Types for carpet hold it on the same principle as a gripper strip, but they have a metal rim which is hammered down to cover the edge. Strips are made in several finishes, and there are types to use where two carpets meet. There are special edging strips without pins for use with foam-backed carpet and others for vinyl and other smooth floorcoverings.

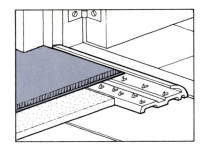

Tools and materials needed
Hacksaw
Screwdriver
Bradawl
Hammer
Scrap wood
Edging strip

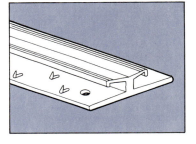

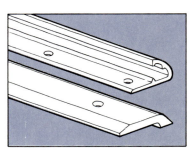

Doorways

Method

1 Cut edging strip to length with hacksaw, removing equal amounts from both ends if necessary to accommodate fixing holes.
2 Screw strip in position so that it will be covered by closed door.
3 With woven carpet, stretch it into place and trim it.
4 Tap the rim of the strip down on to carpet, using a piece of wood under the hammerhead to protect the finish.

On concrete, use a recommended adhesive or masonry pins to fix the strip.

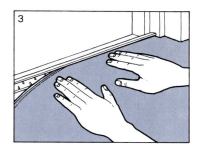

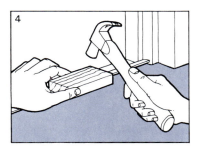

Rush matting

Rush and maize matting – the only soft floorcoverings which can safely be laid over damp concrete or stone – is woven in 30cm (1ft) squares and can be ordered (for additional charge) in any shape which consists of whole squares. You can order it to the nearest 30cm (1ft) undersize and leave a gap around, or it can be made oversize and trimmed to fit with a trimming knife; bind the edges with latex adhesive. The matting is laid loose.

Carpet repairs – joining

When seaming two pieces of carpet, make sure that the pile is in the same direction and the pattern (if any) matches. Avoid having a seam immediately over a join in any underlay.

Woven carpet Sewing can still be used, but preferably only where there are two selvages to be joined. Use carpet thread (waxed if possible) and a carpet needle. Hold the pieces face to face and oversew, taking care not to trap any pile threads.

When finished, lay the carpet face down and tap the seam gently with a hammer to flatten it.

It is easier to use tape. This can be self-adhesive or a carpet-seaming tape which needs to be used with separate adhesive and gives a stronger seam (see below). The wider the tape, the easier it is to use.

Tufted carpet without foam backing is seamed with tape: the self-adhesive kind should be adequate. Apply it along the edge of one piece of carpet, then bring the edge of the second piece up to the first, butting them firmly.

Foam-backed carpet is joined by using double-sided adhesive tape which both seams the carpet and sticks it to the floor (see also page 182). The edge of such carpet is unlikely to be good, so trim one edge carefully with straightedge and sharp knife, then overlap the two pieces of carpet and use the newly cut edge as a template to cut the other piece. Do not try to cut through two thicknesses at once.

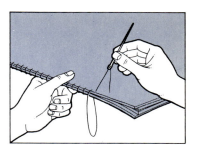

Carpet repairs – joining

Using seaming tape

Tools and materials needed
Trimming knife
Hammer
Carpet seaming tape
Latex adhesive

Methd
1 Lay seaming tape under the edges to be joined.
2 Turn back the edges, temporarily tacking or weighting them.
3 Brush adhesive on to each piece of carpet to half width of tape. Take the adhesive half way up the pile to prevent fraying.
4 Brush tape with adhesive. When it is tacky (after a few minutes), turn carpet edges on to tape, pushing them together.
5 Tap along the seam with a hammer to make good bond.

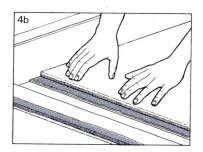

Carpet repairs – patching

Given a spare piece, it is possible to repair carpet by patching. If possible, work from the back. Avoid getting adhesive on the pile.

Tools and materials needed
Trimming knife
Hammer
Straightedge
Measure
Spare carpet
Latex adhesive
Self-adhesive or seaming tape

Method
1 Measure size of patch required and mark it on back of spare carpet.
2 Cut out patch and apply adhesive to half way up tufts to prevent fraying.
3 Use patch as template to cut out damaged area, matching pile direction and pattern. Keep knife vertical. Seal pile round edges of hole with adhesive (as in step 2).

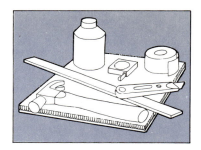

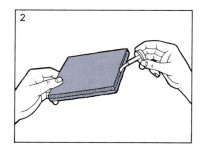

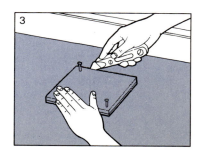

Carpet repairs – patching

4 Cut four strips of tape to fit sides of hole. If not using self-adhesive tape, apply adhesive to tape.
5 Place strips of tape around hole, overlapped by the carpet.
6 Apply adhesive to back of patch round edges. Place patch in position (right way round) and tap with hammer round joins.

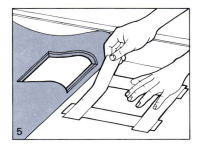

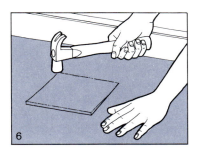

Carpet repairs – lifting

Tacked Starting at the doorway, lever out the tacks with a tack-lifter used between the carpet and the floor. Use pincers where necessary, or a claw hammer. Tapping the back of the carpet with a hammer as you pull the carpet may help. Remove the tacks from the carpet as you go, pushing stubborn ones out from the back with pincers.
Fitted with grippers Lift the carpet off the pins, having undone the edging strip at the doorway first by carefully levering up the turned-over rim. The grippers can be left in place if the carpet is to go back (eg, after decoration).
Taped Start in the corner and pull the tape away from the floor: be careful not to pull the carpet away from the tape, which will tear the foam backing. A scraper may help.

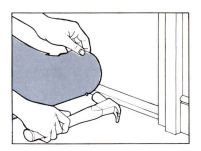

Stairs

Stair carpet can be fitted, or it can be in the form of a runner. A runner is more economical and easier to lay, and it allows the carpet to be moved from time to time to equalise wear and so prolong its life.

Fittings

Apart from stair rods, which can still be used for runners, both fitted stair carpets and runners are now laid with gripper strips of the sort used for floors. They are fitted in pairs – one on the tread and one on the riser, with the pins facing each other. Or there is an angled metal strip which is used one length per stair.

For foam-backed carpet (which must be of a quality suitable for stairs), special pinless grippers have to be used.

With the exception of foam-backed carpet, all stair carpet must be laid on an underlay or it will wear out very rapidly.

Estimating

Check the width of the stairs at several points – it may vary.

On a winding staircase, measure the length on the outside and check with a piece of string.

Allow enough surplus for turning under, and for a runner add 50cm (18in) for moving the carpet periodically.

Choose whichever of the standard widths of carpet will involve least wastage. Check that there is a suitable size of underlay and that there is a length of gripper that will not involve a lot of cutting for straight runs of carpet.

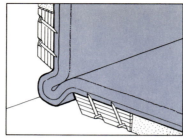
stair grippers

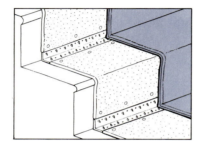

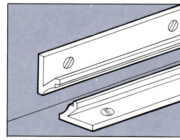
pinless grippers

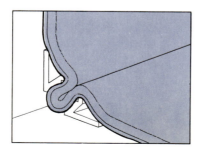

Stairs – laying a runner

Tools and materials needed

Hammer
Punch
Bolster or scrap plywood
Scrap wood
Trimming knife
Knee kicker
Perhaps tenon saw or hacksaw
Rule
Carpet
Underlay
Grippers
Tacks (1cm [$\frac{1}{2}$in] and 1.5cm [$\frac{3}{4}$in])

Method – straight flight

1 Fix the grippers to the base of each riser except the bottom one and the back of each tread, having cut the strips to length if necessary. (Correct length is 4cm [$1\frac{1}{2}$in] less than width of carpet.) They should be about twice the thickness of the carpet apart. Use pieces of scrap wood to save having to measure positions each time.

2 Tack underlay against the edge of the gripper on each tread except the bottom one and trim it to meet the top of the gripper on the riser below. But if using metal grippers, fix them through the underlay.

3 Unroll the carpet on the staircase, making sure that the pile points downwards.

4 At the bottom of the stairs, turn up the spare end of the carpet. Take it on to the bottom tread, where it will serve for underlay. Tack the fold to the bottom of the last riser at 7cm (3in) intervals, starting in the middle and working towards each side. Check that the carpet falls in the middle of the stairs.

5 Stretch the carpet towards the first gripper (on bottom tread), using the knee kicker, and hook it on. Push it between the grippers with a piece of plywood or a bolster.

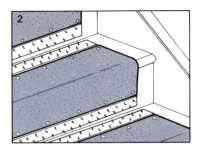

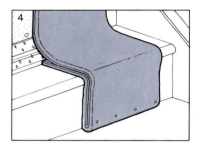

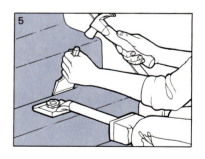

Stairs – laying a runner

6 Continue upwards, making sure that the carpet is straight and central on each stair. The stair carpet should meet the landing carpet at the back of the last riser.

   If you are using foam-backed carpet with special grippers, set the grippers 1½ times the thickness of the carpet apart, and work from the top of the stairs downwards, without using a knee kicker.

Method – bends

If a flight of stairs goes round a corner by means of a half landing, deal with each stretch like a separate flight, taking the carpet from the lower one on to the half landing.

   Where stairs wind, use grippers only on the treads of the angled stairs. Fold surplus carpet tightly, with the fold pointing downwards, and tack it to the risers.

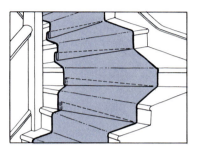

Stairs – laying a fitted carpet

Tools and materials needed
As for runner

Method – straight flight
1 Fit the gripper strips to the full width of the stairs.
2 Put underlay on all stairs.
3 Lay carpet as for a runner, but without the extra length turned up on to bottom stair, trimming to width and round any protuberances as you go.

Method – bends
1 Fit grippers to all risers as well as treads, and also on outsides of treads against walls.
2 Fix underlay on all stairs.
3 Cut separate piece of carpet for each winder, using paper template if convenient. Each piece extends from gripper(s) on one tread to the gripper on the riser below. Stretch each piece into place.

Fitted carpet on the landing should extend as far as the gripper on the first riser of the staircase.

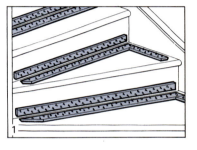

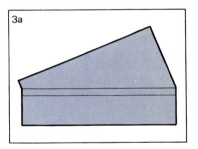

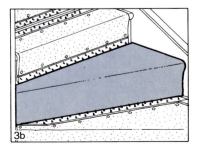

Stairs – moving a runner

You will have to take up a stair runner when redecorating, or to change its position in order to equalise wear. Do this twice during the first year and once a year thereafter.

If the runner has been laid with tacks or with clips which have become faulty, relaying it with grippers will make future moves easier.

Grippers Remove any tacks used at the ends, then ease the carpet off the pins.

Tacks Use a tack-lifter for a carpet laid entirely by means of tacks, working from top to bottom.

Clips and rods Undo these, and check that all screws are sound as you go.

Replacing Brush or vacuum the stairs thoroughly, including the underlay and the tread underneath. If the surplus length of carpet is at the bottom, turn the carpet under by 8–10cm (3–4in) less than before. Tack a 8–10cm (3–4in) strip of underlay (taken from the underlay on the top stair) to the bottom tread so that its edge will meet the end of the carpet.

Relay the runner (as described on pages 184–5 if grippers have been used). At the top, turn the surplus under so that its end meets the edge of the narrow piece of underlay, which you have tacked in place.

At future moves, shift the carpet by a similar amount, rearranging the underlay as necessary.

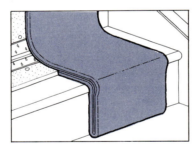

Stairs – laying vinyl

Sheet vinyl can be laid on stairs. (So can tiles, but there is likely to be a lot of waste.)

The easiest way is probably to make a pair of templates, checking them against each riser and tread as you go in case of variation. Deal with risers first, and when making the template for the treads, allow for the thickness of the vinyl on the risers.

Cut strips lengthwise from the roll. Stick the vinyl with adhesive (see page 172), making sure that it is very secure – perhaps by rolling with a wallpaper-seam roller.

You will have to fit metal or other nosings to protect the outside edges of the vinyl. Check whether they are meant to go under or against the edge of the vinyl, and make the templates accordingly.